FUTURE PERFECT

A GLOBAL IDEAS BANK COMPENDIUM

EDITED BY
NICK TEMPLE
STEPHANIE WIENRICH
& RETTA BOWEN

6 Blackstock Mews, London N4 2BT, UK (rhino@dial.pipex.com), 2002, 300pp, ISBN 0 948826 59 2

Published September 1st 2002 by

The Institute for Social Inventions
6 Blackstock Mews
London N4 2BT, UK
tel 020 7359 8391
fax 020 7354 3831
e-mail: rhino@dial.pipex.com
web: www.globalideasbank.org

Further copies of this book are available from
the Institute for £15 incl. p&p.

This compendium is an experimental susbstitute for
Social Inventions journal (Numbers 55-57), ISSN 0954-206X

The Institute for Social Inventions, founded in 1985, is part of an
educational charity, and its aim is to help improve the quality of life by
encouraging the development of imaginative and socially innovatory
ideas and projects

The Social Inventions Awards, with £1,000 in total award money, are
judged each year by the directors of the Institute for Social Inventions.
Members of the public can submit their own ideas and projects (with a
deadline of June 1st each year). The Institute also monitors the media for
good schemes and has a network of correspondents worldwide and sister
Institutes in several other countries. The Assistant Editor in the States is
Roger Knights. Thanks also to Kate Weinberg, Jasmine Jarrett, Yvonne
Ackroyd and, especially, Ben Nash for the illustrations.

British Library Cataloguing-in-Publication Data. A catalogue record for
this book is available from the British Library
ISBN 0 948826 59 2
Printed by Antony Rowe Ltd, Chippenham, Wiltshire

This book is dedicated to Nicholas Albery,
the founder of the Institute for Social Inventions.

Contents

RELATIONSHIPS

HOUSING

TAXATION

WORK AND UNEMPLOYMENT

6 Blackstock Mews, London N4 2BT, UK (rhino@dial.pipex.com), 2002, 300pp, ISBN 0 948826 59 2

ECONOMICS AND BUSINESS

NEW MONEY AND FINANCIAL INNOVATIONS

WELFARE

CRIME AND THE LAW

HEALTH AND THERAPY

6 Blackstock Mews, London N4 2BT, UK (rhino@dial.pipex.com), 2002, 300pp, ISBN 0 948826 59 2

6 Blackstock Mews, London N4 2BT, UK (rhino@dial.pipex.com), 2002, 300pp, ISBN 0 948826 59 2

SPIRITUALITY

OLD AGE

SOCIAL INVENTIONS

6 Blackstock Mews, London N4 2BT, UK (rhino@dial.pipex.com), 2002, 300pp, ISBN 0 948826 59 2

PREFACES

Changing the recipe

Brian Eno

Brian Eno, musician, producer, artist and author, is a patron of the Institute for Social Inventions.

During this June, I watched with fascination and a certain distress as several generations of Englishmen and women followed closely, discussed, screamed at, and missed sleep and work for the World Cup. What impressed me was the sheer vigour and universality of the response, how it engaged everyone and gave complete strangers some sort of basis for conversations. What depressed me was that, in the end, it was only about football. What a world we could be living in, I thought, if only ten per cent of that energy could be redirected towards doing something.

'Energy that people might otherwise use to change the world'

I like sports too, but more and more I come to suspect that the reason governments love them is that they siphon off all the awkward and inconvenient energy that people – particularly males – might otherwise use to change the world. If there weren't lots of sports to watch on TV what would happen to all that energy? We might try to do something useful with it, and that would obviously create chaos for governments everywhere. Whatever they might say, most politicians much prefer it if you leave the politics to them.

In a democracy, of course, that isn't supposed to be how it works. The system isn't supposed to be 'top-down', with policy decisions issuing from government by some mysterious process that doesn't involve the rest of us – except, occasionally, to exercise a crude yes or no at the polling booths. Democratic politics is supposed to be the expression and reconciliation of the concerns and ideas that emerge from society as a whole. But actually this is a description of a process that hardly ever happens. Policy is increasingly made by governments, full stop. People have very little to do with it in any detail and the discourse around it seems almost designed to tell us that we are not particularly welcome. The impression is given that it's all very slow, very complicated, very boring, and largely fruitless. The way it's being done at the moment all that might be true.

Institute for Social Inventions, £15 subs, £17 from abroad by credit card, tel London 020 7359 8391

'Why don't governments tap into that well of creative energy?'

There is, as far as I know, no systematic official way of collecting ideas from ordinary people or for meaningfully inviting them into the process of building the future. What would all the energy of the World Cup fans do if it could somehow be directed towards a project such as 'make our schools nicer places for pupils and teachers'? Why isn't part of the job of government to inspire people, to get them involved, to do everything to tap into that great well of creative energy and enthusiasm that is clearly available? In fact, why isn't that the biggest job of government?

Perhaps these are some of the things Nick Albery was thinking about when he started the Institute for Social Inventions. His vision was to make a place where the natural and generous creativity that people seem so readily to manifest when faced with problems could be collected together and shared. It's pretty amazing to me that a project of such consistently high quality and low running costs hasn't simply been co-opted by government as a resource to be drawn on.

'Nobody wants people coming in and changing the recipe'

But then again, it's not that amazing. We have a media culture in this country that is so intrinsically hostile to any form of cultural or social experimentation that governments resist tampering. Nobody wants to be crucified for trying something that can be ridiculed by those who write for some of our papers. So instead governments seem to content themselves with slightly adjusting the size of the slices of the pie, over and over again. Nobody, it seems, wants people coming in and changing the recipe.

It's getting late. We'd better start doing something. Let's start with some of these ideas. Let's do them. Choose one you like, and get it done.

6 Blackstock Mews, London N4 2BT, UK (rhino@dial.pipex.com), 2002, 300pp, ISBN 0 948826 59 2

Responding, not reflecting

Nick Temple, Retta Bowen and Stephanie Wienrich

Co-editors of the Global Ideas Bank.

The past year is one that will remain marked forever by the events of September 11th. That day was followed by acres of newsprint of reflection and musing, with every columnist, journalist and commentator declaring their views on what it meant for the world, why it happened, and who did it for what reason. The tendency to dwell at such times is an understandable one, when the world seems to have been halted by our own antagonism and negativity. But things do not stop, and nor can we, in our attempts to change things for the better.

As editors of the Global Ideas Bank, we are uniquely placed to receive such breaths of fresh air in the pervading gloom. Shortly after September 2001, hundreds of ideas started to be submitted to the Global Ideas Bank: some were practical ideas on how to avert such a disaster again (airport security, parachutes in tall buildings, dispersing targetable assets), while others concentrated on the root causes of inequality, poverty and disempowerment. It has been particularly noticeable that there have been a significant number of suggestions and ideas focusing on education and the need to communicate concepts of conflict resolution, political democracy and the connected world to the coming generations.

'Positivity translated into action holds the key to our future'

This compendium contains more ideas from individual people submitting to the Global Ideas Bank than ever before, fulfilling the part of our core purpose that is to promote public participation in creative problem-solving. That many of these suggestions have come from people under 25 is another reason to be optimistic for the future: be they a student in Sydney, a teenager in Singapore or a philosophy class in North Carolina, the mindset for positive solution is there. They are not indulging in negative reflection on world events, but responding positively with imaginative schemes, initiatives and projects to help improve society. It is that enduring positivity translated into action that holds the key to all our futures.

Institute for Social Inventions, £15 subs, £17 from abroad by credit card, tel London 020 7359 8391

SOCIAL INNOVATIONS AWARDS 2002

Rewarding the year's best ideas

The Institute for Social Inventions hereby announces its awards for social innovations in 2002. Ideas have flooded into the Institute the whole year, and the flow shows no sign of abating. The award-winners are a small representative of the huge number of ideas which are all worthy of recognition and deserve our support.Be inspired by them.

• *The Institute for Social Inventions, 6 Blackstock Mews, Blackstock Road, London N4 2BT, UK (tel: 020 7359 8391; fax: 020 7354 3831; e-mail: ISI@alberyfoundation.org; web: www.globalideasbank.org).*

Teachers resource pack on non-violent conflict resolution

The £1,000 Social Innovations Award for 2002 goes to the Gandhi Foundation, for its project to create a resource pack for teachers on the theories and practices of non-violent conflict resolution. At present, there is no formal provision for training teachers about this subject, a void which the pack intends to fill.

'Teaching students how to manage and resolve conflicts in their own lives'

The Foundation believes that teaching students how to manage and resolve conflicts in their own lives is crucial to their evolving political and emotional literacy, and to their sense of moral and social responsibility. In a world in which conflicts beget conflicts, and which is beset by divisions, such an educational tool to help students with their own personal conflicts, big and small, is timely. See page 38 for further details.

6 Blackstock Mews, London N4 2BT, UK (rhino@dial.pipex.com), 2002, 300pp, ISBN 0 948826 59 2

Citywide record attempt on learning languages

The Communications Social Innovations Award for 2002 goes to ·Birmingham Council for their Learning Day on March 21st 2002. The council encouraged people to learn five phrases in a new language as part of the biggest simultaneous learning activity ever, and set a new world record. Participants were able to choose from 22 languages spoken in Birmingham, including Somali and Vietnamese, and learn how to say five phrases..

'The city as a learning organism'

The idea is to encourage learning at all levels, show the city as a 'learning organism' and foster understanding between the many different people who live in the city. See page 34 for further details

Student community service instead of tuition fees

The Financial Social Innovations Award for 2002 goes to Alex Jacobs whose proposal is to replace student tuition fees with a student community service. He believes this would save the government a lot of money, improve the economy, increase social capital and facilitate social inclusion of both students and locals.

It would also ground student courses in reality, as students become more aware of problems that are prevalent in society and develop more of a social conscience. Students would also be far less likely to fall into the substantial debts which are presently a feature of the higher education funding system. See page 35 for further details.

Kids teach their elders internet skills, and learn history in return

The Education Social Innovations Award for 2002 goes to a programme initiated by Professor Edna Aphek and carried out in several schools in Israel. The programme aims to reduce the intergenerational gap and the digital divide by having elementary and middle school children tutor senior citizens computer and internet skills and at the same time write together with the seniors a digital 'mini e-book' based on a chapter from the senior's personal history.

'A mutually beneficial exchange of skills and knowledge'

This results in a mutually beneficial exchange of skills and knowledge between the two generations, with the children passing on their technical know-how and the elders passing on their worldly wisdom and stories. See page 42 for further details.

Job references to be supplied by employees, not employers

The Work and Employment Social Innovations Award for 2002 goes to Philip Mcleish for his idea that job references should be supplied by employees not employers. Bullies and bad managers abound because their bosses neither know nor adequately care about their own behaviour, or because they misrepresent conflict between themselves and their underlings. Even if they know, when a bullying person leaves an organisation many employers will still give them a reasonable reference, possibly even to get rid of them.

'Students would develop more of a social conscience'

A very different picture would emerge if it were standard practice for a person seeking a new job to supply names and contact details of everyone who had worked *under* them at their last job. How differently your boss would treat you if his career hinged on your opinion. See page 67 for further details.

Policeman trained in psychology to help mentally ill

The Welfare Social Innovations Award for 2002 goes to Joel Ray, a policeman in San Rafael, California. Joel Ray trained as a psychologist and co-ordinates a project called the Mental Health Liaison Programme (MHLP). The programme was created to try to address the problem of mentally ill people being arrested for minor crimes, jailed, taken off medication and then subsequently released again.

6 Blackstock Mews, London N4 2BT, UK (rhino@dial.pipex.com), 2002, 300pp, ISBN 0 948826 59 2

'The programme brings together policemen and mental health specialists'

The MHLP which brings together law enforcement professionals and representatives from homeless and mental health agencies, has been a great success, and is an example of innovative collaboration. Cases are studied on an individual basis by the MHLP team, and decisions taken on the best course of action. See page 93 for further details.

Village shop owned by its community

The Community Social Innovations Award for 2002 goes to Maiden Bradley, a small village in Wiltshire, UK, which reacted to the possibility of its local shop closing by deciding to buy it themselves. The residents of the village raised money from the government's countryside agency, and over 60 per cent of the village adults contributed sums of between £5 and £500 in return for shares in the shop.

'All proceeds go back into the community'

The shop's future has been assured, and the village now leases out the shop, with all proceeds going back into the community. This piece of direct action has strengthened the community as a whole, because people have an interest in the shop, use it themselves, and it provides a centre for the residents of the village to chat or make contact each day. See page 149 for further details.

Legislating against light pollution

The Environmental Social Innovations Award for 2002 goes to the government of the Czech Republic, which recently introduced legislation to combat light pollution in the whole country. Starting in June 2002, light polluters can be fined up to £3,000 for offences. Lamp posts will have to be shielded from above with curved glass, and billboard lighting will have to face downwards from the top, rather than be uplit.

'Light pollution at night increases sight problems and insomnia'

The reduction in light pollution should help diminish some of the ecological consequences of drowning the night sky with artificial light. Light pollution at night is thought to impair human production of the hormone melatonin, to increase sight problems, to increase cases of insomnia and to damage the immune system. See page 152 for further details.

Exchanging weapons for productive tools, and creating art from the arms

The International Social Innovations Award for 2002 goes to a project run by Christian Aid for the last seven years, which allows the citizens of Mozambique to hand in weapons in exchange for productive tools.

'Creativity is used to render the weapons harmless'

A proportion of the weapons are then given to local artists who transform them into sculptures of harmony and peace, thus using creativity to render them harmless. See page 251 for further details.

Boomerang Day for returning borrowed items

The Wild Card Social Innovations Award for 2002 goes to Tony Paynter for his idea for a 'Boomerang Day'. He suggests we set aside one day a year to search the house for things that don't belong to us (ie borrowed things), and that you've neglected to return, such as a brother's golf clubs or a neighbour's lawnmower. The Boomerang Day would be the day to return those things, and to settle any old grievances. See page 48 for further details.

6 Blackstock Mews, London N4 2BT, UK (rhino@dial.pipex.com), 2002, 300pp, ISBN 0 948826 59 2

SOCIALLY INNOVATIVE VISIONS & SCHEMES

CHILDREN & EDUCATION

Teaching less facts so children can think more creatively

Summarised from an article by Kathryn Tolbert entitled 'Japanese schools will teach less so kids think more', in the Seattle Times (October 7th 2001), monitored for the Global Ideas Bank by Roger Knights. The article originally appeared in the Washington Post.

Japan is reducing its school curricula by a third in an effort to promote creativity and independent individual thinking amongst its children. Although Japanese students are renowned for their grasp of mathematics and science, surveys have revealed that they do not enjoy learning, increasingly dislike subjects as they go through school and, most importantly, are often unable to express individual opinions or conduct research on their own. Education officials decided that the best way to counter this problem is to reduce the amount of information pupils are taught. The new policy has been labelled 'Education with Leeway', but it is more a change of emphasis from passive, spoon-fed learning to involved, active thinking. As well as reducing the amount of material on the curriculum, this approach also includes the introduction of a 'general studies' type class to encourage creative thinking.

'The truancy rate had risen by 12 times in 30 years'

The Japanese education system had been highly regarded for its uniformly high quality, but everyone being taught the same things at the same speed has led to boredom for the brightest students and difficulties for those at the other end of the class. One result of this is that the truancy rate in Japan has been consistently rising, so that the rate is now 12 times what it was in 1970.

Another has been a lack of flexibility and adaptability in students after graduation. The new system aims to treat pupils more as individuals, with classes being divided according to ability and more encouragement for independent thinking. Inevitably, the suggested reduction in the content of what is actually taught has been criticised by parents, who fear it will lead to a lack of basic knowledge amongst the country's youth. However, if happier, more independent and more involved children are the result of the policy, those objections may soon fade away.

International Walk to School Day

Summarised from the International Walk to School Day website (www.iwalktoschool.org), from an original article in Econews of October 2001 by Guy Dauncey. Guy Dauncey, Econews, Sustainable Communities Consultancy, 395 Conway Road, Victoria, BC, V8X 2X1, Canada (tel/fax: +1 250 881 1304; e-mail: guydauncey@earthfuture.com; web: www.earthfuture.com).

The aim of International Walk to School Day, as the name would suggest, is to get children together to walk to school for one day in an effort to make permanent changes to their daily walking routines. The first ever day took place in October 2000 in Canada, Ireland, Cyprus, Gibraltar, Britain, America and the Isle of Man. The following year, 21 countries took part with an estimated three million walking to school on the day. This year's event is scheduled for October 2nd 2002, and the organisers are hoping for even greater numbers to take part.

'It brings environmental issues into children's lives'

The benefits of walking to school are not just limited to reducing traffic congestion, as is often made out to be the case. Certainly that is one main bonus of more children walking to school, but there are several other advantages as well. Walking to school encourages physical fitness and exercise for children, and can be coupled with teaching them road safety rules. It can also help raise the awareness of how walkable a community is, and where local people can lobby for improvements, thereby encouraging a more permanent change in habits.

By its very nature, it also brings environmental issues into children's lives; even if the day only succeeds in provoking children to ask why they should walk to school, then it has been a success. Finally, it also allows parents and children

6 Blackstock Mews, London N4 2BT, UK (rhino@dial.pipex.com), 2002, 300pp, ISBN 0 948826 59 2

to spend quality time together, having a conversation in the morning instead of one concentrating on the road and the other dozing off in the back seat.

• *If you would like your area to get involved, or to get more information, go to www.iwalktoschool.org where there are downloadable resources and advice from successful campaigns from around the globe.*

Student funding by individual contract with universities

Chris Pope

Following recent student protests in Trafalgar Square against the higher and higher debts with which students are graduating, it is quite evident that a solution to university funding is urgently needed. Since higher education is a private good whose benefits are conferred directly on the consumer, without significant externalities, there should be no obstacle to implementing a market-based solution with little need for public money.

There is, however, a need to achieve fairness in such a way which allows everyone the opportunity to a full education. Without equality of opportunity, those at the bottom will be permanently enslaved, and feel oppressed by the capitalist system. When poverty is passed down through generations, whole families find themselves disenfranchised from the economic opportunities available in a free market society. If students must survive on less than £30 per week, then the disincentives to education are strong.

'University graduates earn on average £400,000 more over the course of their lives'

It would, however, be a mistake to react by neglecting the need to equate costs with benefits required for efficient resource allocation. Indeed the key to the dilemma lies in identifying the benefits received from higher education. Most noticeably, university graduates earn on average £400,000 more over the course of their lives than those not going to university. It would be quite perverse for those not enjoying the benefits of education, through the public purse, to pay for others who are. Neither is a 'graduate tax' the option that should be chosen. Government would not provide a flexible incentive-based solution. Indeed, such a tax would just result in graduates emigrating to avoid it. Whilst students should not have to live on £30 per week, welfare is not a solution. Equally, forcing students to spend their time working to earn money should not be considered.

The answer lies not with the coercive powers of government, but in the free market. Students should have the option of signing a contract with universities prior to studying. In return for a significant cost of living allowance and payment of fees, students would pledge a certain percentage of their future incomes to the university. In other words, students would be able to realise a percentage of the present value of an expected stream of future incomes to pay for their fees or to gain enough money to live. (Note the proximity to such a method to that by which firms gain capital to fund expansion by listing on the stock market.)

The simplicity of such a system would be its virtue, which would consequently allow for significant flexibility. Students could decide what proportion of fees they want to pay immediately, and how much they would want to pay as a proportion, or by present value of, future earnings.

Such a system would fully address problems of inequality of opportunity. It would not matter whether one's parents are rich or poor, as availability of higher education would be open to those on the basis of future earning potential, irrespective of family background. Ultimately, such a system could have hugely significant implications for the equality of a society. Since education is one of the most significant means by which inequality is passed through generations, its availability irrespective of current wealth would be a large barrier to this, and may lead to a more wide-ranging acceptance of the free market.

Indeed, the forces of the free market and competition would be felt throughout the educational system. Most likely, prestigious universities would be able to cover the costs of a significantly higher level of service. Prestige of universities would consequently be increasingly valuable, and research would be given a basis in the market as a result of this. No longer would researchers be encouraged by the incentive infrastructure to simply publish in order to best fit into government-dictated pay-per-publication structure, but incentives would encourage high quality research in order to gain prestige.

'A system in which universities compete for a share of students' future earnings'

Such a system, in which universities compete for a 'share' of students' projected future earnings, would also likely have beneficial impacts on the school system. Competition would not be for inflexible school grades, but to directly meet the requirements of the most prestigious universities which would pick students on the basis of their value to academia or the economy as a whole.

A system, which accounts for people's strong self-interest and channels it in a constructive fashion, would be hugely beneficial. No longer would

6 Blackstock Mews, London N4 2BT, UK (rhino@dial.pipex.com), 2002, 300pp, ISBN 0 948826 59 2

universities depend on lobbying governments and special interests for funds, but on the rational decisions and competition between individuals. The significant extra earning potential resulting from going to university would be made available to all, and universities would consequently be able to raise far greater revenues, with efficient allocation of resources meeting the needs of academic research and education.

• *Chris Pope is a student at the London School of Economics (e-mail: c.pope@lse.ac.uk).*

Breakfast club with music and pen-pals

Summarised from an item entitled 'Breakfast Club', in the Community Links Ideas Annual on child poverty, Ground Up *(Community Links, 2001; ISBN 0 9537748 1 3).*

A primary school has gone beyond the normal concept of school breakfast clubs by adding musical instruments and letter-writing to the mix. At Albert Primary School in Penarth, the breakfast club now runs 'Breakfast with Beethoven' and 'European Early-Birds' to encourage not only healthy eating but also music creation and writing to pen-pals across Europe. As well as meeting childcare needs for those with a working day before school hours, the club can improve self-confidence, health and social cohesion amongst pupils.

'Schools have discussion groups based around the morning papers'

Other breakfast clubs across the UK have developed innovative twists to the concept as well. St Edmund's School in King's Lynn actively encourages family participation in their club (rather than it being a substitute for a family breakfast), which has led to greater links and bonds between families and parents, as well as pupils. Other schools have discussion groups over breakfast based around the morning papers, while the Channel High School in Folkestone operates a book-swapping scheme in which pupils exchange favourite books and discover new authors.

• *For more information on school breakfast clubs, contact Tony Apicella, Education Extra, 17 Old Ford Road, London E2 9PL (tel: 020 8709 9900; e-mail: info@educationextra.org.uk; web: www.breakfast-club.co.uk).*

• *For information on Community Links' ideas annuals, contact Richard McKeever, Community Links, 105 Barking Road, Canning Town, London E16 4HQ (tel: 020 7473 2270; fax: 020 7473 6671; e-mail: richard.mckeever@community-links.org; web: www.community-links.org).*

Encouraging philanthropy amongst the wealthy young

Summarised from an article by Jolayne Houtz, entitled 'Young and rich and doing good', in the Seattle Times (July 31st 2001), monitored for the Global Ideas Bank by Roger Knights.

A new group has been set up to encourage wealthy children to give to those less fortunate than themselves. The idea of Social Venture Kids, a new organisation in Seattle, is to get the children involved in doing good in their community. It is also about teaching those who have been born into, or raised with, substantial wealth about what it really means to be able to have and give. Their parents, who helped set up the group, believe it is a way of grounding them and of introducing them to important issues. The members of Social Venture Kids raise money and research causes before deciding where they want that money to go, so those involved also learn about the problems people have and what causes them.

'Reinforcing the principle that with money comes responsibility'

The key tenet is that with money comes responsibility; raising money, researching causes, visiting places in need and then donating that money can only reinforce that notion. The children were surprised at how great the need for funds was, and were reminded of how fortunate they themselves had been. The fear that this process could be viewed as patronising was punctured by the words of a local homeless project co-ordinator: "These weren't typical rich, do-gooder kids – they were learning and interested in people and things beyond themselves". It is that educational part to the programme that should ensure its success, because the children involved end up not only improving the lives of those in need, but also their own through an enriched understanding of the world around them. And it should also instil in them the desire to continue to give to their community throughout the rest of their lives.

• *For more information on the Seattle scheme, see http://www.svpseattle.org/ investee_portfolio/social_venture_kids.htm*

6 Blackstock Mews, London N4 2BT, UK (rhino@dial.pipex.com), 2002, 300pp, ISBN 0 948826 59 2

Green ribbon signifies graduate pledge for future

Summarised from information on the Manchester College website (www.manchester.edu). This item was originally noted in an issue of Econews by Guy Dauncey. Guy Dauncey, Econews, Sustainable Communities Consultancy, 395 Conway Road, Victoria, BC, V8X 2X1, Canada (tel/fax: +1 250 881 1304; e-mail: guydauncey@earthfuture.com; web: www.earthfuture.com).

A new idea is taking off in America's colleges, which involves students taking a pledge of social and environmental responsibility. The pledge scheme, which is based at Manchester College in Indiana, involves the college seniors wearing a green ribbon on their graduation gowns as a public symbol of their support for the idea. Many have also backed up their words with actions, including introducing recycling initiatives, eliminating racist language in a training manual and pushing for greater involvement for women in high school athletics.

At Manchester College, the pledge is as follows:

'I pledge to explore and take into account the social and environmental consequences of any job I consider and will try to improve these aspects of any organisations for which I work'.

Around half the graduates at Manchester wore the symbolic green ribbon at their graduation in May 2002, and over 65 other colleges have now taken up the idea. A further 200 have expressed an interest in doing so. The pledge, which started at Humboldt State University in 1987, has support in both the smallest colleges and the most renowned institutions, including Harvard and Stanford. As Neil Wollman, the scheme's co-ordinator, points out, the pledge "gets at the heart of a good education and can benefit society as a whole. Not only does it remind students of the ethical implications of the knowledge and training they received, but it can help lead to a socially-conscious citizenry and a better world". It can also act as a focal point for awareness campaigns on university campuses or the workplace.

'The pledge is flexible so students can align it with their own worldview'

Taking the pledge is a voluntary one and is flexible, so students can tweak or change the wording to suit their own particular view of what it means to be socially and environmentally responsible. The hope is that the pledge will stay in their minds throughout their working lives, and that they will therefore have a collective positive impact on society. Even if only a fraction of those taking the pledge stick to it for the rest of their lives, they could make a real difference. It is an example that could be followed throughout the world.

• *For more information, contact Neil Wollman, GPA, MC Box 135, Manchester College, 604 E. College Ave., North Manchester, IN 46962, USA (e-mail: NJWollman@manchester.edu; web: http://www.manchester.edu/academic/programs/departments/peace_studies/files/gpa.htm). Downloadable forms and other resources are available online.*

Downloading children's stories to save time for busy parents

Summarised from information on the Storycircus website (www.storycircus.com).

A new project offers parents the opportunity to download bedtime stories from the internet, saving them time and helping them provide a special treat for their children. Storycircus, who are behind the idea, commission the stories, produce them in a portable, downloadable, easily printable format and then license them to other websites who are trying to attract or support parents. Clients so far have included websites of charities, hospitals, supermarkets and book clubs, and the beneficiaries have been the parents, as they can access the stories for free.

'A parent can freely download and print off a story before leaving work, ready to read it to their child at home'

The target audience is parents who don't always have time to get new books out of the library, or can't continually pay for new books, and particularly those who have busy working lives. Through this scheme, a parent can freely download and print off a story before leaving work, ready to read it to their child at home. Or a mother with several children who is unable to leave the house can find another way of keeping them entertained until the rain stops. Even if the family is on holiday, hundreds of miles from any English-language bookshops, a suitable bedtime story can still be found, downloaded and printed within minutes.

Reading to children has long been considered crucial both in terms of fostering parent-child relations and with regard to improving literacy and encouraging reading as an activity. As a supplement to traditional childhood favourites, downloadable stories could prove a real success, particularly as many of them will be brand new and unpublished elsewhere. Other sites offer

6 Blackstock Mews, London N4 2BT, UK (rhino@dial.pipex.com), 2002, 300pp, ISBN 0 948826 59 2

a similar service, with Kidszip (www.kidszip.com), where a subscription entitles you to a number of stories each month, and ABCtales (www.ABCTales.com), where it is free to submit stories and poems, and to read other people's.

• *For more information, contact Storycircus, 106b Shakespeare Walk, London N16 8TA (tel: 020 7275 7000; web: www.storycircus.com).*

• *Also see www.Kidszip.com, www.ABCtales.com and www.youngABCtales.com*

Individual private investment in college students

Eric Simpson

Rather than relying on banks and federal funds to offer student loans to college students, we can privatise this process by giving individuals the opportunity to directly invest in individual students and their educational financing. The way to do this may be by centralising a small company that publishes student information on a web site for potential investors to select from, and which might also handle arbitration issues.

'The student would have to 'sell' his or her potential'

From the student's side, this might not be much different subjectively than existing structures through banks and the federal student loan programme. The main difference, however, might be that the student must 'sell' his or her potential for completing an educational criteria and integrating into the workforce in such a way as to promise repayment of the loan, with interest, in a timely manner.

From the investor's side, risk is balanced by the opportunity to choose his or her own investment. The investor is contributing directly to the economic and social future of his community, and might be rewarded through some sort of tax incentive that equals or exceeds the marginal profit of his educational investment.

• *Eric Simpson (e-mail: ericjamz@aol.com). Eric is a freelance writer, and office clerk, living in Lawrence, Kansas.*

Hotel retreats improve pupil exam results

Summarised from an article by Glen Owen, entitled 'Three-star hotel retreat improves pupil exam scores', in the Times (May 13th 2002). Additional information from TNT magazine (www.tntmagazine.com) and the BBC website (www.bbc.co.uk).

A school in South Yorkshire sends its pupils to a three-star hotel for short breaks before they take their GCSE exams (aged 16), and has seen the number of pupils attaining grades from A* to C rise from 12 per cent in 1997 to 36 per cent in 2001. The break at the hotel includes motivational talks, revision workshops and advice on controlling exam nerves and stress, as well as allowing the pupils a chance for some much needed relaxation. It may well be the latter which is the key to the scheme's success, for the UK education system is now a stressful place to learn, with well over 105 exams currently possible between the ages of five and 18.

'The pupils soak up the rarefied atmosphere and are inspired to perform to a higher level'

The headteacher of Wombwell High School, Irene Dalton, attributes the success of the away-breaks to two other reasons. Firstly, that because the hotel is posh, and the school is not, it "lets [the children] know I think the world of them" and, secondly, that the pupils soak up the rarefied atmosphere and are inspired to perform to a higher level. When combined with the relaxing nature of the hotel breaks and the important revision advice given over the days there, these factors make the scheme an appropriate and effective use of the school's resources.

Other schools have introduced different measures to combat both exam stress and also classroom aggression. St Silas' Primary School in Toxteth in Liverpool has introduced aromatherapy foot and hand massages, and also distributes lavender-soaked tissues to help reduce aggression and stress. The school's scheme also includes a 'quiet place' (a converted classroom) where pupils can wind down and cope with any troublesome situations. The children are also taught relaxation techniques and how to talk about problems as part of the programme. The school's learning mentor, Kate Cassim, says that the initiative has meant that "the children are a lot calmer and it's raised their self-esteem". As well as giving the pupils an atmosphere freer from anxiety and stress, they also learn valuable lessons for the strains of later life.

6 Blackstock Mews, London N4 2BT, UK (rhino@dial.pipex.com), 2002, 300pp, ISBN 0 948826 59 2

An Institute of Simple Learning

Michael Wood

Humankind has produced a lot of 'knowledge'. This includes the common sense wisdom we pick up in everyday life, the more structured visions of the natural and social sciences and mathematics, the arts, and knowledge of the engineering of a multitude of different artifacts. Much of this knowledge is produced by professional researchers, and then packaged and taught in the courses run by educational institutions. The amount of knowledge being created and disseminated by this process is increasing fast. (I'm referring to knowledge as a sort of substance just for convenience; the argument is essentially the same if you view knowledge as a process, or a competence, or any other convenient metaphor.)

There are some fairly obvious criteria by which we can judge how well this system is working. The teaching should be efficient in the sense that learners are generally successful in learning the knowledge. The knowledge produced by the researchers should be judged by its power: the capacity of the artifacts produced to get us to the moon or abolish disease; the extent to which the knowledge tells us the real purpose of life, or the whole truth and nothing but the truth in any area of inquiry.

There is, however, another obvious criterion which tends to fall down the gap between the creators and the disseminators. This is the simplicity of the knowledge: how easy is it to learn and use? Other things being equal, ideas that are easy, and perhaps even fun, to absorb and implement, are obviously preferable to those that are not.

To a large extent simplicity is a substitute (a competitor in marketspeak) for education. If knowledge is simple and fun, the necessity to teach and to assess to check compliance, is much reduced. People will just pick things up as and when they need to or feel like it. This is the extreme scenario: there is obviously a continuum from here to the current situation of viewing learning as hard and nasty work which can only be done under direction and pressure from teachers and assessments systems.

> ## 'Ideally, knowledge would be simplified as far as possible so that the amount of education needed is reduced to a minimum'

In an ideal world, knowledge would be simplified as far as possible so that the amount of education (in the sense of teaching and assessment) needed is reduced to a minimum – or a given amount of education can take people further.

Institute for Social Inventions, £15 subs, £17 from abroad by credit card, tel London 020 7359 8391

Are we living in such an ideal world, or are there opportunities to simplify knowledge further? I believe there are enormous opportunities, many of them relating to the curricula of secondary schools and university courses. This is the area where the interactions between the creators of the knowledge, the disseminators (schools and colleges), and the users (you and I, businesses, and so on) are weakest, so there is little natural market to correct imbalances and idiocies. Let's look at a few examples.

There are many opportunities to simplify mathematics, which is important because mathematics is an essential aspect of so many other branches of knowledge. Particularly with computers, trial and error and simulation methods (build a computer model, run it, and see what happens) are far easier, and often more powerful, than conventional algebraic approaches. This is a particularly powerful possibility with statistics.

Notation systems and concepts can also be redesigned to make them simpler for the uninitiated to appreciate. As a trivial example, the functions ex [exp(x)] and log x on most calculators are two functions for analysing growth at a constant proportional rate. They appear in formulae used in many contexts: eg biology, economics, finance, and reliability analysis. Few people understand much about these functions because this understanding requires a thorough understanding of calculus. However, by slightly redefining the concepts, it is possible to provide a direct link to common sense and bypass logarithms and calculus completely. The revised functions are by no means trivial: they require some hard thought, but nothing like as much as mastering calculus.

'Some fields of learning are complex but useless; they can be simplified by the simple expedient of ignoring them'

There are similar opportunities in other areas. Some strains of sociological theory are expressed in obscure jargon: this could be simplified by removing or changing the jargon. Designing language and notation systems is important in all areas: I remember reading recently of the problems children have with the biological meaning of the word fruit: a runner bean is a biological fruit but not a fruit in the sense of ordinary language. Why not avoid the confusion by inventing another word for the biological concept? Some fields of learning are complex but useless; they can be simplified by the simple expedient of ignoring them.

The English language is another area which might benefit from simplification. Instead of subjecting children to endless hours learning the arbitrary conventions of grammar, spelling and punctuation, why not agree to relax the rules that don't add anything in terms of clarity? I believe there is a tendency

6 Blackstock Mews, London N4 2BT, UK (rhino@dial.pipex.com), 2002, 300pp, ISBN 0 948826 59 2

for languages to get simpler as they evolve: this tendency should be encouraged, not resisted as the education system inevitably does.

I am not sure of the exact extent of the possibilities for simplification. Nobody is, because little effort is devoted to exploring it. Mathematics is invented by mathematicians, for whom, of course, mathematics is the supreme example of simplicity: because they understand it! So the suggestion that the subject could be simplified is, from their point of view, too silly to be worth considering. The same is doubtless true for other areas.

There are obvious and powerful vested interests in preserving the current state of affairs. The subject experts and researchers want to remain experts, and their expertise is likely to be reduced if simpler approaches are discovered. Research in simple areas that anyone can understand is most unlikely to attract the same prestige and money as research in an esoteric area understood by few. Teachers and educational institutions have similar interests in keeping things hard and unpleasant.

There are aspects of life where powerful forces have acted in favour of simplicity. Software designers and makers of documentary programmes on television need to appeal directly to their customers, so they strive hard to make their products as user-friendly as possible. Similarly, manufacturers of cars make their products easy to use (but not to maintain and repair). The difficulties mainly arise in the arena of academic research and education.

In the academic world, simplicity from the learners' point of view is just not on the agenda. It would probably be seen as 'lowering standards'. Does this matter? Yes it does, because of the enormous amount of wasted effort, lost opportunities, and the estrangement of academic knowledge from the people.

'Millions of students are spending years memorising mathematical formulae that are never useful'

Millions of students, all over the world, are spending years memorising mathematical formulae that they never understand in enough detail to be useful, and trying to use academic frameworks which are almost designed to make naive users look stupid. As well as wasting time, this means that opportunities for real progress are lost. There is now so much knowledge out there that without simplification the system will grind to a halt, because there is not enough time to both learn the background and advance the subject. The Einsteins of the next generation need to take every opportunity to simplify things; the education system should be helping this process, not hindering it.

To give a small example of the sort of silliness that half-understood theories can lead to, take the case of a medical researcher who has discovered that one treatment for a disease led to nine out of 12 patients recovering, whereas a second treatment led to six out of 12 recovering. In common sense terms, the first treatment looks better (75 per cent recovery versus 50 per cent for the second treatment) but the sample is small so it would obviously be a good idea to collect more evidence. This is basically what a formal statistical analysis, properly interpreted, would tell us.

Novices (and even some statistics teachers) have a tendency to do the statistical sums correctly but then misinterpret the answer. The statistical test (Fisher exact test using a five per cent significance level) tests the hypothesis that there is no difference between the treatments: the conclusion is that there is insufficient evidence to reject this hypothesis. This is often – incorrectly – taken as accepting the hypothesis that there is no difference.

Unless one is blinded by statistics, this is obviously a silly conclusion. We find that one treatment has a recovery rate of 75 per cent, another has a recovery rate of 50 per cent; we then do a statistical test and find there is no difference! The fact that many people, including good students who would pass their courses comfortably, do not notice this contradiction indicates that the statistical ideas are not integrated into their intuitive view of the world. As such, they are likely to lead to essentially arbitrary decisions, and are unlikely to be a satisfactory basis for further thinking. Statistics will remain as something odd that you do to your results to convince people they are right, not part of a mental toolkit to help come to terms with an unpredictable world.

It is a serious mistake to attribute the problem to the silliness of the less than expert statistician, or the inefficiency of the education system. The problem should be attributed to the user-unfriendliness of statistics. The solution is the redesign of statistics, not more statistics teachers and nastier penalties for failure to absorb the message.

'An Institute would counter the pernicious influence of academic complexification'

My suggestion, then, is to set up an Institute of Simple Learning to counter the pernicious influence of academic complexification. The aim would be to develop and disseminate simple, but powerful, ideas.

This is not something I have thought out in detail. I would welcome comments and suggestions. Initially I envisage it would be some sort of web-based discussion forum or journal. A reviewing system to differentiate the useful ideas from the useless ones would be necessary eventually, but this would have to be sufficiently flexible to take account of the fact that most good ideas start out seeming crazy. Whatever happens, the institute would never, ever, dish out certificates for mastering any aspect of simple learning. This should be as enjoyable and effortless as possible.

• *Michael Wood is a university lecturer living in the south of England; 7 Beacon Square, Emsworth, Hants PO10 7HU (e-mail: mickofemsworth@yahoo.co.uk).*

6 Blackstock Mews, London N4 2BT, UK (rhino@dial.pipex.com), 2002, 300pp, ISBN 0 948826 59 2

Citywide record attempt on learning languages

Summarised from information on the Birmingham Learning Day website (www.bgfl.org/services/learnday/).

As part of Birmingham's Learning Day on March 21st 2002, the council encouraged people to learn five phrases in a new language as part of the biggest simultaneous learning activity ever. Participants were able to choose from 22 languages spoken in Birmingham, including Somali, Vietnamese and sign language, and learn how to say 'hello', 'please', 'thank you', 'goodbye' and 'Birmingham is a great place to learn'. The idea is to encourage learning at all levels, show the city as a 'learning organism' and foster understanding between the many different people who live in the city. It is particularly important in Birmingham, where some schools have up to 39 languages spoken and 95 per cent of pupils with English as a second language.

The record attempt took place at 10.10am for 10 minutes. Each 'class' in the city had to nominate a co-ordinator who recited the phrases; these were then repeated by the learners, and then repeated to each other to show they had learnt the phrase. The co-ordinator recorded the event, noted all those present, confirmed that the phrases had been learnt, and returned the form to the organisers. In this way, the people of Birmingham created a new world record.

'Discounts on coffee for those learning Italian'

The day included a simultaneous learning event in Victoria Square and across the city, a website where people could hear the phrases spoken in each language, discounts on coffee for all those learning Italian, and a 'Pledge to learn' form to be filled in. The latter is again intended to promote the learning ideal, with people encouraged to register their pledge and see it through in the next year. It is all part of the council's attempts to get people learning, and amassing knowledge, be that at home, at work, at school, online or in an adult education class.

• *For more on the day, and the city's learning activities, contact Muhammad Khan at Birmingham City Council (tel: 0121 303 2277; fax: 0121 464 0333; e-mail muhammad_khan@birmingham.gov.uk; web: www.bgfl.org/services/ learnday/).*

Portable fellowships for graduate students

Summarised from an interview, entitled 'Post Scarcity Prophet', in Reason magazine (December 2001 issue), monitored for the Global Ideas Bank by Roger Knights.

In an interview, economist Paul Romer mentioned an idea that could help graduate and postgraduate students in their research. He suggested they could have portable fellowships, which could be used to pay for training in any field of science or engineering at any institution of the student's choice. This would enable the students to break free of what Romer calls the "sometimes parochial research interests of university professors". In essence, it would help students to find courses and programmes that are suited and shaped for their research and career interests, rather than having their research moulded to fit with a particular professor's interest.

'Students could pick and choose supervisors and tutors'

The students could also pick and choose supervisors and tutorials from all over the country, allowing a range of expertise and views to be communicated to them. Romer's idea also equally extends to students in arts subjects, where particular universities are often known for having a particular focus or way of looking at things. To gain a variety of perspectives through the use of a portable fellowship, essentially a tailored funding scheme, would both benefit the students and enrich their work.

Student community service instead of tuition fees

Alex Jacobs

Summary

Idea: To replace student tuition fees with a student community service. This would save the government a lot of money, improve the economy and social capital, and would facilitate social inclusion of both students and locals. It would also ground student courses in reality, as students become more aware of problems that are prevalent in society and develop more of a social

6 Blackstock Mews, London N4 2BT, UK (rhino@dial.pipex.com), 2002, 300pp, ISBN 0 948826 59 2

conscience. Students would also be geared more towards problem-solving rather than pure abstract debate. More senior students can run the system in order to gain management skills and to cut down on organisation costs, enabling the system to be self-administrating and self-policing to a large extent.

Justification

There is much debate and uncertainty about the future of our universities. We are stuck in the middle of an argument which has polarised into two points of view, both of which completely miss the point. Fees or no fees? The proponents of fees point out that university 'adds economic value' to the student and so they can get a better job and earn more money. This is a private gain so they should contribute to it. They tend to play down the idea that the education of our public contributes in both monetary and non-monetary ways to society. Opponents of fees point out that it is very hard for students to get by, even when they don't have to pay fees. They tend to play up the idea that education contributes to society and so students shouldn't have to contribute.

The fact is that our education system fails to contribute to society and in many ways is plainly detrimental to it. People are right to criticise university as being too abstract and for teaching pointless jargon for its own sake. Most subjects treat the idea of social responsibility as if it is some kind of utopian ideal that is nowhere to be found in society. Some display utter contempt to the notion (economics for example). Other subjects, usually science based, claim that it bears no relevance to the course at all. However, social issues affect us all and we collectively have responsibility for them.

'Instead of fees, students have to do a few hours community service each week'

The solution is simple. I thought of this while at university but didn't really know what to do with the idea. Instead of fees, students have to do a few hours community service every week. Firstly it will save the government money in many ways, maybe even exceeding the amount it pays out in tuition fees. Students can visit older members of the community, they can work in homeless shelters, participate in urban regeneration and youth programmes. If they want they could use their subject as a basis of reference. For example architects and landscapers could regenerate local areas. However, one of the most valuable aspects of the scheme would be to give students experience of real life problems that don't immediately and obviously relate to their subject. All subjects and disciplines are interlinked and it is the challenge of the scheme (and indeed life) to discover how you can apply what you are learning in the university to the practical world around you. For too long university has been an ivory tower with students who are involved with the local community as the exception.

I am under no illusion that this scheme would run smoothly all the time. There are bound to be logistical and legal problems but not insurmountable ones. I also take the point that not everyone feels the same measure of social responsibility. However, it is something that is part of human experience, that humans are capable of and consequently deserves to be explored. Those who have problems with contributing (ideological or otherwise) can treat it purely as a work experience venture. The more senior students can get management and administrative experience by actually running the system. There could also be a creative social innovation team or even just a more localised website like this one for suggestions for local problems and new schemes.

We complain about our services and the understaffing of the social component of our existence, yet we are sitting on an army of thousands, many of whom would be more than willing and all of whom would gain from the process. Ideally this system would be a microcosm of the world around it but at the same time integrated into its surroundings. It would be far more experimental and dynamic than its surroundings, and therefore more able and flexible to come up with solutions. What better ideal for a system of education could there be?

'Students challenging their surroundings and testing the foundations of the world around them'

No doubt it would challenge much that we as adults have taken for granted, but it would then be up to us to explain and justify our present habits and actions, or change them. A system of education should involve a degree of students challenging their surroundings and testing the foundations of the world around them. Unfortunately it seems that this is the one thing that our education system is trying to stamp out. Education is more and more being seen as a one-way dissemination of information rather than the complex two way interplay that it really should be.

The benefits and effects of this system are endless and impossible to catalogue here. I feel that the more one thinks about the system, the more benefits and applications appear. I really believe in this idea and I hope that it sparks some interest.

• *Alex Jacobs is a TEFL teacher in London (e-mail: alexjacobs@hotmail.com).*

6 Blackstock Mews, London N4 2BT, UK (rhino@dial.pipex.com), 2002, 300pp, ISBN 0 948826 59 2

Life skills to be taught in school

Marc Steele

In high school in America, you take Driver's Education (at least most people do). Well, they don't really teach you anything, except for maybe the rules of the road, which are pretty evident anyway. But what about the important things involved with automobiles, such as changing tyres? They don't teach you to do that. Let's have a class to teach high school kids about things like that. I'm not just talking car maintenance, I'm talking about all those things everyone expects you to learn on your own. Things that you encounter in life, and most of the time have no idea about. Things like basic first aid, changing a tire, doing your taxes, things like that.

'Teaching people to check oil in their car as well as essay writing techniques'

We could call this class 'Life Skills'. It seems trivial I know, but keep this example in mind. There was an old couple that lived not too far away from me. They used to pick my sister up from school when my mother couldn't. Well sadly, the man died leaving the woman to herself. This was a problem. The man had done everything for the woman. He drove her, he took her to the doctors, he made the appointments, he paid the bills, he did the taxes, he did *everything*. Granted they may have got married in a time where it was socially expected for the man to do everything for the woman. Well, times have changed greatly since then, and shouldn't we teach people to check the oil in their car as well as complicated mathematics and great essay writing techniques? Just a thought....

• *Marc Steele is a student at Elon University (www.elon.edu).*

Teachers resource pack on non-violent conflict resolution

Summarised from material submitted to the Global Ideas Bank by John Rowley, the co-ordinator of the proposal outlined below.

A new proposal from the Gandhi Foundation aims to create a resource pack for teachers on the theories and practices of non-violent conflict resolution. At present, there is no formal provision for training teachers about this subject, a void which the pack intends to fill. The Foundation believes that teaching students how to manage and resolve conflicts in their own lives is crucial to their evolving political and emotional literacy, and to their sense of moral and social responsibility. In a world in which conflicts beget conflicts, and which is beset by divisions, such an educational tool to help students with their own personal conflicts, big and small, is timely.

The pack will aim to:
• describe the key concepts underlying conflict resolution, conciliation and negotiation
• challenge students to examine their own 'values and dispositions' (ie the sources of conflict) and their perceptions of the values and dispositions of others, enabling them to recognise differences (and similarities)

'Demonstrate how conflict emerges from despair brought about by powerlessness'

• demonstrate how anger and conflict often emerge from a despair brought about by powerlessness to change one's life, and that this powerlessness is a consequence of particular social, historical and political contexts
• offer a range of skills and techniques that will enable students to resolve conflicts or negotiate themselves, as they prepare to enter a society in which competition is celebrated at every level and in every sphere
• provide case studies and exercises of direct significance to the students' own lives, families and friends
• show the benefits of managing conflicts and disagreements constructively, be they psychological, social, economic or political

'The pack also focuses on famous figures such as Gandhi, Martin Luther King and Nelson Mandela'

The pack will also look at particular figures famous for their contribution to non-violent conflict resolution, such as Gandhi, Martin Luther King, Nelson Mandela, Aung San Suu Kyi and Lech Walesa. It will also look at organisations and individuals in the UK and abroad who practice negotiation and conciliation, and what lessons can be drawn from their work. It is hoped that the resources pack will be used within the current citizenship requirements on the National Curriculum. Non-violent conflict resolution teaching in schools could certainly be a step in helping the nation's youth become better citizens.

• *For more information on the proposal, contact John Rowley, 73 Carysfort Road, London N16 9AD (tel: 020 7249 4471; e-mail: johnrowley@email.com).*

6 Blackstock Mews, London N4 2BT, UK (rhino@dial.pipex.com), 2002, 300pp, ISBN 0 948826 59 2

Kidscard – a safer, easier system for kids to buy things at school

Kirk Haynes

The 'Kidscard' would be a type of 'credit card' for children, that can have small amounts of money downloaded from their parents' computer. This would cover the costs of school supplies, school lunches, school items etc; it would mean that schoolchildren would not have to carry money, and would not go without if they lost any money they had.

This system would obviously need to be tightly regulated, with the card only being accepted in particular outlets (school canteen, etc) when a child gives a password or code. It could also eliminate the problem of bullying for money – teachers and staff would instantly know if someone was using someone else's card.

Some schools in Las Vegas allow parents to pay for their kids lunches via the website www.myLunchMoney.com with their credit cards, again denying the possibilities of bullying (Newsweek, March 11th 2002).

• *Kirk Haynes (e-mail: havasukirk@yahoo.com). Kirk is a single parent of two children from Lake Havasu City, Arizona.*

Parent mentoring for new and young parents

Philip Averay

'Children do not come with their own instruction manual'

I would like to see a linking of new parents, from any walk of life with mature couples who have already 'successfully' raised their child(ren) to adulthood. The issue is that often new parents either do not have good family support or good parenting role models to assist them with the wonderful challenge and awesome responsibility of raising children. Unfortunately, children do not come with their own instruction manual. The idea is that new parents would be linked with these mentors (experienced parents) to consult with until their child is an adult.

Fortunate people have their own parents to help them, to let them know what is normal for children at various ages. Even the small things that happen in a child's normal development can cause considerable concern and stress to first-time parents. The mentors would be able to reassure these parents about what's normal and what is not normal. I would hope that life long friendships would develop between the two families. This would be a particularly good arrangement for new parents who are either separated from their parents by distance or whose parents are unable to provide this support for whatever reason. New parents could perhaps be linked with mentors through the hospital as part of the discharge planning after the birth of their child, or through their doctor even at the early stages of their pregnancy.

• *Philip Averay (e-mail: p_averay@hotmail.com). Philip lives and works as a social worker in the beautiful city of Adelaide in South Australia, which holds an annual festival of ideas.*

Limited credit card to teach adolescents money-management

Summarised from an e-mail to the Global Ideas Bank from 'Laurena4efas' (January 3rd 2002).

My idea is for a 'financial cushion card' to help adolescents learn how to manage money better. Giving one's offspring a credit card 'for emergencies' does not work, because their view of what is an emergency tends to differ somewhat from their parents' view (desperate need for that latest sweater, urgent case of CD lack, etc). Plus, these cards always have a substantial upper limit, so there is no real control of how much can be spent for a 'real' emergency (being without food, somewhere to stay, petrol, etc far from home).

'A savings card for money that the adolescent gets once a month'

The idea, then, is that there is a 'Savings Card' for money. It's like a credit card but only contains $50 or $100. When it's used up, it's gone. If they don't use it, they can keep it, like a savings account for rainy days. The young person gets one of these a month. If emergencies arise, it would be used. But if the young person is canny, he or she will live within their means and use the card to save for a downpayment on a car or a holiday. It can even be non-transferable in the sense that, like an ATM, a PIN is needed to use it. If lost or stolen, the parent can transfer funds from that card to a new one.

6 Blackstock Mews, London N4 2BT, UK (rhino@dial.pipex.com), 2002, 300pp, ISBN 0 948826 59 2

This idea combines the principle of setting limits without nagging or constant meddling (neither of which are effective). A good coach gets an athlete to repeat what does work and to cease doing what doesn't. The Savings Card would be a remotely-operated incentive for doing both. And the fact that a new card is given monthly would enable the teenagers to learn swiftly from last month's debacle of having great new clothes but no petrol to go to the party to show them off. So the next month, which brings a new card (and a clean slate), they would remember the hard lesson they just learned and show more self-control.

Kids teach their elders internet skills, and learn history in return

This idea was submitted to the Global Ideas Bank by Professor Edna Aphek from Israel. She is a linguist and educational researcher, who specialises in the introduction of computer literacy with a particular interest in educational and social systems. She has designed and implemented virtual learning environments and partnerships for children and senior citizens and has published stories and poetry for children and adults.

A study in reciprocity: bridging the digital divide

This is an ongoing programme initiated by Professor Edna Aphek and carried out in several schools in Israel. The programme aims to reduce the intergenerational gap and the digital divide by having elementary and middle school children tutor senior citizens computer and internet skills and at the same time write together with the seniors a digital 'mini e-book' based on a chapter from the senior's personal history.

The rationale of the programme is based upon the following assumptions:

• The new technologies have created a new situation, previously unknown in human history, wherein young children master a skill much needed by adults in general and seniors in particular.

'In the new high-tech world, children speak the language of IT as their mother tongue'

• In the new high-tech world, where children speak the new language of Information Technology as their mother tongue, it would be most fitting to put their mastery to good use and train them to teach this new language to senior citizens, those unacquainted with the language of the computer and the internet.

• There is a dire need for preserving knowledge at risk of disappearance. Precious knowledge is stored in the heads of senior citizens. Many seniors are 'walking treasures' of history, of folk art (their art work) and of music which is about to disappear.

• *Edna Aphek (e-mail: aphekdr@netision.net.il).*

A 'creative' history course

Raymond Spada

Offer an elective course in historical studies similar to creative writing and fine arts with an emphasis on 'What-if' alternative outcomes in any historical field of interest. This approach could reveal why our ancestors came up with the innovations they did to meet the challenges of their times – challenges that are very similar to the ones which we are facing ourselves – and offer approaches to incorporate into modern-day societal solutions.

'To mine 5,000 years of history as an idea bank and an idea generator'

To mine 5,000 years of accumulated history as an idea bank *and* an idea generator would reinvigorate history class and make it a more palatable subject to students. It would also reinforce the adage 'There is nothing new under the sun', allowing students to gain a wider sense of social and historical perspective.

• *Raymond Spada (e-mail: rspada@webtv.net). Raymond is a lifelong lover of history from Mount Clemens, Michigan, USA.*

Rename and remake museums with children in mind

Aaron Campbell

Museums often have the best stuff for kids and the worst names. In Chicago where I live, the Museum of Science and Industry just screams 'Please Don't Come Here, You'll Be Bored To Death'. Knowing that a museum is the place that supposedly houses the Muses would help a bit, but the kid translation of

6 Blackstock Mews, London N4 2BT, UK (rhino@dial.pipex.com), 2002, 300pp, ISBN 0 948826 59 2

museum is 'Place where I can't touch anything and can't sit down'.

'Children should be consulted in the construction, layout and content of museums'

I suggest to all ideas people that they go to their local museums and come up with some new names. Alternatively, we can instruct our kids that museums are full of magical Muses. Furthermore, kids should have more say in how museums are made and run. Since children are some of the most likely visitors, they should really be consulted in their construction, layout and content.
• *Aaron Campbell (e-mail: aaron@merc.net). Aaron is an innovator from Chicago, and a regular contributor to the Global Ideas Bank.*

Creative tutor network to improve children's self-esteem and positivity

Summarised from information sent to the Global Ideas Bank by Margie McGregor, the founder of Creative Inspirations (www.creative-inspirations.co.uk).

A new nationwide project in the UK aims to encourage children to choose a creative interest which they have longed to take up. This will be done through a network of 'creative tutors', who have been appropriately vetted and trained, who will build a relationship with the child, allowing them to develop a positive, idividual identity. The core principle that lies behind the idea is that failure to achieve a positive identity, to have a necessary level of self-esteem, can lead to many social and behavioral problems later on.

'When the child and adult share an interest, the focus is on the creativity, not the personalities'

The informal network of creative tutors, or, more accurately perhaps, creative mentors, can be used to find the right activity or interest they enjoy in their area, channelling their energy in positive, fulfilling directions. The key to the scheme working effectively is for the child and adult to share the same interest, allowing a focus on the creativity rather than personalities. Margie McGregor, who founded and co-ordinates the project, which is called 'Creative Inspirations', writes that 'the most important gift we can give to our children is to set them free emotionally, encouraging them towards their own goals, not our own'. With careful matching of activities and partnerships, this creative network could have a real impact on children's lives.

• *For more information, contact Margie McGregor, Creative Inspirations, West Wing, Hordley House, Wootton, Woodstock, Oxon OX20 1EP (tel: 01993 812765; e-mail: margie@creative-inspirations.co.uk; web: www.creative-inspirations.co.uk).*

Parents brought into school to administer punishments

Summarised from an item, entitled 'Come in to hit your children', in the Guardian Editor section (February 8th 2002), monitored for the Global Ideas Bank by Yvonne Ackroyd.

A school in New Zealand has got around the regulations banning teachers from administering corporal punishment by inviting the parents of the child to come in and do it. The small, private Christian primary school in Masterton has been calling in parents to physically discipline students because of the 'biblical requirements' for discipline. The acting school principal, Eeuwe Huizinga, said that all parents were in agreement with the policy, and that it was only used in severe cases of disobedience and blasphemy. The Education Review Office in New Zealand recently confirmed that the school *is* complying with regulations, despite corporal punishment having been banned in schools since 1990. Whether one agrees with corporal punishment or not, the scheme certainly encourages parents to get involved directly with their children's education, and to take responsibility for their behaviour.

6 Blackstock Mews, London N4 2BT, UK (rhino@dial.pipex.com), 2002, 300pp, ISBN 0 948826 59 2

RELATIONSHIPS

Indirect complimenting: improving relationships and self-esteem

Anna Carraway

Beyond what is needed for basic survival, what I believe to be most crucial to human happiness is the health and quality of interpersonal relationships. How, then, can we foster happy and mutually beneficial relationships with those we care for? Well, one vital portion of this endeavour should include active and regular attempts to edify and encourage our loved ones, thus spurring them on toward greater character and higher achievements.

> ## 'Most of us have heard our parents compliment us directly a thousand times'

In order to give confidence to our loved ones we often compliment and encourage directly, through either spoken or written words. While this can be a most effective method of edification, it carries inherent and inevitable problems. Most of us have heard our parents, friends, or spouses compliment and encourage us a thousand times directly, and nine hundred of those times it has not penetrated or been effectively absorbed into our souls. Their words are inhibited by the common understanding that it is matter-of-course to compliment face to face, especially to a loved one. They may truly mean what they say, but then again, they may not. Oftentimes we know they compliment us to our faces, then turn around and contradict themselves to others. Their efforts to edify are ineffective, we are not helped, and the relationship is not nurtured.

But what if we happen to overhear a friend generously compliment us to another? Is it not more flattering and effective in encouraging us? I believe so. Thus, it is my proposal that the healthy growth of relationships and individuals in general would significantly benefit from thoughtful, consistent efforts to compliment and encourage our loved ones indirectly – to say to our siblings, "Isn't Mom a great cook?" while our mothers toil in the kitchen, and to declare to the brother of a child we are caring for, "Wow! Your big sister is so good at picking up her toys!" Our loved ones would not only feel better about themselves, they would desire to work even harder to please us and to achieve even greater goals. This indirect edification would not only foster individuals of greater inner strength and motivation, it would nurture the growth of healthy and mutually beneficial relationships. People would be happier and healthier, thus limiting crimes motivated by insecurity or unmet emotional needs, and encouraging widespread growth and advancement through more confident individuals – the world would be a better place.

In pondering needed global improvements and modifications, relationships should not be neglected. Truly loving and nurturing other people should be of utmost importance to all of us – it is clear that many of the world's problems are caused by individuals who either do not know how to love others or have never been truly loved themselves. Let us work fervently to protect and nurture the world's greatest asset: people. Let us learn how to effectively encourage and inspire others around us.

• *Anna Carraway is a student at Elon University in North Carolina, USA (www.elon.edu).*

A mediator in video rental stores to defuse arguments

Summarised from an item in TNT magazine (www.tntmagazine.com), monitored for the Global Ideas Bank by Yvonne Ackroyd.

A video rental shop in Bayswater in London has introduced a 'movie mediator' to prevent couples rowing over which film (or type of film) to take home. Blockbuster commissioned a relationship psychologist, Elaine Spurr, to research the issue, and she discovered that almost half of all renters could not agree on a film to hire when part of a couple or group. She also discovered that women, though using flirting techniques to get what they want, were more flexible and accommodating in the video negotiation process, while men simply tend to resort to sulking.

'Men and women employ different tatics to get their choice of movie'

The mediators will offer tips and advice on the shop floor to try and prevent the, often gender-based, battles. Dr Spurr says that conflict can arise because "men and women employ different tactics to get their choice of movie ...These tactics reflect the gender divide in tyipcal styles of communication". The mediator scheme could help calm these conflicts a little, by recommending films that both can enjoy and through outlining the benefits of flexibility and compromise. If the scheme is successful in Bayswater, there will be further trials in Birmingham, Bristol, London and Manchester.

6 Blackstock Mews, London N4 2BT, UK (rhino@dial.pipex.com), 2002, 300pp, ISBN 0 948826 59 2

Boomerang Day for returning borrowed items

Submitted to the Global Ideas Bank by Tony Paynter, an unemployed thinker who believes that Brisbane, Australia is the best place on earth.

Set aside one day a year where you search your house for things that aren't yours (ie things that you've borrowed), and that you've neglected to return, such as a brother's golf clubs or a neighbour's lawnmower. And then you return them. It can also be a day to set aside any grievances that might have surrounded the offending item. The day would be called Boomerang Day, for obvious reasons.

'I can't remember who lent it to me'

Marriage by yearly contracts

Panya Covington

A common problem in relationships is the fact that they simply don't last very long in today's society. Here's a possible solution:

What if, instead of marriage as it is today, marriages were year-long contracts between two people? At the end of the year, if both people opt to continue the contract they stay married. If one or both persons decide they don't want to stay together, the contract ends, and both parties go their separate ways. Contracts would normally involve how the income of the year would be divided, what would happen to objects bought during the term of the contract, and anything a premarital contract might include.

'If there are children from the marriage, different provisions would have to be made'

If there are children from the marriage, then different provisions must be made. Generally these would be provided in the original contract, but basic laws surrounding marriage contracts could require that the parents would stay together for a minimum of five years after the latest child's birth and after that period designate a particular parent or person to take care of the child or children. That person would not have to be a relative or a parent, simply someone who would be responsible for caring for the child.

This would prevent divorces by first making them disallowed in a sense, and also the reasons for divorce would vanish because no couple would feel obliged to stay together just because of a formal ceremony. Persons who separated due to changes later in life would also have an easier time.

• *Panya Covington is a senior at Elon University (www.elon.edu), majoring in creative writing and minoring in philosophy.*

Cultural sabbaticals at three periods in life

Shelby Clark

Our various world cultures should encourage each of us to live in another, completely different, culture for a year at least three times in our lives. Another culture could be urban vs. rural, a different ethnicity or a different religion. Our first sabbatical would be just after secondary school (at about age 18). The second would be when we were in mid-career, and the last would be just after we 'retired'. I think a year is about the minimum amount of time needed. It's how long it takes for one to go through the pangs of homesickness (they do it all wrong here), to fully embracing (they do it all wrong back home), to an understanding that we all do it right (and wrong) no matter where we are. We are all human, after all.

'When middle-aged, we have difficulty seeing from others' perspectives'

The age component is also important. When we're young, we have the desire but not the skills to change the world. Learning new perspectives can

6 Blackstock Mews, London N4 2BT, UK (rhino@dial.pipex.com), 2002, 300pp, ISBN 0 948826 59 2

only help. When we're middle aged, we have difficulty seeing from others' perspectives. Such an experience could help us truly become a global community (in the best sense of the phrase, not the worst). And, as elderly, such visits would help us regain the respect we once had for the elder members of our communities, a recognition that they are sages, and thus have wisdom to share (and still to gain).

   • *Shelby Clark (e-mail: sdc@toolcity.net). Shelby is a writer living in Western Pennsylvania who 'hopes and prays for better understanding and respect'.*

Relationship compatibility based on equidistance from an androgynous centre

Aaron Campbell

Barbie and Ken. Tim Robbins and Susan Sarandon. Lyle Lovett and Julia Roberts. Which of these relationships doesn't work? Lyle and Julia broke up soon after getting together, but few people were that shocked. Rather, people were shocked when they got together in the first place. I submit that one could guess far in advance the possible success/failure rate of a given relationship.

   I call it the 'Equidistant from Pat' relationship model. Pat in this case is the exceedingly androgynous character from the Saturday Night Live comedy show in the States. He/She is supposedly androgynous to such an extent that nobody knows if he/she is male or female. Hilarity ensues as she/he interacts with people, suitors, co-workers and family, all trying to figure her/him out.

'Relationships work best if they are between people who are equidistant from an androgynous central point'

Here's the premise: relationships work best if they are between people who are equidistant from Pat as seen through the gender role stereotypes that the couple is subject to in their culture. Suppose you have a relationship between a sports-centric male and a cheerleader. The two may tend to adhere more rigidly to gender stereotypes: males play football and act more chauvinistic while females act more submissive and perhaps over-feminine. While we may lament their lack of flexibility and the pressure they feel to 'fit in' to cultural stereotypes, they may very well end up making a great couple. Equidistant from the stereotypical centre of feminine/masculine roles, they like who they are and what they mean to each other.

On the other end of the spectrum, two people who constantly buck the stereotyping they are subjected to may also be a great match. Tim Robbins (The Player, Bob Roberts, Bull Durham) and Susan Sarandon (Thelma & Louise, Rocky Horror Picture Show, Bull Durham) have been happily together (though not married) for years now. They are also equidistant from Pat, only much closer together on the spectrum than Barbie and Ken. They both cross over the centre quite often, taking on the supposed roles of the other's gender, happily sharing their lives with each other.

'The key is being the same distance from the centre of gender role stereotypes'

The relationships that wouldn't work so well (according to the model) are those that feature partners who aren't equidistant from the centre of gender role stereotypes (androgyny). Julia Roberts (Runaway Bride, Steel Magnolias, Pretty Woman), although a fabulous actress and generally nice person, tends to adhere more to current female gender roles than her former partner Lyle Lovett tended to adhere to his gender roles. He crossed over more than she, bucking the macho stereotypes of his native Texas for more sensitive (closer to Pat) and nurturing behaviour. This would put the point where they met kind of off-centre and cause strain in the relationship.

Though there will be those unhappy at thinking that relationships might be more subtly mathematical than spiritual (and I might agree some of the time), I have found that time and again after closer analysis with my pet theory, the relationships that are the strongest and happiest are those that settle into a happy equidistant zone from the androgynous/non-stereotypical centre.

On further reflection, I also noticed that although the Barbie-Ken type relationship may be stronger than a Barbie-Tim Robbins relationship, it is still generally weaker than the Tim Robbins-Susan Sarandon relationship. This observation centres around the idea that those relationships that had their 'meeting point' nearer to the androgynous centre *and* were equidistant at the same time were healthiest. These ideal relationships bucked the stereotypes, but let each partner have their own version of masculine and feminine behaviour that matched the intensity and flexibility of the other partner.

On a final note, I also noticed that the more central *and* centred the partners were, the smarter and more culturally and politically liberal they were in general, but I might need to do some more field research on that note before churning out any more theories. See for yourself: Take a look at the relationships around you and put them to the test. Do they adhere to local cultural gender roles? Does one partner adhere more than the other? Check and see with the handy 'Equidistant from Pat' theory!

• *Aaron Campbell (e-mail: aaron@merc.net). Aaron is a writer and innovator from Chicago, USA.*

6 Blackstock Mews, London N4 2BT, UK (rhino@dial.pipex.com), 2002, 300pp, ISBN 0 948826 59 2

Withholding sex to get running water

Summarised from a Reuters item, entitled 'Women Cut Off Sex to Get Water' (August 14th 2001). This article was first read in the Heads Up e-newsletter (see http://gocreate.com). Additional material from an article by Suzan Fraser, entitled 'No water turn-on means sex turnoff', in the Seattle Times (August 15th 2001), monitored for the Global Ideas Bank by Roger Knights.

A group of women in the village of Sirt in Turkey have banned their husbands from the bedroom in an effort to get running water connected. For several months, the women have had to carry water jugs over long distances, after filling them up at a fountain. Originally, the protest started as a joke, but the few dozen women made the protest real, having been inspired by a 1983 film about women using similar methods to complain about their hard labour. The strategy seems to have had an effect, because the husbands petitioned the government to fix the ailing 27-year-old water system, even offering their own services to speed up the process.

'The men came to him and appealed for pipes and other materials, offering their own labour for free'

Mehmet Carpraz, the local governor in the area, said the men had come to him and appealed for pipes and other materials, offering their own labour for free. As Carpraz makes evident, the issue is now at the top of the priority list for the men in the village: "The men came to us and said 'Please help us, please understand our situation'". The government has since agreed to give the men of the villages enough pipes to tap a nearby water source. The wait may not be over for the men just yet, though: the more hardline of the women have pledged to continue their protest until water comes out of their taps. Water is additionally important to Muslims because Islam says that followers should bathe themselves after sex, so the relationship of the boycott to the problem is not as obtuse as might first appear.

The sex boycott is not a new idea, but targeted in this specific way it seems to be particularly effective. The concept first appeared in Aristophanes' play *Lysistrata*, in which the women of Athens went on a sex strike to coerce their husbands into bringing an end to the Peloponnesian War by achieving peace with Sparta. It worked in that case as well.

State-funded marriage ambassadors to halt rising divorce

Summarised from an article by Peg Tyre, entitled 'Giving Lessons in Love', in Newsweek (February 18th 2002), monitored for the Global Ideas Bank by Roger Knights.

The state of Oklahoma has introduced special marriage counsellors and lecturers for couples having relationship difficulties, in an attempt to lower the divorce rate. Oklahoma has the second-highest divorce rate in America, so the state has introduced a range of measures to try and halt the trend. The main change in emphasis is from people paying marriage counsellors to sort out their problems to the state funding programmes under which people learn about conflict resolution, communication and other relationship issues. The US administration, which has consistently emphasised the importance of marriage for society, has recently put aside $100 million for similar programmes all around the country.

'The ambassadors were paid to give talks and rallies on marriage'

The state hired Les and Leslie Parrott as 'marriage ambassadors', paying them $250,000 a year to give talks and rallies on relationships and marriage on student campuses, as well as setting up a research project on the importance of marriage. Other marriage counsellors in Oklahoma have been trained to offer a workshop called the 'Prevention and Relationship Enhancement Program' which teaches couples how to talk (and fight) more effectively. The workshops are open to the public, and the state encourages those on welfare to go along by linking attendance with their benefits.

The scheme has had no shortage of detractors, saying that the government has no business intervening in people's personal relationships and that having two Christian evangelists (which the Parrotts are) running a public programme is a matter for concern for atheists and followers of other faiths. More damningly, perhaps, there are those who point out that money is being taken from the poorest people to pay people to talk to them, rather than solve the underlying root causes of why marriages are failing (poverty, social exclusion etc). The fact remains, however, that the idea is a radical attempt by the authorities to solve a problem that affects thousands of people, and their children, every year.

6 Blackstock Mews, London N4 2BT, UK (rhino@dial.pipex.com), 2002, 300pp, ISBN 0 948826 59 2

New shared middle names for couples getting married

Antony Weston

I propose that when two people get married they choose for themselves a new, shared middle name. The new name could invoke a favourite memory or place, ancestor, event, or aspiration – or anything, really. John Smith and Mary Jones might choose the name 'Oakwood', for example. They then become John Oakwood Smith and Mary Oakwood Jones. People could choose to use their married middle name in some settings but perhaps not all, just as we do now with our middle names. When children are born or adopted into a family, their last name would be their parents' middle name. John and Mary might have a child Chantal, let's say: her name would be Chantal Oakwood. Children could also be given provisional (ie until marriage) middle names.

'The system avoids reinforcing patriarchy or creating awkward hyphenations'

This system offers a way out of the current naming muddle, for both children and spouses. Right now, we must either reinforce patriarchy once again (using the father's father's...name), or create awkward hyphenated names that cannot last beyond a generation anyway (or use the mother's name mostly for the sake of resistance, or create entirely new names, but these practices are endlessly confusing and have their own problems). The scheme proposed here allows people to keep 'their own names' upon marriage (Mary Jones does not just become Mary Smith) but also to share a name with their spouses (rather than Mary Jones insisting on the 'Jones' and so not sharing a name at all with her partner), as well as allowing both parents to share a (single) name with their own children, and of course also with (both) their parents. No other existing naming system can do these things.

• *Antony Weston (e-mail: weston@elon.edu). Antony teaches philosophy at Elon University in North Carolina, USA.*

HOUSING

Cash for art clause in builders' contracts aids regeneration

Summarised from an article by Gerard Seenan, entitled 'Art thrives among the Gorbals tower blocks', in the Guardian (April 6th 2002).

An inner city regeneration project in Glasgow has been revolutionised by a simple clause in the builders' contracts: one per cent of the total construction costs must be set aside for art. An idea that started in the US and has spread to Europe, the 'per cent for art' scheme has become an integral feature of the regeneration of the Gorbals estate in Glasgow. As well as raising the whole tone of the development, the artwork, which includes a four-storey photograph and a bronze sculpture weighing over a ton and a half, have meant the development has become more attractive to prospective purchasers.

'The key has been the involvement of the artists from the planning stage onwards'

There are problems with such a scheme, including developers being put off by the cost or viewing it as something to consider when they have finished the rest of the building: the art is then added later as an afterthought. The key in the Gorbals project, though, has been the involvement of the artists from the planning stage onwards. This meant that they worked alongside the architects, allowing them to make the art more integral to the design of the whole development. Already, further installations are planned for the next phase of development, including a conversation-producing computer, an inner-city orchard and vast sculptures of birds. While it might not be appropriate for every new development to incorporate art, the cash for art clause could help to revitalise areas in need of imaginative regeneration.

Homesteading to help people on to the property ladder

Summarised from an article by Ros Dodd, entitled 'New life for empty homes', in the Sunday Times (January 27th 2002), monitored for the Global Ideas Bank by Yvonne Ackroyd.

A new 'homesteading' initiative spreading across the north of England aims to make it easier for people to get on to the property ladder and, simultane-

6 Blackstock Mews, London N4 2BT, UK (rhino@dial.pipex.com), 2002, 300pp, ISBN 0 948826 59 2

ously, to rejuvenate struggling urban communities. In some urban areas, the council sell currently unwanted empty properties for half price with the condition that the buyers must spend half of that total again on repairs over a two-year period. In other areas, homes have been sold for as little as 50p in return for commitments to renovating and converting the empty properties. As well as allowing people on low incomes to buy their first property, the scheme also ensures that empty properties are filled, which tends to reduce criminal activity and vandalism. Furthermore, the clauses in the contracts ensure that the houses are not only filled but also improved aesthetically and structurally, lifting the whole atmosphere of the neighbourhood.

'760,000 homes are vacant in England alone'

Thus, in Sheffield, a young couple were able to buy a £24,000 house for £12,000, on the condition that they spent £6,000 over the following two years on new double glazing, roof tiling and other repairs. If that happens with five empty properties along a street, the growing problem of empty houses in that urban community has been reversed, and the downward spiral of the area can be halted. In recent years, there has been an increasing trend for homes in inner city areas to be standing vacant, particularly ones owned by local authorities. Up to 760,000 may be in this state at present in England alone. Vacant, boarded-up homes then attract crime and vandalism which drags the community's status further downward, making the properties even more undesirable. This kind of project helps buck that trend, and also empowers young and low-income home-buyers, rather than leaving them at the financial mercy of landlords or property developers.

• *For more information on the scheme in Sheffield, see www.sheffield.gov.uk*

Landlord ordered to live in his own unsafe apartment block

Summarised from an article by Diane Brooks, entitled 'Landlord in tight corner', in the Seattle Times (August 15th 2001), monitored for the Global Ideas Bank by Roger Knights.

The idea is itself a cliché: a punishment to fit the crime. Yet innovative sentences are few and far-between in today's justice systems. A landlord in Des Moines in the US was on the receiving end of such a judgement when he was given a stark choice of going to jail or living in the apartment block which he had allowed to fall into disrepute. The tenants had had to live in flats with mould, rats and fire damage, all because of the landlord's neglect. So the judge offered him the choice, if he was unable to pay the necessary bills, of living in one of his own flats. He will have to live there under home detention and will be electronically monitored until the safety problems have been fixed.

'There had been no progress on addressing over 30 health and safety violations'

The judge took the unusual step because there had been no progress in seeing to over 30 serious health and safety violations. In the first six months of 2001, there were four fires at the complex, one of which completely destroyed the building's phone system. The situation had deteriorated to the point where many residents stopped paying rent as a protest about their living conditions. The residents, though they would prefer it hadn't reached this stage, feel the judge's decision is a fair one. As Tony Correia, a resident of the building, put it, "It'll give him a taste of what's going on", and it may inspire him to improve the dire state of the apartments.

Lockers with P.O. Box address for homeless

Raj Curry

As a first step to establishing themselves in society, the homeless need a geographical point of reference, for themselves and for those who can or wish to help to contact them. Without much cost, I cannot see why the local authority could not supply a locker with its own key *and*, crucially, its own P.O. Box address. This would provide a means of them keeping in touch with friends and family, and provide a point of reply for prospective employers.

The locks should be combination locks, so that when the lockers are handed on, a key is not an issue. People will disappear from time to time, so they might need to reapply monthly for the free lease of a box. It may not need to be a physical box or locker, but could be done through the Post Office, and recipients could just have a P.O. Box at the local sorting office, paid for by the council. The cost to benefit ratio would be very low for the authorities.

• *Raj Curry (e-mail: TangorePress@onetel.net.uk).*

• *For a similar idea on the Global Ideas Bank, see 'Voice mail-boxes for the homeless' in the Institute's 1993 journal.*

6 Blackstock Mews, London N4 2BT, UK (rhino@dial.pipex.com), 2002, 300pp, ISBN 0 948826 59 2

Mobile home parks as ready-made housing solution

Tony Johnson

Like cars, mobile homes lose their values rapidly, but without losing most of the functionality. While most lack efficient insulation, mobile homes are equivalent to a small flat at a fraction of the cost and will last indefinitely with a little care and maintenance. Secondary insulation can make them more energy efficient.

'An initiative providing small, residential parks with recycled, refurbished mobile homes'

A government backed housing initiative to provide small residential parks nationally with recycled, refurbished mobile homes, could solve the Bed and Breakfast lodger and starter home problem much more rapidly and effectively than permanent buildings. With care and landscaping, these sites could form an attractive alternative to rented accommodation and foster a renewal of community spirit. The used sites could also be more readily returned to other uses including agriculture, as only services and hard standing would be required.

• *Tony Johnson (e-mail: hourhouse@hotmail.com). Living in North Yorkshire, Tony works with computers and has had a practical interest in reuse and recycling for many years.*

Save demolition costs by inviting film companies to explode house

Summarised from an item in the Guardian Editor section (June 8th 2002). The story was originally reported in the South Florida Sun-Sentinel.

The wealthy owners of a Florida mansion have come up with a novel idea for getting their unwanted house demolished: they are offering it to any film companies who might want to have a house explode in one of their films. The 38,000 square-foot property was being built by an heir to the Coca-Cola fortune, but was never finished. To save on demolition costs, Eric Cherry hopes to persuade a film company, presumably making an action picture, to do the work for him. Some neighbours expressed some concern about the effect such a blast might have on their homes, but others showed little worry at all, saying "It won't be atomic. There are people around here". It seems unlikely that the trend will catch on, but there could be an unusual market emerging here: as well as house demolitions, cars going to scrap could be used by TV companies needing cars to wreck in a chase scene. It is a no-lose situation for all concerned.

Parachutes for high rise buildings

Libby Brown

Many lives might have been saved on September 11th if those trapped on upper floors in the World Trade Centres had been able to escape. The same applies for any cause of entrapment in a skyscraper, be this due to fire or serious hostage situations.

In order to provide a final resort for people trapped in such extreme situations, enough parachutes should be provided for all people on each floor, and the people should be taught how to use them, in the same way as is done on passenger flights. In this way perhaps, the safety of those people who work and/or live in high buildings will be vastly increased in cases of fire or any other emergency.

This idea was also suggested by Dave Maughan (Dave.Maughan@btinternet.com) and several others in the wake of September 11th. Neil Bromell (neilb@connectinsure.com) points out that a company already makes 'personal parachutes' which can be kept under desks.

• *Libby Brown (libby.brown@btinternet.com). Libby works for a construction company in the UK.*

Everyone owns their own house: through reallocation and 'rent-to-own'

Gavin Farley

This is a vision for social equity that is so simple it's almost painful given its hitherto non-invention. It is basically, as the title suggests, a vision in which everyone gets to own their own home. The consequential benefits are

6 Blackstock Mews, London N4 2BT, UK (rhino@dial.pipex.com), 2002, 300pp, ISBN 0 948826 59 2

potentially massive. Think about it: as humans we generally look after our own things, we generally put more time into permanent places, we want something to do to put our energy into, to order in some way, we generally don't want to pay for something we aren't going to get to keep.

Some background: It is well known and documented that the free market private property system that dominates under Western 'democratic' capitalism functions as one of the cornerstones maintaining a hierarchical social structure. Given that housing has always been defined as one of the 'basic' needs of humans (along with food, water and clothing), this would appear to be one of the key things that we need to redress.

How it works: Equitable housing allocation requires the fundamental redistribution of properties owned by multiple-property-owners to a public (government) housing pool. People owning more than one house choose one as their residence (their 'favourite') and the public housing pool acquires the others compulsorily for reallocation.

'Non-home owners are able to shop around for a house from the public housing pool'

Non-home owners (currently 'tenants') are able to shop around and choose a house that suits their needs from the abundant public housing pool and inhabit it either temporarily or on a permanent basis. They may do this as either individuals or groups inside of or outside of family structure or other structures defined by age or sexuality.

Accumulative ownership payments – an alternative to 'rent': Non-home owners pay the exact equivalent of 'rent' at a rate that varies on a regular sliding scale with more expensive houses asking a higher weekly 'rent'. However, with the properties owned by a central public housing pool, the 'rent' goes towards paying off the houses acquired by the central pool. Furthermore the 'rent' functions as an 'Accumulative Ownership Payment' (AOP) for the individual or group, that is, a weekly contribution or 'downpayment' to what increasingly becomes their own house or property. (This idea has been put in practice in a policy by the First Nations Cree Housing Corporation in Eastern Canada in their 'Rent to own' scheme (Robin Kearns, 2001. 'Colonised by policy? Housing opportunities for Indigenous Peoples on Collectively-Owned Land in Canada and New Zealand', Australian Canadian Studies Journal, UWS).

Special arrangements for 'AOPs' may be granted to allow low wage earners the opportunity to live in houses beyond their immediate rent-paying capacity (eg in beach areas).

Mobility: People are equally free to move locations and houses and may sell either the house or their 'accumulated ownership' either directly to the new buyer, or back to the public housing pool.

For example, Frank has paid AOP for 10 years at a place X and accumulated approx. $200,000 (10 years at $400/wk). Say he wants to relocate:

He can either 1) sell the stock of the house to a buyer wealthy enough to afford the price (who is then transferred the 10 years/$200 000 ownership); or 2) sell it back to the public housing pool and allow a different non-home-owner to start AOPs from scratch.

Clearly the major obstacle to such a system is in the transition to introduce it, whereby multiple property owners are 'forced' to give up their money-earning second and third properties. The government would also run a substantial deficit if it were to purchase all these properties in one sudden swoop.

Firstly, the governmental housing pool acquisition of all second third and other multiple properties need not occur in a single financial year. Instead, it may be introduced gradually, allowing for both social acceptance of the benefits of the policy and restructuring of lifestyles/professions for those living solely from their position of landowner/property investor. Further-more, over time the recovery of the housing stock value (through AOPs) would balance this deficit alongside the gradual shift towards equitable housing and the laying of a foundation for social equity.

'There needs to be a culture of social equity for the system to be implemented'

Secondly, there needs to be a culture of social equity for the system to be implemented – the question would seem to be whether this would best proceed or follow such a redistributive restructure. That is, whether a government policy enforcing a housing restructuring as significant as this would achieve success outside of a context where social equity is seen as a good thing by society as a whole.

• *Gavin Farley is an urban environmental activist currently working with a food cooperative in Sydney between university tutoring work (e-mail: skiinginthedark@hotmail.com).*

6 Blackstock Mews, London N4 2BT, UK (rhino@dial.pipex.com), 2002, 300pp, ISBN 0 948826 59 2

Protecting tenants' deposits with insurance or special account

Summarised from an article by Nessa MacEarlean, entitled 'Tenants protected', in the Observer Cash section (February 24th 2002) and from information on the Independent Housing Ombudsman's website (www.ihos.org.uk).

A government-funded scheme in the UK helps protect the deposits of tenants renting properties, and helps resolve tenant-landlord disputes. Under the Tenancy Deposit Scheme (TDS), the landlord can either bank the deposit in a building society account or take out insurance guaranteeing repayment of the deposit should the Independent Housing Ombudsman find against them in a dispute. The initiative was introduced because so many students and low-income tenants were losing out on their deposits unfairly: very few have the means to even argue the case, let alone pursue the matter through the courts. The TDS sets out to counter that trend.

'The deposit is put into a building society account overseen by the Independent Housing Ombudsman'

The scheme gives landlords two options. The first, the custodial option, sees the deposit being put into a special Nationwide Building Society account, overseen by the Independent Housing Ombudsman. If there is no dispute at the end of the tenancy, both the landlord (or the agent for the landlord) and tenant sign the withdrawal form to release the money. The form instructs how it should be paid. The landlord can only order the money to be withdrawn under their own signature alone if they instruct that the tenant should get the whole sum. If there is a dispute, there will be no payment until the Ombudsman has made his decision. The Nationwide will then pay out the deposit in accordance with his instructions. The interest gained by the deposits are then used towards the costs of the scheme.

The second path for the landlord, the insured option, is to hold the money in their own bank account. The landlord then pays for insurance from the CGU Guarantee Society to ensure that the deposit will be repaid if there is a dispute and the Ombudsman finds in favour of the tenant. If there is no dispute the landlord will keep or repay the deposit, according to their agreement with the tenant. If there is a dispute and the Ombudsman decides partly or wholly in favour of the tenant, he will instruct the CGU Guarantee Society to make the repayment. The insurance company will then recover the money from the landlord.

'The squabbling over deposits that often occurs at the end of an antagonistic tenancy can be avoided'

Essentially, the scheme assures a fair and just system for both parties, and avoids the incessant (and interminable) squabbling over deposits that often occurs at the end of an antagonistic tenancy. Under the TDS, the Ombudsman will make his decision within just ten working days of receiving the necessary information about a dispute, and if his decision is wholly or partly in favour of the tenant, they will receive the money within a further five working days. It is completely free for tenants, and free for landlords choosing the custodial option. The scheme has been piloted since March 2000 in Brent and Camden, Birmingham, Brighton and Hove, Merseyside and Norfolk, and it may well be extended nationwide in the coming years.

* *For more information, contact the Independent Housing Ombudsman, Norman House, 105-109 Strand, London WC2R 0AA (tel: 0845 601 1200; fax: 020 7836 3900; e-mail: tds@ihos.org.uk; web: www.ihos.org.uk).*

6 Blackstock Mews, London N4 2BT, UK (rhino@dial.pipex.com), 2002, 300pp, ISBN 0 948826 59 2

TAXATION

Tax reductions for participating in elections

Chris G. Kling

The government should offer a flat-rate tax deduction for each and every registered voter. It should then offer a second flat-rate tax deduction to each and every voter that actively participates in each federal and state election. We are now more aware than ever, thanks to the American presidential election in 2000 that every vote counts. Of course, they appear to count more for the winner of the election, but they count, nonetheless, as much to the voter and to the system.

Some may claim that it would be difficult to track this, however I disagree: during the Vice Presidential picking period, amidst the speculation it was easily discovered by the media 1) where Dick Cheney was registered to vote; and 2) how many elections he had voted in during the past X number of years.

'The tax deduction would also encourage good citizenship'

A flat-rate tax deduction would provide a number of benefits, not the least among which would be the rewarding of those who practise good citizenship. Of course, at least in America, only citizens can vote, so, hopefully, it would also encourage non-citizens to work towards their citizenship to earn the right to vote, in order to get that tax deduction.

• *Chris Kling (e-mail: chriskling@hotmail.com). Chris is a "freelance dilettante, currently posing as a lumber and building material salesman". He resides in North Carolina with his wife and three children.*

Website to explain where each individual's tax goes

Jeremy Conrad

The concept of paying tax is one that everyone despises. However, that bitter pill could be made easier to swallow if the government were to introduce an annual letter that was sent to each taxpayer (along with their income tax statement) detailing how and where their money was spent. If they identified how much was paid by each individual and broke it down detailing which sectors each portion of their tax went to – ie 3 per cent of your £11,234.56p (£337.04p) of tax has gone to the education system to help in instances such as increasing the number of teachers per pupil and improving schooling infrastructure; 2.6 per cent (£292.10p) has gone towards the NHS for increasing the numbers of doctors, etc – it may give taxpayers a greater sense of appreciation and understanding as they can quantify how much their tax means to themselves and others.

'It would be like a mini personalised budget plan from the Chancellor to the each citizen'

It would be like a mini personalised budget plan from the Chancellor to the people of Britain. If this was deemed too far-fetched and patronising then people could be directed to a website that would work it out for them and go into greater detail about how the money was used. Visitors to www.wheredoesmytaxgo.gov.uk (for example) would be able to input the amount of income tax they have paid into a converter that then breaks it down for them. Either of these concepts would bring greater transparency to an institutional process that currently frustrates so many people by making them feel they are under-informed.

• *Jeremy Conrad (e-mail: jeremy_conrad@hotmail.com).*

Tax incentives for community service volunteers

Beth Erickson

I propose that tax breaks be given, not only for charitable financial contributions, but also for the amount of time an individual spends yearly donating their time and energy to worthy causes that benefit society. The causes or charities could vary from blood donations, recycling or environmental 'clean-up' efforts, neighbourhood beautification programmes, time spent assisting in shelters or mentoring programs– there are a vast array of possibilities.

'A tax break would be given based on the amount of time spent volunteering'

Volunteers could be provided with a 'receipt' of the time donated. At the year's end, time donated could be totalled and reported on one's taxes,

6 Blackstock Mews, London N4 2BT, UK (rhino@dial.pipex.com), 2002, 300pp, ISBN 0 948826 59 2

resulting in a tax break based on the total amount of time an individual spent 'giving back' to society. The time and energy an individual invests to create a better society should be deemed as valuable as monetary contributions. This would encourage more people to become involved in their communities, foster greater awareness of societal issues, improve the quality of life and give people a greater sense of satisfaction and purpose in their daily lives.

• *Beth Erickson (e-mail: bethjon@bellsouth.net). Beth is a special education teacher working with children who have emotional behaviour disorders and are receiving treatment and stabilisation in a psychiatric facility in southeast Georgia, USA.*

WORK AND UNEMPLOYMENT

Job references to be supplied by employees, not employers

Philip Mcleish

Bullies and bad managers abound because their bosses neither know nor adequately care about their own behaviour, or because they misrepresent conflict between themselves and their underlings. Even if they know, when a bullying person leaves an organisation many employers will still give them a reasonable reference, possibly even to get rid of them.

'How differently a boss would treat his employees if his career hinged on their opinions'

A very different picture would emerge if it were standard practice for a person seeking a new job to supply names and contact details of everyone who had worked *under* them at their last job. The prospective employer would be invited to randomly contact (in absolute confidence) one or several employees to satisfy themselves that the smooth talker at the job interview was actually the team leader she held herself out to be. How differently your boss would treat you if his career hinged on your opinion.

- *Philip Mcleish (e-mail: philmcleish@freeuk.com).*

Companies rewarded for telecommuting workers

Summarised from an item, entitled 'Giving credit for absence', in Green Futures magazine (November/December 2001 issue).

Telecommuting, or working from home, is being promoted in a number of US cities under a scheme run by the Department of Transport. The two-year pilot programme rewards companies who reduce the number of staff travelling into work with smog emissions credits. These credits can then be used against the air quality regulations the company has to comply with, or traded with other companies. The idea is to take the work to the people, rather than bring the people to the work.

6 Blackstock Mews, London N4 2BT, UK (rhino@dial.pipex.com), 2002, 300pp, ISBN 0 948826 59 2

'Telecommuting also tends to reduce absenteeism and sick leave'

Environmental benefits aside, telecommuting also tends to reduce sick leave and absenteeism, give greater flexibility to disabled workers, decrease equipment and space demands at the office, alleviate employee (and family) stress resulting from commuting and, as a consequence of all of these factors, tends to make it easier to attract and retain highly qualified staff. Furthermore, in the unlikely event that all communications and systems in an office break down, telecommuters can help to ensure an uninterrupted service to customers.

- *For more information, see www.dot.gov*

Paid 'Family Days' at work

Janey Holstein

Too many parents these days get too involved in their jobs and not enough with their own family. It is especially important to be involved in their children's lives as much as possible, and some jobs just do not allow time for that. I think there need to be days that someone is allowed to miss work only to spend time with their family, such as going on a field trip with their child, or going away for the day with everyone in their family. Just as everyone gets paid 'sick days' in their job, they should also be allowed two paid 'family days' every six months or so. This could allow parents to spend more time with their children if they have some, and or just with their immediate family. Family is more important than work, and sometimes that is forgotten.

- *Janey Holstein is a sophomore at Elon University (www.elon.edu) in North Carolina, USA.*

Doing one thing at a time saves time; multitasking doesn't

Summarised from an article by William Hathaway, entitled 'One thing at a time saves time', in the Seattle Times (August 7th 2001), monitored for the Global Ideas Bank by Roger Knights. This item originally appeared in the Hartford Courant.

New research has found that multitasking, the buzz-word of 21st century employment, is inefficient and wastes time. Doing one thing at a time, by contrast, leads to a faster and more accurate accomplishment of tasks. This may not come as a great shock to some people who have never been able to rub their stomach and pat their head at the same time, but this is the first time scientific research has lent credence to the theory.

'Those asked to multitask performed up to 50 per cent more poorly'

In the University of Michigan study, Professor David Meyer and his colleagues asked young adults to perform tasks of differing degrees of difficulty and familiarity. Those who were asked to multitask performed much more poorly, taking 50 per cent longer in some cases. Professor Meyer adds that "Not only speed of performance, the accuracy of performance, but what I call the fluency of performance, the gracefulness of the performance, was negatively influenced".

Another study, conducted at Carnegie Mellon University in Pittsburgh, used brain imaging technology to come to the same conclusion. The level of brain activity was found to decrease when two tasks were performed at the same time: essentially, people doing two tasks do neither as well as well as when doing one at a time. The time-saving qualities of multitasking, it would seem, are little more than wishful thinking.

Creating art in the workplace

Chris Panczyk

I think that everyone should have the opportunity during their workday for creative expression. One room in the workplace would be set up as an artist's studio in which the workers could come in and out during the day and express himself through ceramics, drawing, and painting. Workers take smoke breaks. They read paperbacks in the lunchroom. They work out in the Wellness Centre. Why not give workers the opportunity to draw and paint or sculpt? Of course, the company would hire one full-time on-site Workplace Art Facilitator. The Workplace art studio could have easels and tables. Also, there would be an art library. Art films could be shown periodically. And, of course, there would be two art shows every year to display the worker's creations.

• *Chris Panczyk (e-mail: chrisjunkart@worldnet.att.net). Chris is from Denver, and works creatively in a number of areas.*

6 Blackstock Mews, London N4 2BT, UK (rhino@dial.pipex.com), 2002, 300pp, ISBN 0 948826 59 2

Equality of opportunity – a waste of time?

Summarised from an interview with Matt Cavanagh by John Crace, entitled 'Equal wrongs', in the Guardian Education section (March 26th 2002).

A new book by an Oxford-based philosopher argues that striving for equal opportunities is futile, because it is an empty term based on artificial (and ill thought-out) ideals. Matt Cavanagh, who has written the book 'Against Equality of Opportunity', believes that examining the theories behind equality of opportunity (which he pinpoints as meritocracy, equality and discrimination) reveals a lack of any agreement about the details. This has meant that the term 'equality of opportunity' is a vague, near-empty term, which has simply become a sort of shorthand for the method of allocating places, jobs and positions of power, whatever that might actually be.

'Is it fair to force employers to act on a meritocratic basis?'

In a market which is consistently said to be free, is it fair to force employers to act on a meritocratic basis? It may not be the most rational thing to give the job to someone who is not the best person for that job, but jobs are run by (and for) employers, not society as a whole. Cavanagh argues there has to be a place for irrationality in a free market world. He also argues that awarding places on the basis of whom has greater need or would be most affected by such an award is clearly anti-meritocratic; so attempting to allow for (and rectify) differences in background and education, something which might be associated with trying to reach and equality of opportunity, actually conflicts with meritocratic principles.

'People are not equal and not equally deserving'

In terms of equality, Cavanagh's main point is that equality means different things to different people. For some it means everyone starting from the same place, for others it means receiving the same amount of help, and for others it means receiving the same chances in life. But people are not equal, and not equally deserving or needy, so should treating people equally be something to be aimed for? Cavanagh argues that wherever something is scarce there has to be a way of choosing one person over another, and this is always done on the basis of difference rather than equality. The vote can be given freely to everyone, because it is not scarce, but a job has to go to one out of 15 or 20 applicants – how can equality be achieved there?

Finally, he confronts the principle of discrimination, proposing that not all discrimination is wrong, nor indeed irrational. A small company, for example, that chooses not to take on a woman under the age of 40 because she may take maternity leave in the near future, is discriminating against her; but employers are not compensated by government or society for the cost and time lost to such leave, so the company is actually acting quite rationally. Similarly, universities discriminate all the time on the basis of exam grades alone, rather than choosing to interview each candidate separately and judge them as individuals; but their discrimination is, again, a rational one on the grounds that they haven't the time to find out if the candidate with slightly lower results is actually more deserving of the place.

A great deal of this is controversial and, indeed, almost wilfully contrarian, but it is a debate that needs to be had: can positive discrimination and meritocratic principles be reconciled? what is actually meant by equality of opportunity? are inequality and unfairness the same thing? What Mr Cavanagh fails to do, unfortunately, is give any real solutions to changing the present system, beyond saying that there are inherently unfair parts to it which need some sort of positive discrimination to rectify them. He also says, rather enigmatically, "if we are to have quotas to ensure different groups are proportionately represented, I would be interested to know what system would take its place once the quotas were reached". Having now moved from philosophy to management consultancy, though, it would seem that his attention is now diverted away from thinking about what such a system might actually involve.

- *For more, see* Against Equality of Opportunity *by Matt Cavanagh (OUP, 2002, ISBN: 0199243433, £30).*

An ethical careers service

Summarised from an item, entitled 'Careers with a Conscience', in Green Events (June 2002; subs £8 from Green Events, 2nd Floor, 97-99 Seven Sisters Road, London N7 1QP), and from information from the Ethical Careers website (www.ethicalcareers.org).

A new service has been set up by an Oxford-based charity which focuses on ethical careers, opportunities and lifestyles. The intention of the initiative, run by People and Planet, is to help graduates and students make informed choices about socially and environmentally responsible careers. To this end, they provide information, advice, profiles of people in the sector, and highlight the range of opportunities available in charities, not-for-profits and ethical companies. On their website, there are hundreds of links to employers and agencies, but also information on how to make an impact in whatever office

6 Blackstock Mews, London N4 2BT, UK (rhino@dial.pipex.com), 2002, 300pp, ISBN 0 948826 59 2

you are in: green electricity tariffs, fair trade producers, ethical suppliers and recycling information.

For an annual fee of £9, students gain access to the resources online and also receive the organisation's magazine, *yOUR Future*, which includes an ethical advice column, dream job profiles, as well as listings of fairs, seminars, events and vacancies. The people running the service are also keen to stress that their intention is not to preach to students about who they should or should not work for, but to outline issues involved in particular sectors and possibilities for change in all occupations.

• *For more information, contact Ethical Careers Service, People & Planet, 51 Union St, Oxford OX4 1JP (tel: 01865 245678; e-mail: ethical careers@peopleandplanet.org; web: www.ethicalcareers.org).*

Generating and implementing creative ideas in the workplace

A review of The Idea Generator *by Norman Bodek and Bunji Tozawa (published by PCS Press, 2001; ISBN: 0971243687, 377 pages, £37). Reviewed by Nick Temple.*

The aim of this book is to demonstrate to companies and other organisations how they can integrate creative ideas from their employees into their internal structure. In this way, claim the authors, the 'hidden potential' of each employee can be unlocked and 'new excitement and joy' can be brought into the workplace. While some people may find it difficult to imagine excitement and joy ever being brought into our workplace, this book does provide a useful means whereby small, creative solutions can begin to be part of an organisation's day-to-day workings, ensuring continual improvement of working conditions and, in an ideal situation, a greater feeling of involvement and self-esteem on the part of the idea-giving employee.

'The key is the concept of *kaizen*, meaning continuous improvement'

The key to this generation of ideas in the workplace is the concept of 'kaizen', a Japanese term meaning 'continuous improvement'. It is a fluid term, though, and the authors define it here as meaning three things:

• improvement through changes in the method
• small changes, not big changes
• changes within realistic constraints

Norman Bodek, the co-author of the book, was inspired by examples of kaizen he saw in Japanese companies, and vowed to come up with a way of introducing it to American companies. He stresses that this is not a system for introducing cost-savings, but a method of implementing continuous improvements in an organisation in order to improve it for all concerned. This is why he devised his system of 'Quick and Easy Kaizen'.

Quick and Easy Kaizen

There are certain key aspects to Bodek's vision of kaizen that are central to his idea of a workplace system.
* Kaizen is for all employees: everyone is required to submit ideas.
* Kaizen requires each person to write down and implement their own ideas.
* Kaizen is a 'shortcut with a purpose'.
* Kaizen should be put into action within the boundaries of the employee's position, capabilities and experience.
* Kaizen should be used continuously and sustainedly.

'An ongoing process that improves the worker as much as the workplace'

What Bodek is trying to get across with these principles seems to be that kaizen is an ongoing dynamic process of incremental change: one that improves the worker as much as the workplace, and one that utilises the creativity and problem-solving abilities of every person in an organisation. It is also one that shares out responsibility within an organisation, for all people in it have the opportunity to suggest and, crucially, implement new ideas. Kaizen is like introducing a distributed network of creativity and problem-solving within an organisation, which liberates the potential of all involved. Or, so the theory goes.

Examples

The book backs up the theory with examples from companies that have put such a system into practice. It is these examples, however banal and 'common-sensical' they may appear, that bring the concept of kaizen to life. Indeed, the system of quick and easy kaizen welcomes the simple and the obvious improvements, as it is often these that are overlooked. Bodek recounts the example of an employee at a corporation in Oregon who submitted the idea 'Turn off the lights', an idea which went on to save the company thousands of dollars each year. Thus, it is small simple changes that kaizen aims to see put into place, be it repairing the piece of flooring, or teaching a colleague how to use a particular piece of software, or introducing a notice-board to prevent

6 Blackstock Mews, London N4 2BT, UK (rhino@dial.pipex.com), 2002, 300pp, ISBN 0 948826 59 2

over-ordering of goods. Small, obvious solutions to small, nagging problems engender an overall atmosphere of involvement, responsibility and improvement.

Documentation and surfacing

'Surfacing the ideas brings them to everyone's attention'

One question which occurs to mind when reading the book is why does everyone need to document every small idea they implement, even if this is just repairing a door or clearing up cables round a computer. Bodek insists that it is necessary to write these mini-solutions down to ensure what he calls 'surfacing', that is bringing them to everyone else's attention. This visibility shares the information about the improvement, gains the innovator credit, and ensures that kaizen remains in people's minds: that this is a continuous system of total participation, not a half-baked initiative brought in by a bored chief executive. It also makes the implementation of an idea a conscious effort on the part of the employee: s/he has to submit an idea a month, has to submit it and note its effects on the problem it was aiming to solve.

Value

As this is a book (and an idea) intended for corporations and companies, the authors are keen to point out that introducing kaizen need not involve any major level of expenditure, in terms of finance or labour. They refer to the equation Value = Function / Cost, in which 'Function' is the effect of kaizen, and 'Cost' is the sum of money, time and labour. As kaizen is designed to introduce small changes, the cost should be minimal or even non-existent; and it is much easier to experiment with small changes and go back on them if they prove unsuccessful. Indeed, the kaizen system could even be seen as a way of introducing changes and improvements when an organisation does not have the money to do so. Even if economic times are hard, things can still be improved. And the value, as is so often pointed out in the book, is as much in empowering the individual as the actual implementation of a small-scale solution.

Conclusions and comments

All organisations could benefit from such a system, although it will inevitably be those with more employees who will benefit more, both in terms of the number of ideas submitted and because employees in large organisations tend to feel more alienated from their work: the 'cog-in-machine' syndrome. Kaizen could also be an excellent educational tool: imagine a school where every pupil is required to submit one idea to improve something at the school every month, and is allowed to implement it when given the green light. It is instilling this positive outlook, the sense that problems are there to be solved not dwelt upon, that is at the heart of the Institute for Social Inventions' work: encouraging public participation in creative problem-solving.

'Small businesses and charities would seem appropriate places for the system'

I have only a few minor criticisms to offer. The book is well-structured and laid out, and is illustrated effectively by examples of memos from different organisations, but is plagued by unnecessary cartoons. The ideas outlined are all simple and well communicated, with an excellent summary at the end of each chapter, so there is no need for these illustrations: they devalue the book's impact in my opinion. It is here that the mantra of the book, 'Keep it Simple!', has been not followed closely enough. It would also have been nice to have a little more about the history of kaizen and its origins in Japan. While Bodek is open about the inspiration he has taken from Japanese examples, there is little background about the whole theory and how this might relate to the different approaches of different cultures. Finally, it is a pity that the book does not deal with how this system could be implemented and be useful elsewhere. This may be intended as a handbook for executives and managers of businesses, but some beyond the frame thinking would surely show how it can be useful in any number of different organisations, particularly as it is low-cost and small-scale. Small businesses and charities, with little money to spare, would seem particularly appropriate places for such a system, but these merit no mention in the book.

'Changing the mindset of employees'

These are minor quibbles, though, and it is refreshing to read such unbounded enthusiasm for creative idea generation in any sphere. The workplaces of the world, as much as anywhere else, are in need of innovation and invention, and this book demonstrates how this can be done simply, easily and effectively. Its most powerful impact, rather than simply making businesses work better with happier employees, could be the change of mindset that lies behind it: be positive, because each one of you can make things better. That is a lesson that needs to be communicated as widely as possible.

• The Idea Generator *is available in Europe from American Technical Publishers, 27-29 Knowl Piece, Wilbury Way, Hitchin, Herts SG4 0SX, UK. In the US and elsewhere, contact PCS Inc., 809 SE 73rd Avenue, Vancouver, WA 98664 , USA (tel: +1 360 737 1883; fax: +1 360-737-1940; e-mail: bodek@pcspress.com).*

6 Blackstock Mews, London N4 2BT, UK (rhino@dial.pipex.com), 2002, 300pp, ISBN 0 948826 59 2

Group walks during work breaks aid team-building

Summarised from a small item in the Shark Tank column in ComputerWorld magazine (July 23rd 2001), monitored for the Global Ideas Bank by Roger Knights.

A team of employees at an IT firm takes short group walks outdoors during work breaks. Aside from being much healthier than the normal cigarette break, the workers claim that it is excellent for team-building and helps enhance the way they feel about their job. Fresh air and exercise provide a needed physical stimulus after a number of hours at a desk in an enclosed office, and short walks certainly achieve that. The only problem they have come up against is walking past the offices of some senior managers, who complained that they looked "much too happy". Perhaps they should join them next time.

Power-napping improves workers' performance

Summarised from an article by John O'Neil, entitled 'Performance: A Quick Power Nap's Benefits', on the New York Times website (www.nytimes.com; May 28th 2002).

The concept of the 'power nap' to improve performance at work has now been backed up by new research in the journal *Nature Neuroscience*. The researchers put 30 equally rested people through a set of simple tasks (differentiating between shapes that appeared fleetingly on a screen) four times in one day (from 9am to 7pm). The performance of the first group of ten, who stayed awake the whole time, decreased by over 50 per cent. The second group, who had a short nap, managed to retain a consistent level of performance throughout the day, though decreasing slightly. The final group, who had an hour's sleep in the early afternoon, not only maintained the same level of performance but, in some cases, actually improved their performance (in terms of response and accuracy) after their nap.

'The brain needs sleep to make new skills permanent in the memory'

Dr Sara Mednick, of Harvard University, said that these results were consistent with other studies which showed that the brain needs sleep to make new skills permanent in the memory. Her co-author Robert Stickgold, said that "napping may protect brain circuits from overuse until those neurons can consolidate what's been learned about a procedure". He maintains that something similar happens with some musicians who often have a break-through with learning a complex piece of music after a nap or a night's sleep. It may be that the process of sleep refreshes specific neural circuits involved in tasks of perception, essentially letting the mind relax and absorb new informa-tion. What the research shows, though, is that even a small amount of sleep makes a substantial difference, refuting those who regard the power nap as a gimmick for lazy executives; on the contrary, it could be of benefit to everyone.

6 Blackstock Mews, London N4 2BT, UK (rhino@dial.pipex.com), 2002, 300pp, ISBN 0 948826 59 2

ECONOMICS AND BUSINESS

Burgernomics – an alternative way of comparing the world's currencies

Summarised from information on the Economist website. The item about a 'condom index' comes from a letter to the Economist by Jonathan Coppel on May 28th 1994, monitored for the Global Ideas Bank by Roger Knights. (www.economist.com; print subs £86 from 01444 475647 or e-mail: economist.subs@qss-uk.com).

For 16 years, the Economist has been using an alternative method of comparing the rates of countries' currencies: the Big Mac index. The index is based on the theory of purchasing-power parity (PPP) which says that one dollar should buy the same amount in every country in the world. It therefore follows that the exchange rate between any two countries will move towards the rate that equalises prices of goods and services in this way. To measure this price equalisation, an identical 'basket' of goods is needed for comparison, and the Economist use a McDonald's Big Mac as its basket. The Big Mac PPP is the rate that would result in hamburgers costing the same abroad as in America. Economists can then compare this rate to the actual exchange rate and see whether a currency is under- or overvalued.

'The cheapest burger is now in Argentina'

The index has become increasingly useful since its inception in 1986 because McDonald's has become increasingly ubiquitous throughout the world. While this may not be viewed as a good thing by everyone, it has certainly helped economists using the light-hearted index, because they now have 120 countries to compare. The most recent update of the index (in April 2002) showed that the cheapest burger is now in Argentina ($0.78) after its massive financial troubles, with the most expensive being in Switzerland ($3.81). This makes the Argentinian peso the most undervalued currency at the present time, with the Swiss franc being the most overvalued.

The index obviously has some flaws, notably that hamburgers cannot be traded between countries, that national taxes can affect prices, as can rents and other working costs. Despite this, the index has been remarkably accurate in gauging the true level of a currency. When the euro was introduced in 1999, many analysts predicted it would rise because it was undervalued. The Big Mac index disagreed, and was proved correct in the subsequent months. The concept of purchasing-power parity has also been endorsed by several economic studies, which reveal that it can be a particularly good guide to exchange-rate movements in the long term.

A condom index

Jonathan Coppel wrote to the Economist to propose a different index, with the condom as the identical 'basket' to be compared in each country. His argument was that the Big Mac index is flawed because it also includes materials protected by trade tariffs, such as wheat and meat. The condom, on the other hand, is made mostly of rubber which is already traded as a commodity on the international market. Information on contraceptive prices could then be used in the same way as detailed above to work out whether currencies are over- or undervalued.

• *For a number of articles on the Big Mac index, see http://www.economist.com/ markets/bigmac/index.cfm*

Make the small print as big as the rest of the text

George Rogers

Everyone complains that contracts and agreements use small print as get-outs because people either don't notice or can't be bothered to read through great swathes of written material.

'Encouraging companies to reduce their exclusions'

Why not enforce or lobby for a change so that all contractual material (exclusions,etc) has to be the same size of print as the rest of the text? This would encourage (or even force) companies to reduce their exclusions, or make them very clear, because of the otherwise colossal size of legal documents. It would also make clearer to everyone what they are entering into when they put their pen to paper.

• *George Rogers (e-mail: george.w.rogers@mailcity.com). George is retired and lives in Cheshire in the UK.*

6 Blackstock Mews, London N4 2BT, UK (rhino@dial.pipex.com), 2002, 300pp, ISBN 0 948826 59 2

Label products to show how much is profit and for whom

Robert Hallett

Compulsory labelling of all goods and commodities with exactly how much of the purchase price to the consumer is actually profit and for whom. The mark up on goods (for example cars and CDs in the UK) is huge but the culture of secrecy prevents consumers from being able to see exactly how greedy the producers/vendors actually are. This idea would inevitably require legislation both nationally and internationally, but would increase consumer choice and information and provide a truly level playing field of competition across industries, producers and countries.

* *Robert Hallett (e-mail: robonly@tinyworld.co.uk). Robert is a professional working in mental health in the UK for many years.*

Gross National Happiness and altruistic economics

Summarised from a paper by Sander Tideman, entitled 'Gross National Happiness: Towards Buddhist Economics', on the New Economics Foundation website (www.neweconomics.org), and from information on Charles Onyango-Obbo's website (www.charlesobbo.com).

The Bhutan initiative

Led by its young king, King Jigme Singye Wangchuck, the kingdom of Bhutan is the only country in the world to measure its wellbeing by Gross National Happiness (GNH) instead of Gross National Product (GNP). This unorthodox approach is a serious attempt to question the values of unbridled economic progress, and foreground the importance of maintaining a balance between tradition and modernisation. Bhutan has followed a cautious path of development since the 1960s, with the intention of preserving its heritage and culture and protecting its environment.

'Anyone with a grievance can get a hearing with the king'

GNH is an official policy of the kingdom, having been passed in parliament, and it is perhaps best illustrated by some examples from Bhutan which prove that happiness really does take precedence over economic prosperity there. The country limits the number of tourists that are able to visit it, because the Bhutanese had complained that the environment was being affected and sacred lands were being spoiled. The limiting was therefore aimed at increasing the 'happiness' of these people. Similarly, demonstrating that the concept of GNH is inextricably connected to accountability, anyone with a grievance can go to the king himself and get a hearing.

The policy of GNH, as well as focusing on cultural promotion and good governance, also aims to put an end to 'spiritual hunger'. Material and technological progress is not rejected or banned, but it must not be to the detriment of the value of human life, and humanity's soul. So the new policy has a spiritual aspect to it, as well as an eminently sensible accountability aspect. Mental and psychological wealth are genuine considerations in Bhutan. Happiness is more important than monetary wealth.

The flaws of Gross National Product

The concept of GNH was introduced by the leaders of Bhutan as a means of placing their Buddhist principles at the heart of life, replacing the conventional measure of a nation's economic performance, the GNP. Essentially, the idea of GNH is to encourage a rethinking of what is important in people's lives: should the success of a nation be judged by its ability to produce and consume, or should it be based on the quality of life in that country, the happiness of its people, however difficult that might be to measure in practice?

'Economic calculations ignore the value of fresh water and green forests'

It is also intended to provoke discussion about how altruism, or spiritual and moral beliefs, can be integrated into economics. That is, it is intended to question the basis on which modern economics is founded, where wellbeing is judged on the acquisition of material things, consumption and production. Economics has limited itself to things which can be measured monetarily, and this is its weakness as well as its (empirical) strength. As Sander Tideman points out, in his paper 'Gross National Happiness: Towards Buddhist Economics', it is the qualitative distinctions that are lost in this measuring of quantity: "economic calculations ignore the value of things such as fresh water, green forests, clean air, traditional ways of life", merely because they cannot be easily quantified.

Similarly, for example, money from logs is counted as part of a country's income, but the depreciation of the forest as a result is nowhere calculated. The unpaid volunteering, caring and nurturing sector, the informal 'Compassionate Economy', is also noticeably absent, despite some studies saying it

6 Blackstock Mews, London N4 2BT, UK (rhino@dial.pipex.com), 2002, 300pp, ISBN 0 948826 59 2

represents 50 per cent of all productive work in societies. And while the GNP measures an increase in production and consumption, and labels it as a symbol of success, there is no proportional increase in waste mentioned, nor the fact that environmental resources are finite, not a free good.

Incorporating altruism

So how can these kind of factors be incorporated into an economics? And can a spiritual dimension lead the way, as in Bhutan? In Buddhism, happiness is not determined by what we have and own (although this can be useful in alleviating poverty and allowing generosity), but also by our knowledge, our living skills and our imagination: by being, not having. Compassion and co-operation are as important to achieving happiness as competition. And developing our minds could be the key to all of these changes.

'Defining development by free provision of education and healthcare'

There has been increasing awareness in economic studies of the need to incorporate previously unquantifiable factors, such as emotional intelligence, and the need to base development on more than just material production and consumption: Amartya Sen, for example, defines economic development in terms of the freedom of basic necessities such as education and healthcare. Thus an ethical dimension begins to be restored to economics. There has also been an increasing trend for corporations and companies to demonstrate 'social responsibility' due to public pressure. All of these factors point to the need for, and trend towards, an altruistic economics taking account of all factors concerning wellbeing, not just financial ones.

Steps in this direction include the World Bank's 'Wealth Index' (which includes the concepts of human capital and environmental capital), the UN Human Development Index (which measures things like education provision, human rights records and life-expectancy) and, most interestingly, the 'Calvert-Henderson Quality of Life Indicators' which also incorporate cultural values and activities of self-improvement and group participation.

A change of emphasis

What Sander Tideman suggests is that initiatives like Bhutan's GNH "point us to the need to base development on spiritual values, transmitted through culture, rather than merely material values". An economics incorporating environmental and human factors does not deal with the essential problem for Tideman, which is that material development should only ever be seen as a means for people to devote themselves to spiritual development: that mind should always come over matter, as it were.

'Buddhist economics deals with the totality of life, not just finance'

This is a kind of Buddhist economics, where material factors might only be measured for the amount of time they allow followers to develop their minds and inner selves. This, the argument goes, is dealing with the totality of life, not just its financial aspects. This still leaves the thorny task of quantifying the unquantifiable: those aspects of life and wealth that cannot be dealt with by maths or rational logic. And it is here that there is a lack of solutions. Altruistic economics may be possible, and one with a spiritual dimension might also, but as yet, Gross National Happiness is a policy and an ideal, not a quantifiable economic system. Which is not to say that the example of Bhutan should not be followed, only that it should be improved upon.

• *A copy of Sander Tideman's paper, entitled 'Gross National Happiness: Towards Buddhist Economics', can be downloaded for free from the website of the New Economics Foundation at www.neweconomics.org*

• *For examples and information on the Calvert-Henderson Quality of Life Indicators, see www.calvert-henderson.com*

• *Another interesting book to look at on this topic is Lester Brown's* Eco-Economy: Building an Economy for the Earth *(Norton, 2001; ISBN: 0393321932, 224 pages, $16) which argues that the ecological costs of economic activities should be incorporated into the market prices of products and services. These additional costs could be offset, he suggests, by a reduction in income tax.*

A third world designer label

Jeremy Hillyard

This would be a designer label to be proud of: a third world designer label. The trend in today's street fashions is for designer gear which is usually quite expensive and often made in third world countries by people on very low levels of pay. How about a designer label where the profits would go to the people making the clothes? (this is similar in concept to fair trade coffee) That would surely be a range of clothing people would want to wear. Well known designers could donate designs for clothes for the label as well, ensuring it has credible appeal.

• *Jeremy Hillyard (e-mail: jez625@hotmail.com). Jeremy is a singer living in the Lincolnshire Wolds.*

• *See also www.nosweatshoplabel.com*

6 Blackstock Mews, London N4 2BT, UK (rhino@dial.pipex.com), 2002, 300pp, ISBN 0 948826 59 2

NEW MONEY AND FINANCIAL INNOVATIONS

Donate unwanted shares to charity and reap the rewards

Summarised from an article by Tony Levene, entitled 'Why not share in the giving', in the Guardian Jobs and Money section (March 2nd 2002), and from information on the Giving Campaign website (www.givingcampaign.org.uk).

The Giving Campaign, a new organisation set up in the UK, encourages people to donate unwanted shares to the charity of their choice. This is not a new idea, but one made relevant by the new Gift Aid and tax relief measures introduced by the government. Many people in the UK have received minute amounts of shares from mergers, privatisations and other 'free' share hand-outs. The cost of selling these small numbers of shares is often as great as the value of the shares themselves, and they can be more bother than they are worth when it comes to filling out tax assessment forms and the like. Charities, on the other hand, can sell the shares at much lower rates and receive the benefit of 28 per cent Gift Aid on top. And the donor can claim tax relief equal to the market value of the shares on the day the gift is made, together with any associated costs.

'Any shares left to charities in wills avoid inheritance tax'

It is hoped that, as well as those with small holdings, larger investors will participate in the scheme, either for ethical reasons or to avoid capital gains tax (which can be as much as 40 per cent). Any shares left to charities in wills also avoid inheritance tax, making them a very sensible way of leaving a legacy. The Giving Campaign estimate that two-thirds of the 12 million shareholders in the country did nothing with their shares in 2001: even if only a small proportion of those were to donate some shares in 2002, the effect will be substantial.

Pooling small share bundles

Summarised from an article by Fran Littlewood in The Times (August 4th 2001).

Sharegift is a share donation scheme based on the premise that all around the UK there are shareholders who are sitting on small, unwanted piles of shares. Many people have or inherit small handfuls of shares that can be more of a nuisance than anything else, whilst others regard constant correspondence regarding their shares as nothing more than junk mail or a stream of unwanted documentation. For the elderly, and those with little financial experience, it can be bewildering and upsetting.

'They wait to amass a certain number of shares before cashing them'

Shares of a total value that is less than twenty pounds are rarely much by the time you have paid the brokers chargers and paid a capital gain. Instead, Sharegift will wait until they have amassed a certain amount to cash them, and the proceeds are donated to charity. Masterminded by Viscountess Mackintosh, this scheme charges no cover costs and, furthermore, allows the donors to claim income tax relief on the value of the donations.

• *For more information see: www.givingcampaign.org.uk or www.allaboutgiving.org*

• *Sharegift can be contacted on 020 7337 0551 or www.sharegift.org*

Units of labour or work as a global currency

Summarised from two submissions to the Global Ideas Bank by Aaron Campbell and Mike Saavedra.

Introduction

Alternative currencies is something the Institute for Social Inventions has often focused on in the past, ranging from Ithaca Hours to Energy Dollars, and it is a topic that continues to energise people around the world, particularly as the phenomenon of globalisation extends its reach. The following two ideas were submitted to the Global Ideas Bank within days of each other, completely independently, and both focus on the possibilities of building a universal currency based on labour or work. Aaron Campbell believes this will occur inexorably over time, as the world's currencies meld together, and that this trend should be taken advantage of as an equalising force. Mike Saavedra, meanwhile, believes labour units could be freelyexchanged in direct substitution of money without any central control, on a more local level.

6 Blackstock Mews, London N4 2BT, UK (rhino@dial.pipex.com), 2002, 300pp, ISBN 0 948826 59 2

A dollar is a work unit
Aaron Campbell

Watching CNN and MSNBC, I realised that there is a great deal of money made simply with money, and that money was originally intended to represent a unit of physical value (ie an ounce of gold or silver). Over time, the unit of money came to represent a unit of Gross National Product, related more to how productive or profitable a nation was, rather than to any physical representation of value. Money is made by simply gathering something (raw material, raw labour) in quantity and selling it to someone who either doesn't have access to it, or doesn't have enough time to make it themselves. Often, money can even be traded for different money and in a flash of a ticker become more valuable.

A dollar will eventually become a (universal) Dollar. Globalisation is not a myth, it's the way of the world. Eventually, the strongest currencies will meld into one recognised unit of value. This will occur when enough people place the value of certain stock items (loaf of bread, can of beans, gallon of milk, pound of coffee) at a particular minimally-fluctuating price. This is occurring whether we like it or not. Soon, a loaf of bread will 'cost' three euros and that number will get more and more inflexible.

'The labour needed to create a loaf of bread will become increasingly constant'

It may then follow that the labour needed to create that one loaf of bread will be increasingly constant as well. Fifteen minutes will eventually yield a loaf of bread, globally. At the moment, this is not the case, and that's what causes populations to become enslaved. Their labour is valued less, and they are paid wages that do not exchange across borders in the same way that money and goods do.

A Dollar (or whatever its name will be) will eventually equal a work unit. Over time, the more trade that opens up, the more countries will learn to manage their natural resources without outside coercion, the more wage slaves will be given real opportunity and value-based pay, and the more chance our world will have of knowing peace. Peace will come when the value of each activity (say, 15 minutes of bread kneading) will have an intrinsic worth. Global minimum wages are being established with or without our input. If we make a public point of establishing a minimum wage or value for each work unit, then nations with more working people will be able to truly rise.

I therefore suggest that the world proactively establish a matrix of values for work units. An hour of social work is worth (x) Dollars, a loaf of bread takes (x) work units to create and therefore is equal to (x per cent) of Dollars. With

Institute for Social Inventions, £15 subs, £17 from abroad by credit card, tel London 020 7359 8391

enough input (the way the Global Ideas Bank gathers input, over the internet using simple databases) by enough people, the World will begin to narrow down the range that a work unit can be worth. Since corporations are already doing this without much input by their employees, we need to get cracking as soon as possible. If we put the engine in place to assign true equity to each person's work unit value regardless of location, age, race, gender, size, colour, lifestyle, etc, then true equality can be established as the world connects to itself. I, for one, suggest that the euro (with its cross-cultural, cross-country breadth) be the base for a global monetary unit, but the world has to vote on it in the end. Let's make the global economy a real tool for peace and resource management, and make sure the workers have a real say in it.

• *Contact Aaron Campbell at aaron@merc.net*

A currency based on labour for the world
Mike Saavedra

I have been observing the recent events in Argentina, the devaluation of their currency and their attempts to find a new currency. I have shared this idea with others, and wonder if a new model for currency is warranted. I thought of a currency based on labour. For example: one 'LABOUR' = one hour of labour. This currency can be exchanged freely between individuals without central control (like a mini-contract) or can be used by co-operatives as a tool to exchange goods and services. It can be used as an interim currency and help bridge the gap between the poor and the rich using the great equalizer, labour. Poorer countries can use this to exchange labour and goods among themselves and to counteract a global 'market' currency with a global 'labour' currency.

'It would place greater value on the labour of products rather than the materials involved'

Other social economists may look upon this as a stop-gap measure, and perhaps with some polish, a different economic model. It would place greater value on the labour of products rather than the materials involved. Scarcity of raw materials and environmental concerns can be used to adjust the price (in LABOURS) of products. Automation would lower the prices since less labour is involved. Manufactured goods would be priced according to the LABOUR involved primarily. It can also help communities become more self-sufficient and independent from foreign money that comes with strings attached. Jobs that are needed, scarce, dangerous, or unwanted can warrant a higher rate with an acceptable upper limit (for example a doctor could get a rate of two and a half times the hourly rate and so on).

6 Blackstock Mews, London N4 2BT, UK (rhino@dial.pipex.com), 2002, 300pp, ISBN 0 948826 59 2

If this idea has been examined before, it is worth a second look. With some adjustments it may become a tool to help equalise the quality of life among our brothers and sisters worldwide. I would ask those who study economics, social science and history to explore this idea as well. It may be something with which we can start to make a change.

- *Contact Mike Saavedra at taodo@yahoo.com*
- *An excellent new book on the whole subject of alternative currencies is* Money: Understanding and Creating Alternatives to Legal Tender *by Thomas H. Greco (Chelsea Green, 2002, ISBN: 1890132373, 295 pages, $19.95). As well as looking at alternative currencies such as Ithaca Hours and Toronto Dollars, Greco details corrective measures for their flaws, and suggests ways in which local currencies could be extended over a wider geographical area.*

A 'green credits' system protecting the environment within capitalism

Justin T. O'Conor Sloane

A system of 'green credits' designed to protect the environment while preserving an unrestricted free market enterprise system could be applied to any nation's economy. The beauty of the green credits system is that it utilises the mechanisms of free market enterprise to financially reward consumers who take personal responsibility for protecting the environment, thus providing a strong incentive to do so. Simultaneously, it allows other consumers to do as they please, but at a monetary cost; this is akin to the higher taxes associated with alcohol, tobacco, etc in the US and elsewhere, and to the higher fuel taxes paid by drivers when state governments wish to encourage carsharing.

The green credits system works in much the same way for the individual consumer as carbon credits do for industry. Here is a very simple outline of how it could work:

'All consumers are issued a certain number of annual green credits'

All consumers are issued a certain number of green credits per year by the government. The consumers who do not use all of their green credits can sell them to consumers who need more. So, for example, if a consumer has used all of his green credits for the year but decides to buy a sport utility vehicle anyway, he may purchase the number of green credits he needs from another consumer.

If everybody happens to use their entire allotment of green credits then more can be purchased from the government with proceeds directly funding environmental protection measures. All consumer goods, services and utilities would be indexed as being worth a certain number of green credits. Activities like planting trees could earn a consumer additional green credits.

Hopefully, as a result of green credits, most consumers would modify their habits of consumerism. A modification reflected in the marketplace (ie more hybrid cars produced, less sport utility vehicles produced, etc), without a curtailment in economic growth. Very importantly, this modification in consumerism would contribute to sustainable development, conservation of natural resources and protection of our global environment.

• *Justin O'Conor Sloane (e-mail: KingOConor@yahoo.com). Justin is an AmeriCorps Volunteer living in Seattle, Washington, USA.*

Text messages to combat credit card fraud

Summarised from an article by Joia Shillingford, entitled 'Texting 2 the rescue' in the Guardian online section (April 4th 2002), and from a news item by Andy McCue, entitled 'UK banks tackle credit card fraud', on the Yahoo! news website (May 29th 2002; www.yahoo.co.uk).

One of the most innovative uses of text messaging to mobile phones could prove to be combating credit card fraud, if new schemes proposed by British companies are implemented. Logica's scheme allows banks and other financial institutions to alert cardholders to any suspect card transactions via a text message, anywhere in the world. It then asks the customer to verify a transaction as valid (or not), making it quicker, more reliable and more efficient than chasing cardholders by telephone or mail. Meanwhile, Mastercard's Ariston service will supply a similar service, as well as giving the customer the option of receiving alerts by e-mail.

'As soon as an unusual transaction is noted, the text alert is despatched'

Both systems work through traditional fraud management systems which note exceptions, oddities (such as a merchant swiping a card twice within a few minutes) or purchases outside parameters set by the cardholder. As soon as an exception is noted (or a parameter broken), the text alert is sent off instantly.

6 Blackstock Mews, London N4 2BT, UK (rhino@dial.pipex.com), 2002, 300pp, ISBN 0 948826 59 2

As well as helping to combat card fraud more speedily, thus saving everyone money, the companies claim that it will enable the card issuer to have a closer, and more interactive, relationship with their customer. In the initial stages, customers will not be charged for fraud alerts to which they do not reply, although this may change as the scheme is more widely introduced.

Logica's scheme was recently piloted in Rio de Janeiro, where fraudulent credit card transactions account for 26 per cent of all card use. Customers of Unibanco can now opt to receive the text message alerts every time their card is used; a phone number at the end of the message lets them know who to call if they don't recognise the transaction.

• *For more information, see www.logica.com and www.mastercard.com*

Alternative local currency backed by Canadian dollars

Summarised from information on the Salt Spring Dollars website (http:// saltspring.gulfislands.com/money/welcome.htm), and from an article, entitled 'Salt Spring Island Prints Dollars', in Positive News (Spring 2002 edition; subs £12.50 by calling 01588 640022, e-mail office@positivenews.org.uk or see web: www.positivenews.org.uk).

A new local currency scheme set up on a Canadian island has avoided the problems of other alternative currency initiatives through a number of innovative measures. These include special artwork for the notes, involving the local banks and credit union, and making the notes fully redeemable with Canadian dollars. All of these have contributed to a large take-up of the new money on the island, with over 95 per cent of local businesses now accepting the Salt Spring dollar.

The Salt Spring Island Monetary Foundation (SSIMF) was created specifically to design, issue and maintain a local currency for Salt Spring Island with the goal of raising funds for worthwhile community projects whilst also promoting local commerce and goodwill. During its research into other currencies (such as Toronto Dollars, LETS schemes and Ithaca Hours), it found that the take up had not been substantial because of two main problems: firstly, and primarily, that the local currencies were not fully redeemable with the national currency, and secondly that the local currency project was often separate from local financial institutions.

'The notes have an expiry date of two years'

To solve the first problem, the SSIMF gave the notes an expiry date of two years. This meant that they could make 'profit' on any notes kept as souvenirs by tourists, collected for their artwork, or simply lost. In addition to the interest on the Canadian dollars exchanged for Salt Spring dollars (which are kept in a special reserve fund), this profit on unredeemed notes covers the scheme's administrative costs. Any excess then goes to community projects on the island. This is a fundamental difference from previous local currencies, in that locals feel more secure in the knowledge that the money is 'worth' exactly the same as the national currency, and that they can exchange one for the other at any time. The innovation of putting limited edition artwork on the backs of the notes has also helped to ensure their collectibility with tourists and locals alike.

The second problem, that of local financial institutions not being involved in operating the currencies, was solved by involving the Island Savings Credit Union, the Chamber of Commerce and two major Canadian banks in the project. With their backing, the Salt Spring dollar could then be distributed and exchanged for the Canadian dollar on the island. In legal terms, the Salt Spring dollars are gift certificates, but have been such a success that cash machines on the island will soon begin issuing the notes. Since their first introduction to the island on September 15th 2001, the response has been impressive. Even just two weeks later, major businesses were accepting the new currency without a problem, and the local people have been suitably encouraged to spend locally and, therefore, to put money back into their own community.

• *For more information, contact Salt Spring Island Monetary Foundation, c/ o 147 Robinson Road, Salt Spring Island, British Columbia, V8K 1R6, Canada (e-mail: dollars@freesaltspring.com; web: http://saltspring.gulfislands.com/ money/welcome.htm)*

6 Blackstock Mews, London N4 2BT, UK (rhino@dial.pipex.com), 2002, 300pp, ISBN 0 948826 59 2

Auctioning a mother's wisdom and thoughts

Summarised from an item in the Heads Up! e-newsletter (see http://gocreate.com), entitled 'Proud son offers eBay auction on his mother's wisdom and thoughts' (March 31st 2002).

Dan Baber, a 32 year-old businessman from Michigan, has such pride in his mother that he auctioned her wisdom on the internet. The item up for sale on eBay (www.eBay.com) was entitled 'Best Mother in the World – Her Thoughts', and read as follows:

"All I know is that I have the best mother in the world. ... All proceeds will go to her so she can spoil her grandchildren and teach me how to be as good of a father as she was a mother".

'The winning bid was for $610'

Baber's mother ran across the tribute while surfing the net, and found it incredibly touching. Originally, Baber had put up one day of his mother's attention for sale, saying she would e-mail the highest bidder for a whole day and make them feel like "you are the most special person on Earth". The internet auction site took this down because of potential misrepresentation and safety issues, so the sale of his mother's wisdom went up instead. Rather than being viewed as a rather soft-hearted paean to a mother, though, people began seriously bidding for the lot. Within a few days, 40 bids had been submitted, the highest being $165, and the bidding finally closed with the winning bid of $610.

Some might decry the auction as a symbol of the continuing commercialisation of the world, with everything having a price. Others might feel that it shows a refreshing repudiation of commercial instincts: the most valuable thing to Dan Baber was his mother's wisdom, and that was something he wanted to share for a day with someone else. Perhaps this lateral way of thinking could even lead to an alternative kind of auction site where people exchange advice, acts of kindness and wisdom in a currency-free environment.

WELFARE

Policeman trained in psychology to help mentally ill

Summarised from an article by Cherine Badawi, entitled 'Doc Cop', in the Whole Earth magazine (Spring 2002 issue; subscribe at www.wholeearthmag.com).

In San Rafael, California, a policeman who is also a psychologist co-ordinates a project called the Mental Health Liaison Programme (MHLP). Joel Fay decided that the majority of his police work actually involved the use of psychology, rather than self-defence or chasing criminals down the street. He also noticed that there were a significant number of people who were mentally ill who were having difficulty with the police. To try to address the problem of mentally ill people being arrested for minor crimes, jailed, taken off medication and then subsequently released again, Officer Fay went back to school to study psychology. He then founded the MHLP which brings together law enforcement professionals and representatives from homeless and mental health agencies. Cases are studied on an individual basis by the MHLP team, and decisions taken on the best course of action. The team then meet the following month to evaluate progress of the individual, and so on.

'The collaboration helps both camps find a middle ground'

Officer Fay has found that the collaboration process has helped both camps find a middle ground. Previously, police were keen to deal with problems quickly, while the mental health agencies took a much more considered approach, weighing up the information available. Now the two have started to work together, effective action is taken quickly, but not at the expense of looking at a range of options for each individual. Thus, for example, a mentally ill homeless man could be jailed for a few days to get him off his drugs, before being put on a medication and outreach programme. Then people can be helped to find permanent housing where their treatment can be monitored.

'The team has a 50 per cent success rate in getting individuals into housing'

Thus far, none of those integrated into housing and treatment have been rearrested, and the team has a 50 per cent success rate on getting individual cases off the street. The police department in Marin County, which includes

6 Blackstock Mews, London N4 2BT, UK (rhino@dial.pipex.com), 2002, 300pp, ISBN 0 948826 59 2

San Rafel, believes in the success of the scheme to the extent that it is giving 15 per cent of its officers 40 hours of training to enable them to make rough diagnoses about mentally ill people, and a further two officers will be sent to study for advanced degrees in psychology. The key has been cooperation across normal lines of involvement and a willingness to not prejudge any particular cases. It is an example others could easily follow.

• *For more information, see www.srpd.org or contact Joel Fay at joel.fay@srpd.org*

Drive-in brothels to control prostitution

Summarised from an item noted in the Heads Up e-newsletter (see http:// gocreate.com), entitled 'Cologne, Germany sets up drive-in brothels' (October 7th 2002).

The city of Cologne, in Germany, has set up drive-in brothels in an effort to further control prostitution in the city. The complex, on the outskirts of the city, has an 'approach zone' where clients make their selection and a covered parking space which is adjacent to a bedroom with a shower. The idea was originally put into practice in an effort to move the red-light district away from the city's beautiful cathedral, but it has also helped regulate prostitution in the city. Police and city officials are always at the site, as is a charity which provides support to the prostitutes.

'Several Dutch local authorities have set up special drive-in bays'

Prostitution is legal in Germany, but this is the first example of a publicly-funded scheme of this nature, and it is costing the German taxpayer 830,000 marks (over £250,000). The Netherlands, which legalised brothels in October 1999, has also tried to control the trade in a similar way. Several local governments have set up special legal 'drive-in' bays for customers' cars, again enabling a close monitoring of any potentially problematic situations. What these schemes do not do is deal with the problem of prostitution itself, and some may justifiably feel that these initiatives only serve to encourage men to use prostitutes, as they appear to condone their activities to some extent.

Cab drivers to counsel domestic violence victims

Summarised from an article by Gaby Hinsliff, entitled 'Britain's biggest mouths learn to shut up and listen', in the Observer (May 26th 2002), and from information on the government's Women and Equality Unit's website (www.womens-unit.gov.uk). The US item is summarised from an article by Rene Sanchez, entitled 'Hair salons enlisted to aid war on abuse', in the Seattle Times (November 22nd 2001), monitored for the Global Ideas Bank by Roger Knights.

'It acts as something of a modern-day confessional'

Cab drivers have been selected to offer help to victims of domestic violence, under a new project backed by the UK government. Research has revealed that women fleeing from their violent husbands or partners tend to open up more in the back of a taxi than they would do normally: it acts as something of a modern-day confessional. A taxi is often the first port of call for a woman trying to get away from domestic abuse, and this makes the initiative all the more important. Taxi drivers may be trained in giving sensitive and thoughtful answers if the subject is raised, and advised on the best ways of lending a sympathetic ear. Taxi receipts will carry helpline numbers for domestic violence, and adverts with further information will be carried on the tip-up seats in the back of the cab.

'The support could get to victims faster'

Domestic violence accounts for a quarter of all violent crimes in the UK, and two women die as a result of it each week. In addition, it is estimated that the annual economic cost of domestic violence in London alone is over £250 million, when court time, working days lost and everything else is included; and the emotional and psychological cost to families is incalculable. This new initiative could help get to the victims faster than is normally the case, by providing support in an unexpected way, although it is in no way meant to replace the professional services already in existence.

As well as with the cab drivers, the Government is working with the TUC (Trades Union Congress) and the CBI (Confederation of British Industry) to raise the profile of the role that the workplace can play in terms of supporting domestic violence victims. In the long term, it is also hoped that the scheme will reduce society's acceptance of violence against women. The only barrier to the project's success may be achieving what many a passenger has found impossible: getting the cab driver to listen instead of talk.

6 Blackstock Mews, London N4 2BT, UK (rhino@dial.pipex.com), 2002, 300pp, ISBN 0 948826 59 2

Hairdressers also enlisted to help

'Hairdressers can notice bruising on the face or neck'

In a striking parallel to the UK scheme detailed above, San Francisco social workers and prosecutors have enlisted hairdressers to help women suffering from domestic abuse. As with cab drivers, hairdressers are another sector of the population with whom people often talk more openly. Therefore, they hear stories that even the victims' family and friends may not be aware of. Hairdressers are also in a position where they can spot bruising or other signs of assault to the face or neck. As a result, officials in San Francisco have begun training hairdressers to look out for these signs of abuse, to offer careful (and considered) counselling, and to encourage, where appropriate, women to report crimes or go to shelters to get help.

As with the cab drivers, the risk is that these are not trained professionals, but if they act subtly to give information and motivation, the authorities believe they could make a real difference to helping abate one of the most underreported crimes. It is a measure of how difficult domestic violence is to tackle that legal agencies and social workers are looking at these kind of radical, unorthodox projects.

* *For more information on the Hairdressers Against Domestic Violence Project, or to receive a copy of The Hairdresser Project Guidelines (available for $15), contact Sue O'Toole via phone: +1 860/535-2100 or via e-mail: susiespeddingotoole@yahoo.com*
* *Or see the San Francisco District Attorney's website at www.ci.sf.ca.us/da/*
* *For more information on the cab driver scheme in the UK, see www.womens-unit.gov.uk*

An improvised homeless village

Summarised from an article by Carol Estes, entitled 'A place for dignity', in YES! A Journal of Positive Futures (Spring 2002 issue, subscriptions $24 + postage from Positive Futures Network, P.O. Box 10818, Bainbridge Island, WA 98110-0818, USA; tel: +1 206 842-0216; fax: +1 206 842-5208; web: www.yesmagazine.org).

In Portland, Oregon, an innovative village for the homeless has sprung up, in an effort to help those living on the streets break the cycle of jail to shelter to streets to jail. In cities like Portland, shelters provide a necessary but flawed service: three out of four people seeking shelter cannot be accommodated, and places are allocated randomly or on a first-come-first-served basis. Homeless people therefore find themselves concentrating all their efforts on finding shelter, taking care of their possessions and generally surviving. Job interviews and housing applications are not high on the agenda, nor often even possible. The village aims to change all this, by helping homeless people to look after themselves and each other.

'500 village graduates have found jobs and apartments in the past year'

The community, of about 60 people at any one time, is self-governing, with rules made by consensus, and has a strict drugs and alcohol ban on the premises. The residents build their own shelters, with the help of volunteers, from whatever they can lay their hands on in terms of donated and recycled material. Everyone is required to help with chores (such as recycling all rubbish) and there are unofficial systems to help people find jobs and places to live. 500 ex-village residents, or 'graduates' as they are called, have found jobs and apartments since early 2001, with others kicking drug habits or regaining custody of their children.

'Pulling their own weight encourages self-reliance and self-respect'

The key to the village's success, according to its founder Ibrahim Mubarek, is that everyone has to pull their weight, which encourages the growth of self-reliance and self-respect. Rather than being spoon-fed short-term solutions, the homeless are encouraged to help themselves by being given the stability and opportunity to change their circumstances. Now, despite seven different locations in the past year, the villagers look like they may have a chance of a permanent site for their community, as the local council has agreed to help them in a pilot project. The aim is to have a sustainable urban village, democratically run, and, on the basis of what has been achieved so far, it might just happen.

• *For more information, contact Dignity Village, c/o Sisters of the Road, 133 NW Sixth Avenue, Portland, Oregon 97209, USA (tel: +1 971 570 0220; fax: +1 503 295 7747; e-mail dignity@dignityvillage.org).*

• *You can also buy Dignity Village merchandise or support the village directly by donating money online at www.dignityvillage.org*

6 Blackstock Mews, London N4 2BT, UK (rhino@dial.pipex.com), 2002, 300pp, ISBN 0 948826 59 2

Taxi firm hands out free condoms

Summarised from an item, entitled 'Taxis score with free condom safe-sex drive',
on Yahoo News online (June 6th 2002; http://daily.news.yahoo.com).

A Norwegian taxi firm has been handing out free condoms to any client of any age who asks, and many have been taking up the opportunity. In two weeks, 300 condoms were given out from the firm's 20 taxis, thanks to a sign on the back of the seat reading 'Forgot condom? Ask the driver!'. The Norwegian health authorities, who came up with the idea, decided that taxis could play a part in the safe-sex drive they were undertaking, in an effort to reduce the number of unwanted pregnancies and cases of sexually transmitted diseases. Jon Hilmar Iversen, promotions director with the health authority, said, "We want to give easy access to condoms to people where they are when they need it". Taxis are the perfect place, and the Norwegian public have not been shy in using the service.

Online resource kiosks for the homeless

Summarised from an article, entitled 'Help for the homeless at the touch of a
button', in West End Extra (June 14th 2002), monitored for the Global Ideas
Bank by Yvonne Ackroyd.

A new service has been launched in London which gives homeless people access to thousands of services, including information and advice on accommodation and employment. 250 of the online kiosks will be up and running in the city by the end of the year, allowing anyone free access to travel news, housing information, job vacancies and other useful information. The kiosks also have a free e-mail facility integrated into them, meaning users can send e-mail to any address, and can nominate their own e-mail address for replies. An inbox facility will soon be added, so that users will be able to check their mail accounts from any kiosk.

It has also been suggested that the kiosks could prove useful for victims of domestic violence, because it allows them instant and anonymous access to support and advice services. Many victims of domestic violence have internet and phone access controlled by their abusive partner.

CRIME & THE LAW

Fining judges for crimes committed by released defendants

Summarised from an article by Steven Landsburg, entitled 'A modest proposal to improve judicial incentives', in Entrepreneurial Economics, *edited by Alexander Tabarrok (OUP, 2002; 328 pages, $39.95; ISBN 0195145038).*

Steven Landsburg's suggestion for improving the judicial system is a novel one. In order to reduce the number of crimes committed by defendants released on bail, he suggests that judges should be fined when this occurs. In essence, the judge is made personally liable for any criminal damage resulting from his decision to release the accused criminal. The theory is that the judge then focuses more closely on what the right decision is for the criminal and the community, because he has a personal (financial) incentive to get it right.

Clearly, introducing the fining system alone would not work, because judges would simply never release anyone out on bail to avoid the possibilities of fines. Landsburg therefore proposes that there be 'a simultaneous countervailing incentive' in the form of a cash payment to the judge for every defendant he releases. In this way, the introduction of financial incentives could be used to make judges directly liable for their decisions: liable to benefit if they get it right, and liable to be fined if they get it wrong. The level of cash incentives (and fines) could be adjusted depending on the wishes of the particular legislature: if it was a judicial area marked by a public favouring rehabilitation and leniency, the incentives for release could be increased. If the opposite was true, the level of possible fines could be increased. And the public could judge their lawmakers on the line they choose to walk along between safety and freedom.

Offering burglars holidays to prevent repeat robberies

Summarised from an item, entitled 'Company boss offers two-month holiday to burglars', on the Ananova news website (June 17th 2002; www.ananova.com).

A Norwegian company plagued by burglars continually breaking in has offered them a two-month holiday, plus spending money. The boss of the energy firm, Bill Schjelderup, decided that offering the vacations would be

6 Blackstock Mews, London N4 2BT, UK (rhino@dial.pipex.com), 2002, 300pp, ISBN 0 948826 59 2

more cost-effective than being burgled every two weeks. Recent burglaries have cost the company nearly £90,000. The cost of a holiday for the burglars would be significantly less than installing continual security on top of the financial losses from things taken. Mr Schjelderup, who believes the same burglars are responsible for the break-ins, said the firm couldn't "take any more", a feeling which prompted his radical suggestion.

Goods and property seized from criminals used to fund the police directly

Dereck Thomson

When the police break a gang network and seize property, goods and money, then they should be able to use those resources for investing into their own force instead of it going into the central pot and being used elsewhere. This would encourage local police forces to double their efforts at solving crimes, as they would have a financial incentive for doing so.

  • *Dereck Thomson (e-mail: nosmoht.kcered@ulonline.co.uk). Dereck lives in East Yorkshire in the UK, and works as an accounts manager.*

Prisoners to pay for their upkeep with work done inside

Sarah Reeve

It costs approximately £35,000 (Note 1) to house one prisoner per year (in an uncrowded prison place). This means that for the 68,000 people in prison in the UK (Note 2), the taxpayer has to foot a bill of £2,380 million, or £79 per person per year (Note 3).

'Prisoner loans to be paid off through work done in jail'

I accept that society has to deal with offenders, but we could place a monetary punishment on offenders as well as placing them in institutions to remove them from society. Just as there are student loans, let there be prisoner loans. If a person is sent to prison for one year, let him be given an automatic debt of £12,500 to pay towards his accommodation. This can either be worked off through offering jobs in the prison, or he can carry it forward to when he leaves. After he leaves the prison, he will be charged interest at base rate (less than any other debt he may have) until he pays it off. This would go on his credit rating, making it difficult for him to get other loans/credit cards etc unless he paid it off. To encourage the offenders to pay off the debt, there should be work on offer inside the prisons which will allow an offender to raise the amount of his debt in the time of his sentence.

I accept that there are two possible problems with this. Firstly, the very rich who commit crimes would be able to easily afford this debt. The debt should then be scaled for disposable income, or on some other means-tested basis. However multiple offenders would soon find the debt rising quicker than they could pay it off.

For the very poor, exceptions would have to be made. They should be actively encouraged to work in the prison to pay off their debt, and debt counselling should be offered. Offenders showing a total inability to pay should be allowed to have the debt cancelled, rather than be put in a position where they have to re-offend to pay for their previous debt. However, this should be strictly monitored, to ensure that offenders do not hide possible sources of money from the prison service. Certain things should be exempt, such as the offender's main property. Possibly they could be forced to take in lodgers to provide money for the loan during their prison term.

This would have a number of good outcomes. The amount of money it costs society to imprison people would be cut, offenders who earn money by crime would be given the opportunity to learn to work and earn money honestly, and prisoners would not become 'bored' in prison.

All in all, it would certainly change the meaning of the old adage of 'paying their debt to society'.

[Notes:
1. Target cost of the HM Prison Service 2000 annual report (www.hmprisonservice.gov.uk)
2. Prison population as at 02/11/2001 from HM Prison Services (www.hmprisonservice.gov.uk)
3. Population estimate for mid-2000 from national statistics (www.statistics.gov.uk). Assumes 50 per cent of population is paying taxes.
One way of avoiding there being a hierarchy in jail under this scheme (whereby the richer prisoners would just pay off their debt when they got out) could be to make the debt *only* payable through work done in jail. This would level the financial playing field for all prisoners.]

• *Sarah Reeve (e-mail: sarah.reeve@ntlworld.com). Sarah lives in London and works at an accounting firm.*

6 Blackstock Mews, London N4 2BT, UK (rhino@dial.pipex.com), 2002, 300pp, ISBN 0 948826 59 2

Emergency text messaging service for the deaf

Summarised from an article by Jane Bird, entitled 'When it's handsets to the rescue', in the Times (March 28th 2002), monitored for the Global Ideas Bank by Yvonne Ackroyd.

In another example of the way in which new technology is being used innovatively to overcome problems in society, West Midlands Police are launching a new text messaging scheme to allow the deaf, hard-of-hearing and speech-impaired to contact them more easily. While most police forces have minicom systems that allow hearing-impaired people to type in messages by telephone, the text messaging service will allow them to communicate with the police in urgent cases or as a witness out on the road, without the need for an intermediary.

'The service may be extended to the fire and ambulance services'

After introducing the service, the police are consulting with the ambulance and fire brigade to look at the possibilities of extending it to include them. The service was launched on July 15th 2002 and is available to all people living in the West Midlands.

 • *See www.west-midlands.police.uk for more details.*

Playing TV cop theme tunes reduces petrol stealing from garages

Summarised from an item in the Guardian Editor, entitled 'Drive-offs', on September 1st 2001.

The supermarket chain Tesco have been playing theme tunes from popular TV police shows in order to reduce those driving away without paying for their petrol. They are claiming a 20-30 per cent reduction since introducing the unusual music. A spokesperson for the supermarket said, "It seems to prick people's consciences and make them think of the police".

Opera drives away unwanted gangs of youths

Summarised from an item, entitled 'No-go aria', in the Guardian Society section (March 13th 2002).

A Lancashire shopkeeper has managed to drive away youths loitering outside his shop by playing opera music at high volume. As soon as the arias and cantatas started to blare out from the loudspeakers specially erected on the roof of the shop, the gangs began to disperse.

'Janacek's sparse glissandi tempestuosi really bug me!'

A similar project in Essex has met with greater difficulties. First Great Eastern had launched a project piping classical music at six stations in the county, in an effort to deter youths from causing trouble, but the station at Frinton on Sea had its speakers vandalised. The company is repairing the system and plans to continue the scheme, which it claims has been effective in preventing teenagers congregating and causing damage at stations.

6 Blackstock Mews, London N4 2BT, UK (rhino@dial.pipex.com), 2002, 300pp, ISBN 0 948826 59 2

Tasteless but nutritious loaves for misbehaving inmates

Summarised from an article, entitled 'Misbehave, and you'll get food for thought', in the Seattle Times (April 4th 2002), monitored for the Global Ideas Bank by Roger Knights.

Prisons in the US state of Maryland have introduced a tasteless and leaden loaf for inmates who are flouting prison rules. The loaves, which weigh one pound, are low in fat and cholesterol and contain recommended daily allowances of Vitamin C, calcium, iron and other nutrients, but their taste is unpalatable enough to bring hardened prisoners into line. Especially when it is served to them for breakfast, lunch and dinner with only water to wash it down.

Michael Jackson, a Baltimore inmate who's been on the bread diet twice, described it as smelling "kind of foul", before adding, "the first few days are the worst. I can't even describe it. It's awful". Others merely describe it as bland beyond belief, but all have noticed an effect on those having to eat it. Maryland prison officials have said that adding the bread to other disciplinary measures doesn't usually last long, because it has such a noticeable impact on the prisoner's behaviour. And because the loaf provides everything you get in a well-balanced diet, the prison is not harming or depriving those under its control.

'The bread is a low-cost, low-tech tool for controlling prisoners'

This millennial Maryland version of medieval bread and water includes: dehydrated potato flakes, finely grated imitation cheese, powdered milk, raisins, carrots, tomato paste, six slices of wheat bread, two cups of beans and a can of spinach. This mixture is then moulded into a loaf-shape and baked for just under an hour. And there you have it: the new low-tech tool for controlling prisoners – the 'special management meal'.

[Please note that other American states add variety into this mix: in Pennsylvania, the 'breakfast loaf' contains prunes, eggs, hash browns, toast and orange juice; in Texas, inmates are given 'food loaf', a bread made up from the previous day's leftovers; and in California, they simply call it 'the brick'.]

A Pacific Island paradise prison experiment

Summarised from an article by Mary Jordan, entitled 'No cells, bars at Mexican prison 'paradise'', in the Washington Post (February 5th 2002). The article was featured in the Guardian Editor section (February 16th 2002) and the Seattle Times (February 17th 2002); the latter item was monitored for the Global Ideas Bank by Roger Knights.

A new Mexican prison takes the principle of rehabilitation to its extremes – it is a beautiful Pacific island on which inmates live with their families. There are no bars, no cells, no uniforms and only 36 (unarmed) prison guards for the 3,000 inmates. The concept behind the Isla Maria experiment is that if prisoners are going to have to return to everyday life at some point, why not let them live in a community that simulates that everyday life? Only inmates who have shown a willingness to reform are allowed on the island, with the warden weeding out those who he thinks are less suited to the unique circumstances of the prison. The island also has its own bakery, church and dance hall, while the inmates live in ordinary houses and work on farms.

The island prison is all the more remarkable because it started out as a kind of Mexican Alcatraz for the most hard-bitten criminals in the country, a place renowned for its harsh treatment of inmates. Although Mexico has quite a liberal judicial system (neither the death penalty nor life imprisonment are allowed by law), some prisons have become infamous for bribery and illegal punishments. Therefore, on Isla Maria, much of the power has been taken out of the hands of the guards to try to avoid anything similar occurring there.

'The prisons help keep families intact – a key factor in rehabilitation'

There are those who criticise the expense of the prison (three times more per prisoner than a normal prison) and the apparent laxness of its regime. The island's inmates are mostly drug traffickers, but also include a few who have committed assault and murder. In its first nine months, 93 prisoners had to be transferred to the mainland, with others being punished by banishment to the other side of the island (away from music, television and their family). There are also concerns over children being raised in a community of criminals, although this happens in other Mexican prisons and helps to keep families intact, which is another key factor in rehabilitation. Furthermore, the neighbourhoods and housing are often safer and of a better standard than those which the families left behind on the Mexican mainland.

One woman, Lorena Avila Suarez, came to the island with her father (a convicted murderer) when she was eight, but still lives there, having fallen in

6 Blackstock Mews, London N4 2BT, UK (rhino@dial.pipex.com), 2002, 300pp, ISBN 0 948826 59 2

love with a cocaine trafficker who has another 18 years left to serve. Her father has long since left, but she could now be there until she is 43. Her mother, Mrs Suarez Ilago, praises the island's rehabilitative effect, though, pointing out that her husband received schooling on the island, worked diligently on a farm, and has been in no sort of trouble since his release. And, she adds, "I never forgot for a moment that I was in jail".

Arraignments and hearings by videoconference

Summarised from an article by Craig Savoye, entitled 'Lawyers can now call witnesses by remote control', on the Christian Science Monitor website (www.csmonitor.com).

A courthouse in the US has introduced videoconferencing for charging prisoners and for pre-trial hearings. The technology has speeded up the process hugely, and made it more secure. Previously, prisoners would have to be taken from their cells, searched, handcuffed and transported by bus to the courthouse where they could be charged: this could take up to two hours. With the videoconferencing technology in place, the whole process can be over in less than ten minutes, and there are no attendant security problems of transporting those in custody from the prison to the court.

'Giving evidence via videoconferencing saves transport and accommodation costs'

Sheriff Ted Boehm, of the Boone County Courthouse, acknowledges that the initial outlay (of $80,000) is substantial but claims that it has paid for itself in under three years in saved time and transport costs. And as the technology becomes cheaper, so the use of it will inevitably increase in other areas too. Courts have been using video technology for juvenile witnesses for some time to prevent them being intimidated by the courtroom atmosphere, but it could also help reduce costs for people travelling to give evidence. One doctor scheduled to appear at a malpractice trial in West Virginia couldn't make it because of flight problems: instead, he gave evidence via videoconferencing facilities, thus taking a full part in the trial and for a tenth of the cost of flying him in for a few days.

Those who oppose the introduction of such technology tend to argue that it affects the way testimony is given and received: that a defendant being charged while still in prison may have his rights compromised compared to a defendant appearing in the flesh in court. Up till now, the opposition has been minimal, though, with prisoners, lawyers and court officials alike endorsing the use of videoconferencing technology for saving time and money.

More on videoconferencing

Summarised from an item, entitled 'The Teleconference Agenda', in Green Futures magazine (November/December 2001 issue).

Since the events of September 11th, there has been a huge upsurge of interest in phone- and videoconferencing, as businessmen and women suddenly became extremely reluctant to fly everywhere. Though the reason for the increase in the uptake is not one that anyone wished for, the benefits to the environment in terms of reductions in number of flights are manifold. Similarly, the inconvenience, wasted time and (now) insecurity of flying can all be avoided with the use of videoconferencing technology. Every meeting that replaces a face-to-face one saves time, money, carbon emissions from car or aeroplane fuel and, often, a great deal of aggravation or congestion.

'Phone conferencing effectively reduces carbon emissions'

British Telecom, which increased its use of phone conferencing by 45 per cent in 2001, has estimated that, over that year, it saved 12 million litres of petrol, 1,800 years of time, 220 million miles of travel and 54,000 tonnes of carbon dioxide emissions, never mind the saving to the company itself. Obviously BT has an interest in pitching videoconferencing to other businesses, but the figures are undeniably impressive, and using the new technology appears to benefit everyone. The only downside is in the loss of face-to-face contact between individuals.

Good behaviour contracts bring troublemaking youths into line

Summarised from an article by Maria McHale, entitled 'Stop or go', in the Guardian Society section (August 29th 2001).

A new initiative in North London aims to cut down crime committed by youngsters by making them sign 'acceptable behaviour contracts' (or ABCs). These agreements lay out rules which the youths must abide by; any breach of the rules could result in their families facing eviction from their housing association home. The contracts had a much greater effect than any other means of cutting down on graffiti, vandalism and harassment in the area, because the parents suddenly had a direct interest in what their kids were up

6 Blackstock Mews, London N4 2BT, UK (rhino@dial.pipex.com), 2002, 300pp, ISBN 0 948826 59 2

to, and the youths became aware that their actions could make their family homeless. Arresting the youths had had little effect, because being arrested had come to be viewed as something of a badge of honour, hence the introduction of the ABCs.

'Under the contracts, the whole family has an interest in ensuring good behaviour'

The contracts were drawn up on an individual basis with the community police officer, the area housing manager and the young people involved, and they were then monitored for three months. 62 contracts were initially issued, and only three were breached. No families were evicted, as they were either rehoused or sent their child to live with relatives more able to cope. The key to the success of the scheme appears to have been getting the parents involved in the welfare and behaviour of their child: if the whole family has something to lose, the whole family has an interest in ensuring their family's good behaviour. The liaising between the police and the housing authorities also seems to have paid dividends; interviews of youths with their parents took place not in a police station, but at a local housing office, to reduce any suspicion and scepticism on the part of the families involved (and to eliminate the need for solicitors to be present).

The scheme has now been introduced in Southampton, Lincolnshire, Manchester and the Midlands, with two further pilots taking place in London. The founders of the Islington scheme are also hoping to bring in other partners to help tackle the problems, including mental health professionals, and they are keen to make ties with local schools as well, ensuring that all relevant parties know what is happening and why and, most importantly, what the result will be if they step out of line.

• *See www.homeoffice.gov.uk for more information.*

Painting gardening tools pink to deter criminals

Summarised from an article by Andy Mann, entitled 'Paint your mower', in the Burton Mail (May 22nd 2002).

Police in Burton-on-Trent in Staffordshire are recommending residents paint their garden tools garish colours to make them less attractive to thieves. The 'Paint it Pink' scheme suggests that painting gardening equipment, such as lawn mowers and strimmers, will deter crooks because they will find it difficult to sell on. PC Nigel Fermor said that "Criminals will not want the bother of having to re-paint the items and I doubt they will able to re-sell them whilst they are pink". And if the implements are stolen, the colours will also make identifying the stolen goods signifcantly easier. PC Fermor was keen to point out that the recommended technique was not intended to replace more obvious security measures, such as locks on sheds, but could prove a useful additional method of crime prevention.

• *For more on the scheme, contact PC Fermor, Burton-on-Trent police, on 01283 565011 ext 4718.*

6 Blackstock Mews, London N4 2BT, UK (rhino@dial.pipex.com), 2002, 300pp, ISBN 0 948826 59 2

HEALTH AND THERAPY

Health Tips of 2002 from recent medical research

The following is an update supplementing the far more comprehensive book published by the Institute for Social Inventions, entitled **1,001 Health Tips – from recent medical research** *(£6.99 inc p&p from www.globalideasbank.org/ bookorder.html). These updates are summarised from literature and cuttings sent to the Institute by correspondents in the UK and the USA. Wherever the correspondent remembered to provide a date and source, this has also been included. The focus here is not on the latest drugs or treatments but on tips that empower the average person, enabling them to do something for themselves about staying healthy or about regaining their health.*

Food & diet

• An **apple** a day will help alleviate diarrhoea, promote the elimination of excess fluids and toxicity, speed recovery from coughs and colds, reduce inflammation and regulate blood sugar (Healthy You, Jan/Feb 2002).

 • **Lemon juice** can assist in the prevention of **'economy class syndrome'**, by improving circulation during long flights. If taken once every five hours, it should significantly reduce the risk of blood clots forming (the Guardian Editor, September 1st 2002).

 • Eating a portion of **broccoli** every day reduces the risk of **colon cancer** by 46 per cent, a study at Liverpool University has shown. Broccoli contains a sugar called galactose which prevents cancer-causing proteins from becoming attached to the colon lining. The six-year study concluded that while eating a high-fibre diet made negligible difference, eating greens promoted colonic health (the Week, June 22nd 2002).

'Habitual tea drinking preserves bone density'

 • Researchers have found yet more reasons why the nation's favourite drink is good for us. A team from the National Cheng Kung University Hospital in Tainan, Taiwan, found that **habitual tea drinking** over many years preserves **bone density** in men and women, possibly because of tea's high fluoride content, especially the green variety. They believe it is not the quantity of tea drunk which matters, but for how long the person has been a habitual tea drinker (BBC News Online: Health, May 13th 2002).

 • **Cider** contains high levels of **antioxidants**, which 'mop up' the free radicals which cause cell damage, claims Dr Caroline Walker of Brewing

Research International in Surrey. The level is roughly equivalent to that found in red wine (from the Week, June 8th 2002).

• Eating **cereal** for breakfast can reduce the chance of catching a **cold or influenza** by more than 50 per cent. Research at Cardiff University has shown that people who eat regular breakfasts, particularly cereals fortified with vitamins and micronutrients, are far less likely to get a cold than those who abstain. Andy Smith, who headed the study, noted that a good breakfast also alleviates the patient's symptoms when they do succumb to a cold or 'flu, dubbing the foodstuff "one of the best preventive medicines out there" (the Times, March 6th 2002).

'Eating less prolongs life'

• Scientists have confirmed that **eating less prolongs life**. 'Calorific restriction' has extended the life of almost every animal tested by up to 50 per cent. The lifespan of monkeys fed on a normal low-fat diet remained the same, whereas those who were fed 30 per cent less seemed to live longer and were less susceptible to diseases such as cancer, heart disease and diabetes (New Scientist, June 2002).

• The risk of developing **colonic cancer** doubles if an immediate family member has suffered from the disease. However, recent findings indicate that a daily dose of 400 milligrams of **folic acid, fewer than two alcoholic beverages a day, and methionine**, can significantly reduce the risks. (Methionine has been linked to heart disease, so some might be best advised to concentrate on the first two). Charles Fuchs, a medical oncologist at the Dana-Farber Cancer Institute in Boston lead the study of over 89,000 women over a 16-year period (US News & World Report, March 25th, 2002).

• Recent findings, published in the 'American Journal of Medicine', indicate that **folic acid supplements** may keep blood vessels working better and **prevent heart disease,** a daily dose reducing the risk by up to 20 per cent. Foods rich in folic acid include **broccoli, tomatoes, leafy green vegetables such as spinach, kidney beans, liver and some citrus fruits** (BBC News Online: Health May 13th 2002).

• **Wild mushrooms** throughout Europe and beyond may still be unfit to eat following the Chernobyl nuclear disaster in 1986. Wild mushrooms absorb **radioactive caesium,** and wild animals which feed on them have shown elevated levels of radiation in their bodies. Pavel Kalac of the University of South Bohemia in the Czech Republic, who studied the reports, advises against consuming them but suggests radiation can be reduced by drying the mushrooms and cooking them in salted water (New Scientist, September 29th 2001).

• A diet rich in **polyunsaturated margarines and cooking oils** may double a child's risk of developing **childhood asthma**, report Australian researchers.

6 Blackstock Mews, London N4 2BT, UK (rhino@dial.pipex.com), 2002, 300pp, ISBN 0 948826 59 2

The team, led by Michelle Haby of the Royal Children's Hospital in Melbourne, does not yet know "whether changing the diet will reduce the risk or severity of asthma. That is the subject of ongoing investigation" (New Scientist, July 28th 2001).

• Eating **fish** once a week can significantly reduce a woman's risk of developing **heart disease**, say doctors from the Hereford School of Public Health. They monitored the health of nearly 85,000 nurses since 1980 and discovered that the benefits of fish in combating heart disease can be enjoyed from eating just one fish supper a week (the Times, April 10th 2002).

'Eating fish three times a week helps combat depression'

• Eating **fish** three times a week or taking daily **fish oil capsules** helps to combat **depression**, states a report published in the International Journal of Clinical Practice. EPA, an omega-3 fatty acid found in fish oil, was found to reduce even severe forms of depression by normalising brain chemistry (the National Enquirer, February 10th 2002).

• **A diet low in salt and very low in protein** (about 4 oz daily), with a normal intake of calcium, is the best way to prevent a recurrence of **kidney stones**. The Italian researchers who discovered this have refuted the received wisdom that a low-calcium diet reduces the risk, claiming it may do exactly the opposite (Time, January 21st 2002).

• A diet rich in **sugars and refined carbohydrates**, including bread and cereals, may be to blame for the high incidence of **short-sightedness**, or myopia in Western society, says Professor Loren Cordain of Colorado State University. These foods raise insulin levels which in turn leads to high levels of growth factors: this process has a bearing on the development of the eyeball in childhood. While there is no undoing damage already done, the research may prevent further degeneration. Cordain's team found that increasing the levels of proteins in the diets of myopic children (and thereby reducing or balancing the carbohydrates consumed), slowed the progress of myopia (the Times, May 7th 2002).

'Fruit juice is best drunk at lunchtime'

• **Fruit juice** is best drunk at lunchtime, and a mix of juices may be more beneficial than one. Fructose, the fruit sugar is swiftly absorbed and raises blood sugar levels quickly, thereby stimulating insulin production. The subsequent fall in blood sugar level stimulates low density lipoprotein fats to be released by the liver, which are damaging to the artery. The effects of a dose of fructose are greater first thing in the morning (the Times, May 2nd 2002).

Institute for Social Inventions, £15 subs, £17 from abroad by credit card, tel London 020 7359 8391

• Recent evidence suggests that **chewing gum** enhances **mental perform-ance**. Dr Scholey, Director of the Human Cognitive Neuroscience Unit at the University of Northumbria, and his team studied the performance of 25 people carrying out computer tests whilst chewing sugar-free gum. The gum-chewers performed significantly better than the group who mimed chewing and those who did not chew at all, outperforming them particularly in their long and short-term recall ability. This may be because chewing gum releases insulin into the body which then assists the brain in memory formation. Dr Scholey claimed that although it might help people to revise for and pass exams, it would not necessarily work for everyone, and he was against advocating gum chewing in the classroom (the Times, March 14th 2002)

• These findings come in tandem with recent research demonstrating that very small quantities of **alcohol can assist recall**, particularly of words or dance steps. It is counterproductive to drink alcohol before learning, said Dr Scholey, "but if you consume a very small amount immediately after learning something, often it will help" (the Times, March 14th 2002).

• Certain flavours of **herbal tea** can cause **tooth rot**, according to a study at the Manchester University Dental Hospital. Researchers found that teas containing fruits such as blackcurrant, lemon and raspberry can dissolve tooth enamel, and affect teeth to a much greater extent than ordinary tea (the Week, December 1st 2001).

• Drinking **coffee** late in the day can reduce your chance of a good night's **sleep**, say researchers in Israel. It can take many hours to expel caffeine from the body, and caffeinated coffee is not only a stimulant, but also halves the body's levels of melatonin, the hormone that sends people to sleep (the Week, April 27th 2002).

'One to three alcoholic drinks a day reduces the risk of getting Alzheimer's'

• Having one to three **alcoholic drinks** a day reduces the risk of getting **Alzheimer's disease** and dementia by up to 40 per cent, a Dutch study has found. Scientists posit that alcohol thins the blood and thus reduces the likelihood of clots blocking blood flow to the brain (Healthy You, April 2002).

• **Bread, chips and crisps** contain high levels of acrylamide, a substance believed to cause **cancer**, according to a study by Swedish scientists. Chips from Burger King and McDonald's were found to contain 100 times more acrylamide than the maximum the World Health Organisation allows in drinking water, while a bag of crisps contains 500 times this limit. Acrylamide is formed when foods rich in carbohydrates – such as rice and potatoes – are baked or fried, and can cause gene mutations which may lead to stomach tumours (Metro, April 25th 2002).

6 Blackstock Mews, London N4 2BT, UK (rhino@dial.pipex.com), 2002, 300pp, ISBN 0 948826 59 2

• **Vitamin E**, a powerful antioxidant abundant in leafy green vegetables, nuts and seeds, may help protect the brain from ravaging diseases such as **Alzheimer's** (the Times, December 18th 2001)

• Dieters have been warned by doctors marking Salt Awareness Day that **so-called healthy foods** can be **dangerously high in salt**, and that low-calorie meals often contain the same levels of salt as high-fat foods. A high-fibre cereal for breakfast, soup and wholemeal bread for lunch and a dinner of lasagne and salad contains more than 13 grams of salt, twice the recommended daily intake. High salt intake has been linked to heart disease, strokes, high blood pressure, gastric cancer and osteoporosis (Metro, January 30th 2002).

Tips to make your summer healthier:

• The solution to increased **air pollution** during the summer months is to eat plenty of **strawberries**, which, like raspberries and grapes, are packed with pollution-busting ellagic acid. Asthma sufferers will benefit from the Vitamin C found in strawberries, raspberries, peppers and citrus fruits.

'Hay fever sufferers should eat plenty of apples, onions, and leeks'

• **Hay fever** sufferers should eat plenty of a**pples, onions, lollo ross lettuces, endives and leeks**, all of which are rich in quercetin, which supposedly acts as an anti-histamine. Omega 3 fatty acids, found in **oily fish**, can help **reduce inflammation** in both hay fever and asthma.

• Those likely to swim in swimming pools should **chew gum** containing xylitol, which protects the throat and ears from **infections** caused by water-borne bacteria.

• Eating **mangoes, sweet potatoes, carrots and apricots** can help boost the **skin's immunity** to the sun's harmful rays (although high factor suncream should always be worn). All are rich in betacarotene, a pigment which accumulates in the fatty layers of the skin, providing mild protection. (From Amanda Ursell in the Sunday Times, summarised by The Week, June 15th 2002)

Lifestyle

• It is possible to **increase muscle strength by visualising** a muscle working without actually flexing it, according to scientists at the Cleveland Clinic Foundation in Ohio. After only a few weeks, volunteers who visualised exercising their pectoral muscles showed a 13.5 increase in strength (the Times, November 11th 2001).

• A team led by Gavin Cleary, a specialist registrar at Great Ormond Street Children's Hospital, claim a link between prolonged use of **vibrating com-**

puter games and a condition known as **hand-arm vibration syndrome**. Symptoms include hands becoming white and swollen when exposed to cold, and red and painful when warm. Cleary has called for such vibrating computer games to carry "statutory health warnings to advise users and parents" (the Times, February 1st 2002).

• A new report in the 'Annals of Behavioural Medicine' has pooh-poohed supposed evidence linking **faith** to **better health**. Richard Sloan and colleagues reviewed all 266 articles written on the subject and found the vast majority had serious flaws in their methodology (US News & World Report, March 25th 2002).

'Visualising a relaxing scene is an effective cure for insomnia'

• **Visualising** a relaxing scene is a more effective cure for **insomnia** than counting sheep, say researchers at Oxford University. The study showed that volunteers who were asked to conjure up an engaging scene such as a waterfall or being on holiday fell asleep 20 minutes earlier than usual, whilst those counting sheep took longer than normal to fall asleep on the nights of the experiment (Healthy You, April 2002).

• Tips to counteract **insomnia**:

* avoid coffee, tea, late-night meals. A night cap, such as a small whiskey, is fine, but any more than two glasses of wine will be detrimental to sleep.

* Keep your bedroom uncluttered; too many possessions, including books, diaries, etc, mean that the associations between the bedroom and sleep are lost.

* Try banishing those vindictively repetitive thoughts by repeating a mantra, such as 'Om Om Om'.

* Set yourself the task of remaining awake until 2am – once you stop worrying you will find it difficult *not* to sleep.

* If all else fails, you can spend the red-eyed hours wisely by visiting www.britishsleepfoundation.org.uk for solace and advice (the Times, January 22nd 2002).

• **Smoking** may cause **mental illness**, claims Sophie Petit Zeman in an article in New Scientist. Depressives are twice as likely to smoke, and up to 88 per cent of those with psychotic conditions such as schizophrenia are smokers. The tobacco industry has traditionally taken the line that the illness came first, with sufferers taking up smoking to alleviate their distress. However, a 1998 study shows that of 1,000 people tracked over five years, those who smoked were twice as likely to develop depression during that period than non-smokers (the Week, April 27th 2002).

• Physicists in Japan have found that when a group of commuters all use their **mobile phones** at the same time in a confined space, the levels of

6 Blackstock Mews, London N4 2BT, UK (rhino@dial.pipex.com), 2002, 300pp, ISBN 0 948826 59 2

electromagnetic radiation generated far exceeds the recommended levels as determined by international guidelines. They found that in a standard train carriage with a maximum capacity of 151 persons, it took only 30 people talking or surfing on their phones to exceed this level (New Scientist, May 2002).

* **Tips to reduce the risks posed by mobile phone use:**

* Keep **calls** as **short** as possible.

* Ensure the **antenna** is as far as possible from the head and hand.

* Avoid handsets with **internal antenna**, as these usually increase radiation levels in the brain and the hand.

* Avoid using your phone when it has less than four or five bars of **signal strength.** Radiation varies 100-fold according to availability of reception.

* If you are using your phone indoors, **stand by a window,** (and have the handset on the window side) where the signal strength can be up to ten times greater and thereby reduces the amount of power generated by the phone

* **Use a hands-free kit,** which does, contrary to belief, reduce radiation. But exercise caution about where the phone is on your body

* Use some form of **protective device.** For a comparison of the different devices, read Simon Best's article, 'Mobile Phones: the pressure and the evidence continue to mount', in *PROOF* magazine vol 5/1 (call [+44] (0)20 8944 9555 to obtain a copy). (Adapted from the Ecologist, Vol. 31 No. 8, October 2001.)

'A daytime nap improves decision-making by 50 per cent'

* Scientists at Nasa have reported that a **daytime nap** can **increase alertness**, improving your performance by 35 per cent and your ability to make the right decision by 50 per cent (the Times, March 20th 2002).

* Claims that **ecstasy** causes long-term brain damage are based on 'bad science', states an article in New Scientist. A study in 1998 which used scans to prove damage to serotonin transporters in the brains of drug users has led to the notion that regular ecstasy use can lead to serious mental illness in later life. However, two independent experts have declared this study flawed and unreliable. Most tests of mental performance have also shown that ecstasy users performed just as well as non-users. Ecstasy can cause mild depression in the short term, and while it has proved fatal in certain circumstances, casualties are relatively low: more people in Britain die in skiing accidents (the Week, April 27th 2002).

* **Golfers** hoping to lower their handicap may be wasting their time out on the course. Sports psychologists at Manchester Metropolitan University have discovered that players who repeatedly watch a video of their game, listen to an audio tape or read about golf succeed in taking up to nine shots off their

handicap. Dave Smith, who headed the research, found the technique to be more effective than pre-shot visualisation techniques; players who had imagined putting whilst **watching a video of their game** during the six-week trial improved their putting performance by as much as 57 per cent (the Times, March 14th 2002).

'Fitness is the single most significant factor in determining longevity'

• **Fitness** would appear be the single most significant factor in determining **longevity**, concludes a study of 6,000 middle-aged persons conducted at the Veterans Affairs Health Care System at Stanford University. Dr Ken Cooper, a fitness expert, added: "You are better off being fat and fit than skinny and sedentary" and added that just taking a walk every day makes a big difference (www.msnbc.com/news; March 2002 www.msnbc.com/news).

• Regularly taking an **over-the-counter medicine** could greatly reduce your risk of developing **Alzheimer's** disease. Researchers led by Bruno Stricker at the Erasmus Medical Centre in Rotterdam found that taking an average of two anti-inflammatory pills per week cut an elderly person's risk of developing the disease by 80 per cent. These drugs have not been promoted in the past because regular use of non-steroidal anti-inflammatories can cause severe stomach problems or intestinal bleeding. However, a new type of pill called a Cox-2 inhibitor has been developed, which has anti-inflammatory properties without gastric side-effects. These drugs have been said to break up the amyloid plaques that build up in the brains of Alzheimer's sufferers, and it is thought their properties may also defend healthy brain cells from attack by immune cells (New Scientist, December 1st 2001).

Workplace

• Giving people **more control at work** can leave them healthier, and so help relieve the burden on health services, according to research by Daniel Ganster of the University of Arkansas in Fayetteville. He monitored the stress levels and healthcare costs of 105 nurses over five years, and found that those with high-stress jobs but little control spent more on healthcare than those with equally demanding jobs but more control (New Scientist, November 24th 2001).

• Research has found that seven million people suffer from **allergies caused by work:** up to 300 toxic substances have been found in offices which can lead to headaches, breathing problems, itchy skin and lethargy. irritants include chemicals used by cleaners, as well as high levels of indoor ozone emitted by computers, fax machines and photocopiers (the Evening Standard, March 18th 2002).

6 Blackstock Mews, London N4 2BT, UK (rhino@dial.pipex.com), 2002, 300pp, ISBN 0 948826 59 2

• **Nausea, headaches and dizziness** in the workplace may be caused by **old carpets** emitting noxious odours which subconsciously affect workers, rendering them less productive (Metro April 4th 2002).

• Staff who nod off at their desks should not be reprimanded, as **napping may raise** their **productivity** by up to 35 per cent, claims Mark Rosekind, chief scientist of California-based Alertness solutions. However, kipping for longer than 45 minutes will leave the person groggy and less effective. He also advises preventing jet lag by having two solid nights of eight hours' sleep prior to departure, whilst business travellers should not book meetings in the 3-5am and 3-5pm periods in their 'home time' when they will be sleepiest; maximum alertness is usually achieved between 9-11am and 9-11pm (the Times, March 18th 2002).

'Plants in the workplace boost productivity'

• **Plants** may not only improve the aesthetics of a workplace and improve air quality, but have also been proven to **boost productivity** and reduce the amount of sick leave taken by staff. A recent study carried out by Professor Virginia Lohr, of Washington State University, found that reaction time was 12 per cent faster in workers who had plants on their desks. Plants' ability to process and reduce the volatile organic chemicals (VOCs) prevalent in the atmosphere, has a direct influence on stress levels and health in the workplace. The best plants for the job are those which require lots of watering, or have a high leaf area to pot size ration. See www.plants-for-people.org for more tips (the Times, June 11th 2002).

Men

• Increasing the rate of **male circumcision** could dramatically reduce cases of **cervical cancer in women**, according to research led by Xavier Castellsague at Llobregat Hospital in Barcelona. His team reviewed studies of almost 2,000 couples, and found that women with 'high-risk' partners – men who had more than six sexual partners – were 58 per cent less likely to develop cervical cancer if their partner had been circumcised. They also found that Human Papilloma Virus, which is sexually transmitted and contributes to most cases of cervical cancer, was present in under six per cent of circumcised men as opposed to nearly 20 per cent of uncircumcised men. Circumcision involves the removal of the inner lining of the foreskin, which is believed to be especially vulnerable to infection (NewScientist.com, April 16th 2002).

• **Men whose waist measurement exceeds 37 inches** are at a greater risk of **a premature death**, while those with a waist measurement over 40 inches are likely to suffer clinical obesity. Dr Ian Campbell, a specialist in men's health and weight control, exhorts those who fall into this category to slim urgently. He has set up a website (www.fatslim.com or e-mail at:

enquiries@fmshealthcare.com) which, at a reasonable cost, will provide men with the necessary structure and support to lose weight at home (the Times, March 28th 2002).

• **Men who smoke** are almost three times **less likely to make their partners pregnant** through IVF than non-smokers, according to research led by Michael Zitzmann, from the Institute of Reproductive Medicine in Munster, Germany. He believes smoking probably has an adverse affect during fertilisation and also damages the DNA in sperm (the Guardian, July 3rd 2002).

'Doses of folic acid may increase sperm production'

• A study of 100 subfertile men has shown that taking daily doses of **folic acid** with zinc may increase healthy **sperm production** by as much as 74 per cent (with a slight increase in abnormal sperm), but they do not yet know whether this translates to better odds of conceiving. The research, led by Dr Wai Wong of the University Medical Centre Nijmegen in the Netherlands (and published in the March issue of the journal 'Fertility and Sterility'), found no significant alteration in the sperm count of fertile men (http://hvlib.integris-health.com/HealthNews, March 14th 2002).

Women

• The World Health Organisation has found that women who take **the Pill** for longer than five years may be at nearly twice the risk of developing **cervical cancer**. The WHO asserts that Pill users expose themselves to sexually transmitted diseases such as human papillomavirus which, left untreated, can lead to cervical cancer – however, they also claim that the cervical screening programme is cutting the number of cases (Metro, March 27th 2002).

• **Hormone replacement therapy** may increase the risk of **ovarian cancer**, a study in The Journal of the National Cancer Institute has shown. Scientists found that women who take HRT for more than ten years are at greatest risk (the Times, April 3rd 2002).

'Hormone replacement therapy could halve hardening of the arteries'

• **Hormone replacement therapy** could halve hardening of the arteries, which reduces the risk of heart attacks and strokes, scientists have found (Metro, April 4th 2002).

• Despite the recent criticism over **breast cancer screening**, the recent World Health Organisation (24 experts from 11 countries) findings show

6 Blackstock Mews, London N4 2BT, UK (rhino@dial.pipex.com), 2002, 300pp, ISBN 0 948826 59 2

that, from a sample of 1,000 healthy British women aged 50 to 69, 20 would get breast cancer after a decade, and about six would die from the disease. With screenings, however, only four would die. False diagnosis remains a possibility, but while it causes needless anxiety, it is not life-threatening. The experts concluded, however, that there was as yet insufficient evidence to recommend screenings for women aged under 50 or over 70.

Self examination also did not appear to help in the detection of cancer. A large study of Chinese women who had been taught to self-check, found that regular checking did not limit the numbers of women dying from the disease. There was also no evidence to suggest that a doctor checking was effective. Valerie Beral, a professor of epidemiology at Oxford University and chairwoman of the National Advisory committee on Breast Cancer Screening in the NHS advised: "A formal programme of self-examination does not work, but women should still be aware of their breasts and if they find a lump, go to their doctor, even if they have just been screened" (the Times, March 19th 2002).

• A study by the International Agency for Research on Cancer has found that women who have the human papilloma virus (HPV), a common **genital infection**, and who are long-time **Pill users** are three times more likely to develop **cervical cancer**. The research looked at 1,900 women who were either healthy or were being treated for cervical cancer, and found that 94 per cent of those with invasive cervical cancer were infected with HPV. Women who had been using the Pill for five to nine years were three times more likely to have cervical cancer than those not using oral contraceptives. However, there was no evidence that long-term use of the Pill increased the risk of cancer in the absence of HPV, and the Family Planning Association pointed out that the Pill "reduces the risk of both cancer of the ovaries and womb" (the Times, March 27th 2002).

• Meanwhile, a new study has found that the chances of missing early detection of breast cancer more than doubles when the breast is poorly positioned during a **mammogram**. The study, published in April's edition of the American Journal of Roentgenology recommends a woman should lean in as far as possible and the author, Stephen Taplin of Group Health Cooperative's Center for Health studies, suggests furthermore: "You need to feel the [edge of the compressing surfaces] against your chest wall ... You shouldn't have to twist and stand on your tippy-toes to be in the machine ... it should come to you" (US News & World Report, April 8th 2002).

'Having children late in life reduces the chance of developing ovarian cancer'

• Women who have **children late in life** may be significantly reducing the chances of developing **cervical cancer**, suggests a new study in 'The Lancet'. "The risk of ovarian cancer decreased by about 10 per cent for each five year increment in age at first childbirth", said Dr Hans-Olov Adami. The study confirmed reports that the greater the number of pregnancies a woman has, the less likely she is to develop the disease, and discovered that a woman planning to have just one child would reduce her risk of contracting cervical cancer by 50 per cent if she delayed pregnancy from the age of 20 to 45 (from the Week, April 6th 2002).

• **Tips to relieve menopausal symptoms:**

* Limit alcohol and caffeine intake, particularly before bed.

* Increase consumption of foods rich in phytoestrogens, eg soyabean products (tofu, miso), apples, broccoli, chickpeas, lentils, linseeds, oatmeal, peas, pumpkin seeds, potato.

* Limit consumption of hot spices, sour fruits such as rhubarb, citrus and berries, as well as salty foods.

* Take regular exercise.

* Stop smoking.

(from the Times, November 27th 2001)

Conception, Childbirth and Pregnancy

• A study has found that women who gain more than 50 lbs during pregnancy and do not lose it after birth can triple their risk of **breast cancer**. The study, presented to the American Association for Cancer Research in San Francisco, observed over 27,000 breast cancer patients and found that each 2.2 lbs (1kg) increase raised the breast cancer risk by 3.9 per cent. Scientists stressed, however, that gaining 25 to 50lbs during pregnancy is normal and not associated with any increase in risk.

• Babies conceived by **IVF** are more than twice as likely to suffer **birth defects** as babies conceived naturally, claim researchers at the University of Western Australia. The study revealed that nine per cent of IVF babies had major defects, compared with just 4.2 per amongst those conceived naturally. It is not known whether the defects are caused by aspects of IVF, or the factors that make couples infertile, or both (New Scientist, March 16th 2002).

• A link has been asserted between **ultrasounds** and possible **brain damage** to foetuses, in the largest study yet conducted on the subject. Professor Juni Palmgren, a member of the Swedish team which conducted the research, found that men who were genetically predisposed to right-handedness may have become left-handed as a consequence of ultrasound, but urged people not to refuse them, as the possibility of damage was slight (the Sunday Times, December 9th 2002).

• Pregnant women who have a diet rich in **fish** are almost four times less likely to have a **premature delivery**. Danish scientists reporting in the British Medical Journal found that of 8,700 pregnant women, 7.1 per cent who never ate fish gave birth prematurely, while only 1.9 per cent of those who ate fish regularly did (the Times, February 22nd 2002).

6 Blackstock Mews, London N4 2BT, UK (rhino@dial.pipex.com), 2002, 300pp, ISBN 0 948826 59 2

• However, pregnant women (and children under 16) should avoid eating **marlin, shark and swordfish**, due to their high mercury content. The UK Food Standards Agency, which issued the warning, said that a tingling sensation in the skin was an early sign of **mercury poisoning**, but stressed that these effects were highly unlikely to be more than transient (the Week, May 13th 2002).

'There is a correlation between poor oral health and premature birth'

• Researchers at the Alabama University School of Dentistry have uncovered a correlation between **poor oral health** and **premature birth**. The team examined women's mouths when they were between 21 and 24 weeks pregnant and found that those with gum disease were between four and seven times more likely to deliver their babies early. They are continuing their investigation to ascertain whether gum disease is itself a symptom connected to premature births (New Scientist, July 28th 2001).

• High levels of **chemicals in public swimming pools** may be linked to **miscarriage and birth defects**, suggest a team of scientists at Imperial College, London. Chloroform, created when chlorine reacts with organic matter such as skin cells, can be easily absorbed by swimmers who swallow it or inhale it as it evaporates. Dr Mark Nieuwenhuijsen has called for the levels of chemicals in pools to be reduced "as far as possible while maintaining effective control against water-borne diseases" (Metro, April 4th 2002).

• **Mothers who 'lie in'** with their babies have a lower risk of **postnatal depression** according to professor Dominic Lee, a psychiatrist at the Chinese University of Hong Kong, who is studying ancient postnatal customs.

• A team led by Professor Vivette Glover at Imperial College, London claim to have found a link between **stress during pregnancy** and **hyperactivity** in young children. They discovered that women who had high stress levels during pregnancy were 50 per cent more likely to have children who suffer from hyperactivity or other behavioural problems; Glover suggested that an unborn baby's brain could be affected by the stress hormone cortisol (the Week, September 15th 2001).

• A seven-day **contraceptive patch** for women could soon become available in Britain. The patches have a 99 per cent effectiveness rate, similar to that of the Pill, and have been approved by the European Medicines Agency; but the approval must now be confirmed by the European Commission.

• A child is five times more likely to develop **diabetes** if its mother **smokes during pregnancy**, according to researchers at the Karolinksa Institute in Stockholm. They followed 5,000 British births from 1958 through to adulthood, and found that 32 per cent of those who developed diabetes had a mother who smoked heavily. Research fellow Dr Scott Montgomery believes that smoking damages the receptors which deal with fat: "The foetus is programmed to believe it is being born into an environment of malnutrition ... so the child is ready to preserve as much fat as possible", which leads to obesity and diabetes (Metro, January 4th 2002).

• Drinking even a small amount of **alcohol during pregnancy** increases your child's chances of developing **behavioural problems** later in life. A study reported in 'Pediatrics' compared teetotallers and women who drank the equivalent of one cocktail a week during pregnancy, and found that the latter were three times more likely to have a child with problems such as delinquent behaviour, aggression and attention deficit disorder (Healthy You, February 2002).

• Children who are **breast-fed** are 32 per cent less likely to suffer **obesity** in later life than their formula-fed counterparts, according to a study published in 'The Lancet'. Human milk boosts immunity but also limits the growth of fat cells, while mothers using formula milk often overfeed their babies, establishing poor habits for later on (the Week, June 22nd 2002).

• Furthermore, babies who are **breast-fed** for at least six months are up to five times less likely to develop **pneumonia**, and suffer from fewer colds and ear infections (the Week, May 18th 2002).

Children

• Children who have suffered several **serious illnesses** may be at greater risk of developing **anorexia nervosa**, according to a team led by Beth Watkins at St George's Hospital Medical School in London. They studied 90 children with eating disorders and found that those with anorexia were more likely to have a history of serious illness than healthy people (New Scientist, September 29th 2001)

• **Toxic fumes from incinerators** may be impairing the **sexual development** of children, a report in the Lancet has suggested. Medical research has found that teenagers living near incinerators had small sexual organs compared to those in rural areas; their bodies contained high levels of toxic chemicals already linked to cancer, heart disease and breathing difficulties (Healthy You, August 2001).

'Household pets double the risk of childhood asthma'

• Household **pets** can double the risk of children developing **asthma**, according to researchers from the Children's Hospital Medical Center in Cincinnati. Studies showed that asthma rates in children aged between six and 17 years were reduced by 45 per cent once animals were removed from the home (Healthy you, August 2001).

6 Blackstock Mews, London N4 2BT, UK (rhino@dial.pipex.com), 2002, 300pp, ISBN 0 948826 59 2

• A supposedly healthy diet high in **polyunsaturated fats,** found in margarines and vegetable oil, may double the risk of **asthma** in pre-school children. However, Michelle Haby of the Royal Children's Hospital in Melbourne who led the research, claimed that increased bottle feeding might account for 16 per cent of the higher asthma rate. Other studies have shown that while polyunsaturated fats are essential for health, excessive reliance on them to the exclusion of others may also lead to cancer (the Times, July 19th 2001).

• Watching **Thomas the Tank Engine** TV programme aids the development of children with **autism and Asperger's syndrome**, says a report by the National Autistic Society. Autistic children have difficulty understanding and communicating emotions, but the characters' exaggerated fixed facial expressions help them to intuit the emotion being felt. Bold colours and simple scenery also help autistic children who find changes in sound and movement distracting (the Times, March 5th 2002).

• People who have **problems with basic maths** may be suffering from a genetic disorder called **discalculia**. A report in the Sunday Telegraph draws attention to the little-known disorder, which renders sufferers baffled by such basic concepts as 2+2=4. Scientists believe that up to six per cent of the population are affected by discalculia, and that thousands of children may be falling behind with their schoolwork because the condition is not recognised. Professor Brian Butterworth of University College, London has designed a discalculia test to identify sufferers, which will be introduced in schools throughout the country in September (the Week, April 27th 2002).

'Watching television does cause aggression'

• A comprehensive study of 707 New York families over 18 years has confirmed that **watching TV** does cause **aggression**. Professor Jeffrey Johnson of Columbia University, who led the research, found that of teenage boys who watched three hours of TV per day, 45 per cent went on to commit an aggressive act against another person, compared with nine per cent of those who watched less than an hour. Less hardened TV watchers – those who watched an hour or more TV per day aged 14 were also more likely to commit aggressive acts than those who watched the box for less than an hour (from the Week, April 13th 2002).

• New research has found that children who attend **nursery school** or day care early in life are less likely to suffer from **leukaemia**, as exposure to a variety of infections assists in the development of a healthy immune system. Professor Patricia Buffler, who headed the study at the University of California, Berkeley, added: "As well as attending nursery there are many ways in which the immune system can receive developmental stimulation, such as vaccination and exposure to siblings and friends" (the Week, May 18th 2002).

Miscellaneous

• A trial by Cancer Research UK has shown that a single **bowel cancer examination** at the age of 60 could save 2,000 lives a year in Britain. The test, called sigmoidoscopy, allows polyps which might develop into cancer to be detected and, if necessary, removed. Researchers found that screening could cut bowel cancer incidence and death rates by 40 per cent (the Times, April 12th 2002).

• A persistent **chesty cough** could be an early warning of **lung disease**, say doctors of the British Thoracic Society. This affliction may be a sign of chronic obstructive pulmonary disease, which kills 30,000 people a year; other symptoms include frequent heavy colds and breathlessness (Metro, January 7th 2002).

'Playing the harmonica can help lung disease sufferers'

• A team headed by Jeff Fraser at Florida Hospital is helping to rehabilitate patients suffering from **lung disease** and breathing problems by teaching them to play the **harmonica**. The breathing technique used to play the harmonica can help to exercise respiratory and abdominal muscles and increase the strength of the diaphragm, whose muscles can become weak or flattened by lung disease (Green Events, March 2002).

• Hospital patients about to undergo **surgery** have been urged to make sure the **doctor marks the correct site in ink** before performing the operation. The Joint Commission on Accreditation of Healthcare Organizations cites a rise in surgeries on the wrong body parts, surgery on the wrong patient or the wrong surgical procedure as the reason for this alert (Newsday, December 6th 2001).

• **Vaccinations** against tetanus, diphtheria and polio may **reduce your chance of developing Alzheimer's** in later life, according to a study at Laval University in Quebec. Rene Verrault, head of the research, offers two possible explanations: either boosting the immune system helps the brain to fight amyloid plaques, or beating childhood illnesses leads to better mental health in old age (New Scientist, December 1st 2001).

• Lit **incense sticks** emit dangerous carcinogens thought to trigger **lung cancer**. However, Dr Ta Chan Li, who led the investigation, is not yet certain to what extent these airborne carcinogens are inhaled into the lungs (Metro, August 2nd 2001)

6 Blackstock Mews, London N4 2BT, UK (rhino@dial.pipex.com), 2002, 300pp, ISBN 0 948826 59 2

Text messages to help people giving up smoking

Summarised from an article on the BUPA website, entitled 'Text messages help smokers quit in the New Year' (www.bupa.co.uk/health_news/ 291200smoke.html), and from an item entitled 'Bound to happen', in On magazine in Spring 2001 (www.onmagazine.com), monitored for the Global Ideas Bank by Roger Knights.

A new internet company sends out three months' worth of morale-boosting text messages to people trying to give up smoking. MyAlert.com provide the free service to any smoker with a mobile phone and access to a computer, and as soon as a person has signed on, the messaging can begin. As well as supportive messages to boost morale, tips to help give up smoking are also sent out.

'The company sends out messages to divert the smoker's attention'

A company in Switzerland are also providing a text messaging service to help those trying to give up smoking. Any time the person feels the urge to light up, they can look at messages sent by the company to divert their thoughts and attention. Before they know it, the attempted habit-kicker might be pondering which three people they would most like to be marooned on a desert island with rather than what brand to buy. So if the gum, patch, inhaler and old-fashioned willpower have all failed, mobile phone owners can take the text-messaging approach, even if that might just mean swapping one habit for another.

Blood group information on hand for emergencies

Stan Hayward

Everyone should have their blood group listed as part of their identity on passports and other documents, so that in an emergency this information is readily available. This could save crucial time in emergency situations, particularly as some people are unaware of what blood group they are.

• *Stan Hayward, 25 Walm Lane, London NW2 5SH (e-mail: stan@hccat.demon.co.uk). Stan runs film workshops for children and young people.*

Massage on the school curriculum reduces stress and anxiety

Solveig Berggren

Since 1996, I have worked with introducing massage on the curriculum in schools. Now it is on the curriculum every week in Sweden, and it is very popular. As a massage therapist I know how massage can help people, and children are no exception. Our schools today have a lot of problems with overcrowded classrooms, anxiety, bullying, testing and children not getting enough attention. We adults maybe do not have the time for our children that they are in need of.

The aim of the massage is to relieve stress and create a relaxed peaceful atmosphere. For the small children I start with massage stories, the next level is different strokes with relaxing music in the background, (this is all with clothes on of course). This goes on for about five to eight minutes for each child.

For the older children it is more about ergonomics (working with computers), preventing stress, stretching and other relaxation techniques. This really helps the children, improving the mood and reducing aggression of pupils. I also talk about respect for each other, not hurting, private zones and the right to say no to unwanted touch.

This 'positive touch' seems to give children a sense of attention and validation, as well as having a beneficial impact on their levels of concentration and relaxation. Touch has been shown to result in the secretion of oxytocin, the 'calming hormone', and to decrease the secretion of cortisol, the 'stress hormone'.

[Another suggestion, from Retta Bowen from the Institute for Social Inventions, is that children could be taught to massage each other as well, ensuring a whole generation knows the positive power of touch, and its relaxing properties. Obviously, there would have to be strict guidelines and supervision laid out, as Solveig implies above]

In June 2002, primary school students at Cochrane Castle Primary School in Johnstone, Renfrewshire, were taught basic massage techniques aimed at both reducing aggression and improving concentration. The five-week course taught the pupils the basic strokes of Swedish massage.

• *Solveig has been a skilled sports massage therapist since 1991 and has worked with introducing massage on the curriculum since 1996. He also does workshops with nurses and teachers about the effects of massage for children.'*

• *Solveig Berggren (e-mail: solveig@mailbox.calypso.net).*

6 Blackstock Mews, London N4 2BT, UK (rhino@dial.pipex.com), 2002, 300pp, ISBN 0 948826 59 2

Short 'first aid' adverts before popular programmes

Martin Curtis

This is quite a basic idea really, though I think it would not only interest but also benefit all viewers. The idea is to have a 30 or 60 second slot on BBC or ITV before such programmes as Eastenders or Coronation Street, basically those programmes with high viewing figures. On each occasion, a different first aid tip would be shown. For example, how to give first aid to a heart attack victim or electric shock victim. The series of adverts could give five key points on how to save someone else's life.

They could maybe run for a week, once every one or two months. The BBC would be most suitable as they have no advertising to contend with. They could also be made with a fun or humorous element which I'm sure would make it more easy to remember. Celebrities could be asked to be involved to give the adverts more of an impact with those watching. It would be a new, useful twist on the old public information broadcasts of the 50s and 60s.

• *Martin Curtis (e-mail: mgc@thecrez.fsnet.co.uk). Martin lives in Richmond, North Yorkshire.*

Taxing pharmaceutical and food adverts to fund independent 'truth' adverts

Summarised from an article by Norman Solomon, entitled 'A modest proposal for media reform', on the independent media website, www.alternet.org (June 21st 2002).

In order to counter the advertising impact of the pharmaceutical companies and fast food giants, Norman Solomon proposes taxing their adverts to fund alternative, independently researched 'truth' adverts dispensing health information. The problem, in America and elsewhere, is that the public is besieged by an onslaught of advertising telling us what to put in our mouths, both to feed us and cure us. This is never balanced by a similar stream of objective, scientific information. Taxing all food and drug adverts would create a pool of money to pay for adverts created by an independent 'truth commission', who could keep the public informed on the latest research on the risks, and benefits, of such products.

Institute for Social Inventions, £15 subs, £17 from abroad by credit card, tel London 020 7359 8391

'A third of Americans talk to their doctor about a drug they have seen advertised'

A recent survey in the US, by the Henry J. Kaiser Family Foundation, found that almost a third of all Americans talk to their doctor about a drug they have seen advertised, and that almost half of those people end up receiving the drug, whatever it might be. Such medications are not only expensive, but may have side effects or other associated risks. The same is true of food advertising: imagine if every McDonald's or Burger King advert was followed by statistics on obesity and life expectancy. 'Truth commission' adverts would fill in the gaps about this information, and help introduce facts and rationality to counter the hype of those selling their products. It might also encourage more public scepticism to claims made in adverts.

Family support co-ordinators help patients' deal with underlying problems

Summarised from an article by David Brindle, entitled 'Help without stigma', in the Guardian Society section (July 18th 2001).

In an effort to tackle the underlying social problems behind medical complaints, a scheme has been initiated in which family support co-ordinators are attached to doctors' practices and health centres. The WellFamily project works by doctors and health workers referring patients to the family support co-ordinators, who then try and deal with the more general issues that could be root causes of the health problems.

'60 per cent of those referred went on to receive counselling'

Of over 1,200 referrals (over a period of two and a half years), 53 per cent had emotional or psychological problems, 41 per cent had material or financial problems and 34 per cent had family problems. 60 per cent of those referred went on to receive counselling, while 41 per cent were put in touch with other agencies. The key to the scheme's success was its informality and its speed: nearly a quarter of people were seen the same day as being referred, and more than half were seen in the same week. The co-ordinators, though trained in a range of areas such as social work, housing and counselling, were seen as more open and friendly than those representatives of the standard health services.

6 Blackstock Mews, London N4 2BT, UK (rhino@dial.pipex.com), 2002, 300pp, ISBN 0 948826 59 2

It is an excellent example of how a holistic approach to health problems can help everyone involved. A typical example given by the scheme is that of a woman complaining of headaches and lack of sleep. The family support co-ordinator to whom the woman is referred discovers that the cause of these problems is the behaviour of her son. On further investigation, the son is found to be being bullied at school, a problem which can then be addressed. As well as the direct benefits for, in this case, the mother and the son, there are indirect benefits for the overworked health system. Imagine if five per cent of all minor health problems could be solved in this way: the savings in time and cost for doctors would be huge.

• *For further information on the scheme, contact the Family Welfare Association, 501-505 Kingsland Road, London E8 4AU (tel: 020 7254 6251; fax: 020 7249 5443). The Association have also put together a report on the scheme and a practice guide for people wishing to implement the model; this is available from them for £10 including p&p.*

New fathers permitted to stay the night in hospital

Summarised from an article by Nigel Hawkes, entitled 'New dads will stay night in hospital', in the Times (June 11th 2002).

Nottingham City Hospital has introduced a 'patients' hotel' where parents (and siblings) of newborn children can stay together after the delivery. The 'hotel' is one of a number of initiatives aimed at involving fathers more in the child's upbringing at an early stage, and also allows the new parents to stay together on one of the most memorable evenings of their lives. It is another blow to the stereotypical image of the father who is not prepared to go in the delivery room, never mind stay the night.

'Evening bathtimes to encourage fathers to be more involved'

Some hospitals have encouraged fathers to take their shirts off in order to get 'skin-to-skin' contact with their babies, while others have introduced evening baths for the babies so fathers can be more involved. Double beds have also been introduced in some maternity wards, so that couples can stay together for the whole period of the mother's stay in the hospital. Like the 'hotel', the double beds allow the parents to be close to each other at an important time, a time when the relationship between the two can be quite fraught and emotional.

• *For more information, see www.fathersdirect.com*

Online message centres for patients to contact their GPs

Summarised from an item in 'New Age' (November/December 2001), monitored for the Global Ideas Bank by Roger Knights.

A website in the US has opened up a new, hassle-free way of contacting your doctor for non-urgent cases. Instead of wasting time and money on phonecalls (especially when calling from abroad), the patient can contact their doctor online through a new site.

'The website acts as a network of message centres for doctors across America'

The website acts as a network of 'Message Centres' for 400,000 doctors across the country, allowing the patient to send non-urgent messages through the site's server. Once the message has been sent, it is then forwarded to the relevant doctor or delivers it by fax if the medical practice doesn't have Internet access.

- *See www.MDhub.com for more information.*

MDMA as a treatment for post-traumatic stress disorder

Summarised from an article by Andrew Gumbel, entitled 'Ecstasy to be tested as trauma treatment', in the Independent (November 9th 2001), and from information in the MAPS bulletin (volume XI, number 2; Fall 2001).

The American government has given the go-ahead for clinical trials to be held looking at MDMA (better known as ecstasy) as a treatment for post-traumatic stress disorder (PTSD). There has been a substantial amount of research and investigation into the drug's potential use as a treatment for schizophrenia, depression and general pain relief, but this research will be much more specific, focusing on patients with chronic PTSD. The psychiatrists and academics behind the research believe that ecstasy will prove more effective than standard anti-depression drugs such as Prozac and Zoloft which have failed to have any effect on some sufferers.

'MDMA facilitates the processing of trauma'

Dr Julie Holland, a world expert on the medical benefits of ecstasy, said that the idea for the research came about because of "strong anecdotal evidence

6 Blackstock Mews, London N4 2BT, UK (rhino@dial.pipex.com), 2002, 300pp, ISBN 0 948826 59 2

that ... MDMA provides an opportunity to process a trauma in a more comfortable atmosphere". Just as an anaesthetic allows major physical surgery to proceed, so ecstasy assists in the processing and treatment of emotional and psychological trauma, according to Dr Holland. Allowing clinical trials also signals a belief at the highest level that, despite widespread illicit use and concern at long-term side effects, ecstasy does have positive, therapeutic potential.

The Multidisciplinary Association for Psychedelic Studies are also hoping to extend the MDMA-PTSD research to include patients in Israel who are suffering from the disorder due to terrorism and war. Again, the intention would be to use MDMA-assisted psychotherapy with one group alongside a control group given a placebo in place of ecstasy.

• *For more information, contact MAPS, 2105 Robinson Avenue, Sarasota, FL 34232 (tel: +1 941 924 6277; fax: +1 941 924 6265; e-mail: info@maps.org; web: www.maps.org). MAPS is always looking for more support and funds to continue its research.*

• *A useful new book on the subject is* Ecstasy: the complete guide *edited by Julie Holland (Park Street Press, 2001; ISBN: 0892818573, 464 pages, $19.95). It looks at the risks and benefits of the drug, and also includes an interesting piece by Douglas Rushkoff on ecstasy and social cohesion.*

Pre-book by phone into emergency for minor injuries and ailments

Stephen Boyle

Waiting times in Accident and Emergency units in the UK are very long. Why not ring the department first where those in need can be sorted by telephone and given an attendance time? Then the person can wait at home until the allotted time comes round, rather than sitting in a stressful and packed waiting room.

• *Stephen Boyle (e-mail: helensteveboyle@hotmail.com). Stephen has been in nursing for 15 years and is currently a Senior Charge Nurse in Intensive Care in Cheshire, UK.*

Photographic warnings on cigarette packets

Summarised from an item in the Heads Up e-newsletter (subscribe at http:// gocreate.com) and from the Canadian Government Health website (www.hc-sc.gc.ca).

Since December 2000, photographic health warnings have been placed on cigarette packets in Canada to try and make the warnings more effective in encouraging smokers to give up. The regulations allow for a variety of different photographs, including lung cancers, bleeding gums, mouth disease, congested blood vessels and damaged brains, and these are in addition to the statutory written health warnings required by Canadian law (which include 'Don't poison us' and 'Tobacco smoke hurts babies'). The Health Minister at the time, Allan Rock, said that "studies have shown that these warnings are 60 times more persuasive when accompanied by photographs".

'Photographs get the message across in areas where literacy is low'

Beyond the shock value of the graphic warnings, the photo-laden packets could have a more interesting use elsewhere. In developing countries, where literacy is a substantial obstacle to communicating important health messages, photographs could be an important medium for doing so. For the smoker who cannot read the amounts of tar and nicotine, or the written health warnings on the packet, a photograph of a cancerous lung could have a much greater impact.

Night-shift working women at greater risk of breast cancer

Summarised from an article, entitled 'Light at night and working the graveyard shift linked to increase risk of breast cancer', on the Fred Hutchinson Cancer Research Center website (www.fhcrc.org). Additional information from an article by Sylvia Pagan Westphal, entitled 'Safely tucked up', in New Scientist (October 27th 2001; New Scientist subs £99 or $140, call 01444 475636 or e-mail ns.subs@qss-uk.com).

A new study has shown that women who work the night shift may face an increased risk of breast cancer of up to 60 per cent. The research, conducted by the Fred Hutchinson Cancer Research Center, in association with the

6 Blackstock Mews, London N4 2BT, UK (rhino@dial.pipex.com), 2002, 300pp, ISBN 0 948826 59 2

National Cancer Institute, looked at night-shift work and light at night as specific risk factors for breast cancer. Over 800 women who had been diagnosed with breast cancer were interviewed, and their history of shift work, sleeping patterns and exposure to light at night was compared to a control group of the same number. The findings are astonishing: women who had worked the graveyard shift at least once in the decade before diagnosis had a 60 per cent increased risk of breast cancer compared with those who had not. In addition, the risk of breast cancer increased further still with each additional hour of night-shift work.

The researchers, led by Scott Davis, believe that the results of the study may be due to a hormone called melatonin. Sleep deprivation and exposure to light at night may interrupt melatonin production, thereby stimulating the body to produce more oestrogen, which is a known hormonal promoter of breast cancer. This theory is also supported by other research that found that blind women have a reduced risk of breast cancer compared to sighted women; the thesis goes that blind women are immune to the fluctuations in light, so their melatonin levels remain constant.

'Any disruption of the circadian biology of the body may affect hormone production'

The study does not aim to draw any specific conclusions about any intervention or behaviour modification, and is looking to do further research focusing on nurses who work day and night shifts. The findings should also be placed in a more general context; as Davis points out, "more important is to focus on the general notion that anything that disrupts the normal circadian biology of the body might affect hormones that influence cancer risk". Along with exposure to light at night and sleep deprivation, this might also include the greater stress that is often involved with night-shift jobs (police workers, nurses etc) and other disruptions to the normal routine.

Research done at the Brigham and Women's Hospital in Boston has reinforced the findings described above. In a study of nurses working night shifts, those who had been working at nights for more than 30 years had an increased risk of breast cancer of 36 per cent. Researchers point out that this only translates to one or two more cases per 100,000 50 year-old women, but do advise that women interrupt their night shifts for periods of time if they are concerned.

Computer games help stroke victims regain muscle control

Summarised from an article by Eugenie Samuel, entitled 'Play to win', in New Scientist (Ocotber 27th 2001; New Scientist subs £99 or $140, call 01444 475636 or e-mail ns.subs@qss-uk.com).

Playing computer games with specially adapted joysticks could help stroke victims regain control of disabled muscles more quickly than conventional techniques. In America alone, a quarter of a million people survive strokes with some sort of disability, which may mean months of physiotherapy to recover any control over their limbs. The beauty of the computer game-joystick technique is that it retrains the limbs rather than training the patient to cope with their lack of muscle control. In this sense, it could prove an effective tool for hundreds of thousands of stroke sufferers all over the world.

'The game increases resistance as the patient grows stronger'

Therapists do not generally attempt to retrain disabled limbs because it is immensely time-consuming and difficult, as they have to pick up on minute movements. The joysticks and pedals of the new machine detect these movements and encourage further use through a feedback system. In addition, Hermano Krebs, the inventor of the new technique, has devised several new computer games specifically focused on particular muscle injuries. For a person who has lost movement in a wrist, a game is played in which the player scores points by moving icons towards targets. The joystick system increases the resistance to moving towards the target as it senses the patient getting stronger, thus ensuring an upward turn in the use of the limb and associated muscle. In his study, Krebs found that those using his system regained twice as much control over disabled muscles than a control group, over the space of just three months.

• *Hermano Krebs' homepage at MIT is www-me.mit.edu/people/personal/hikrebs.htm*

6 Blackstock Mews, London N4 2BT, UK (rhino@dial.pipex.com), 2002, 300pp, ISBN 0 948826 59 2

Leeches alleviate arthritis suffering

Summarised from an item, entitled 'Leeches take the bite out of arthritis', on the Yahoo News website (June 14th 2002; http://story.news.yahoo.com).

New research by a group of Russian scientists has found that leeches can be successfully used to treat rheumatoid and osteoarthritis. The researchers gave leech therapy to 105 arthritis sufferers, focusing particularly on the muscles surrounding the joints. All of the patients had clinical improvements, including the decrease (or even disappearance) of muscle pain and a reduction in early morning stiffness. In many of the patients, the range of movement allowed by joints also increased. The saliva of leeches has analgesic and anaesthetic qualities, and also contains hirudin, an anti-blood clotting agent.

'There were no side effects after the leech treatment'

The researchers believe that leeches could be a low-cost, effective and safe treatment for arthritis sufferers, particularly in countries with little extra funds to buy the latest drug remedies. They also noted that there were no noticeable side effects after the leech treatment, something which can not always be said for new drugs. Before medicine became more technically advanced, leeches were regularly used to treat a whole number of different ailments, and it appears that they may begin to do so again.

• *The research was done at Kazan State Medical University, 49 Butlerova Str., Kazan, NA 420012, Russia.*

Paging reminders to pill-takers

Greg Wright

Pill-takers who need to be reminded to take their medicines could benefit from this innovation: a patient's customised drug-regimen schedule being transmitted to them by a phone or pager. The hi-tech reminder could have a particular tone or vibration, so the patient knows it is a reminder to take their medicine. A product that combines a pill-case with a pager could even be devised.

Recent studies have shown that nagging and prompting has a valuable part to play in ensuring patients take the medicine they require, particularly those who have a whole cocktail to remember doses and times for. It could also prove useful for those more elderly patients with failing memories. I believe that the cellphone and pager-based Drug Tele-Reminder system should be created and operated by a partnership of the health and telecommunications industries: it would provide a further revenue stream for them, and a valuable service to individual pill-taking patients.

• *Greg Wright (wright@sunutility.com) is the founder of Wright Thinking, and the winner of an Social Inventions award for his idea for a Global Suggestion Box, which became the Global Ideas Bank.*

Cycling on bumpy roads improves bone density

Summarised from an item, entitled 'Bumpy rides build better bones', in the New Scientist (January 19th 2002; New Scientist subs £99 or $140, call 01444 475636 or e-mail ns.subs@qss-uk.com).

'Cycling off-road makes bones less prone to fracture'

New research has shown that cycling on bumpier terrain improves the bone density of the cyclist. Scientists at the Uiversity of Utah measured the bone density of a group of mountain bikers and compared it to the bone density of road-racing cyclists. Those who cycled off-road had denser bones, which makes them less prone to breaking and fracturing. Janet Shaw, who led the research team, said that the results could be explained by the fact that "the skeleton responds to things out of the ordinary", meaning the off-road spills and thrills of the mountain bikers had actually helped improve their bones, when some might have thought the opposite would be the case.

Second and third siblings less likely to have allergies

Summarised from an article by Anil Ananthaswamy, entitled 'Best to be last', in New Scientist (November 17th 2001; New Scientist subs £99 or $140, call 01444 475636 or e-mail ns.subs@qss-uk.com).

First-borns are more likely to suffer from allergies, including hayfever and asthma, making it healthier to be a younger brother or sister. Previous research had thought that this phenomenon might be due to the so-called 'hygiene

6 Blackstock Mews, London N4 2BT, UK (rhino@dial.pipex.com), 2002, 300pp, ISBN 0 948826 59 2

hypothesis', that being around sniffling, grubby older children helps expose younger siblings to those health challenges. A new study, however, has revealed evidence that this may in fact be due to hormonal changes in women for different pregnancies, meaning the differences occur in the womb rather than the outside environment.

'Being the youngest could mean better health'

The research team at Michigan State University found that the level of a particular immune protein, one associated with allergies, was higher in firstborns than in subsequent brothers and sisters. This implies that something within the pregnancy itself is producing what has become known as the 'sibling effect'. Other scientists have welcomed the new theory, but also pointed out that it is more likely to be a combination of the pregnancy hormone change *and* the grubbier environment that causes second and third siblings to have fewer allergies. Being the youngest is no longer something to moan about, but something to celebrate: it could mean better health.

• *The original research is from the American Journal of Epidemiology (volume 154, p. 909).*

Train commuters taught first aid

Summarised from an article, entitled 'Commuters taught first aid', on the BBC website (March 20th; www.bbc.co.uk).

A group of commuters from the south of England decided to train themselves in basic first aid, after a passenger collapsed on the way to London over the Christmas period of 2001. Brighton Line Commuters set up the scheme in the belief that finding someone with first aid training on board a train could prove to be the difference between life and death. As commuting can be extremely stressful, the possibility of a collapse or attack of some sort is arguably higher than elsewhere during the day. It is also often difficult to obtain swift medical help to someone who has fallen ill aboard a moving train.

So the commuters organised courses with a local charity, Brighton Heartguard to teach passengers the basic rudiments of first aid. A single call over the train's public address system will now bring a number of trained individuals to the scene from elsewhere on the train. The initiative has also won the backing of the train companies, who would like to see it spread throughout the country.

NEIGHBOURHOOD

Home zones for community-building and safer streets

Summarised from an article by Christian Wolmar, entitled 'Street life', in Search magazine (Issue 36, Winter 2001/2; the Joseph Rowntree Foundation), and from information on various websites.

Home Zones are an attempt to reclaim the streets from cars for the pedestrians who live on them, in an attempt to make the streets safer and to improve community cohesion. A home zone is a 'residential street where the living environment clearly predominates over any provision fo traffic': essentially, the traditional domination of the car driver is challenged. Strategies for creating such a zone include the same surfacing for pedestrians and cars, traffic calming measures, tree planting and the introduction of benches and play equipment. In effect, the car passing through becomes a guest of the neighbourhood, rather than the road owner. Such zones reduce traffic accidents, encourage children to play outside more and exercise, create a greater sense of community and help foster a sense of togetherness and community ownership.

'Over 6,500 home zones in the Netherlands'

The concept, then called 'woonerf', originated in the Netherlands in the 1970s, and there are now over six and a half thousand zones there. They have also been introduced with no little success in Germany, Denmark and Sweden. Now the UK is starting to look at the possibilities of the zones, not primarily as a transport solution, but as a community-building solution with by product benefits: as part of urban renaissance. It has become apparent that traffic-calming humps alone do not affect the speed of cars, or the feel of an urban neighbourhood, enough to make any substantial change. A fully-implemented and planned home zone, by contrast, can radically change the whole feel of an area, encouraging not only children to play, but neighbours to converse, and local people to cycle and walk in their locality.

'Emergency service access has to be considered'

Planning and design are the keys to a successful zone. Emergency service access, traffic congestion and child safety issues all have to be considered as well as creating a greater sense of community and peace. If traffic is slowed

6 Blackstock Mews, London N4 2BT, UK (rhino@dial.pipex.com), 2002, 300pp, ISBN 0 948826 59 2

down so there are queues throughout a zone belching fumes at playing children, residents will soon question the wisdom of its introduction. It is important, therefore, that a home zone is part of an integrated local plan, but the need for careful planning should not obscure the potential benefits of such a scheme.

• *See* Home Zones: a planning and design handbook *by Mark Biddulph (The Policy Press/JRF, 2001; ISBN: 1 86134 371 X, £13.95).*

• *For background information on Home Zones, and schemes underway in the UK and Europe, see www.homezones.org.uk or www.homezones.org*

Cuban neighbourhood transformation workshops

Summarised from an article by Neal R. Peirce, entitled 'Neighbourhood democracy in (gasp) the land of Fidel', in the Seattle Times (January 21st 2002), monitored for the Global Ideas Bank by Roger Knights.

To solve local problems at a local level, and with the participation of local people, a Cuban organisation has been setting up and running neighbourhood transformation workshops for a number of years. The Group for the Integral Development of Havana, which mostly consists of architects and planners, set up the workshops to enable residents to make more decisions rather than waiting for government action. Architects, social workers and engineers are brought in to advise the locals taking part in the workshops, who confront problems of housing, environment and employment. The citizens are then encouraged to develop plans for their neighbourhood, with suggested solutions and revenue sources to implement those solutions.

'Officials are now encouraged to collaborate with the neighbourhood groups'

Officials in the various municipal areas of Havana are now encouraged to collaborate with these neighbourhood groups, as there is increasing recognition that these bottom-up solutions are having more effect than any from the centralised government. Local, participatory, ecologically sound neighbourhood transformation workshops with (qualified) government approval: Havana could be a model for cities around the world.

• *Contact Migul Coyula, Grupo para el Desarrollo Integral de la Capital, Calle 28 #113 entre 1 y 3, Miramar, Playa, Ciudad de la Habana, Cuba (tel: +53 722 7303, fax: +53 724 2661; e-mail: gdic@ceniai.inf.cu; web: http:// www.cosg.supanet.com/gdic.html).*

'Yard Of The Week' contest to regenerate communities

Clif Judy

In three of the more downtrodden neighbourhoods we could find here in South Carolina, we announced that we would have a spring planting contest. Prizes were to be given each week and signs noting winners were placed in yards. In a given year, there are eighty signs for a neighbourhood of some 250 to 300 houses. Of eight prizes per week, seven are given based on effort.

After several weeks, the places come alive. The benefits are not only in the appearance of the gardens and yards in the community, either. People who have never won anything discover they can be rewarded for personal efforts. A function of self esteem, the winning feeling then feeds into the house, and through to the family as a whole.

We have been doing the competitions for six years in one area, five years in another and four years in another. It is a private contest with me paying the cost of the signs and ten gold Dollar Prizes. The people pay for everything else! And it works wonders for the communities and those who live in them. We are now looking to expand the idea on a national basis.

• *See www.yardoftheweek.org for more details, or contact Clif Judy (e-mail: clifjudy@mindspring.com). Clif aims to "redefine notions people have that impede their progress, entrap their being, and disrupt their lives".*

How to transform public spaces into community places

Summarised from an article on the Project for Public Spaces website, entitled 'Eleven Principles for Transforming Public Spaces into Great Community Spaces' (www.pps.org). This item was originally noted in the January issue of Utne Reader (subscribe by calling +1-800-736-UTNE or see www.utne.com).

The Project for Public Spaces (PPS), a nonprofit organisation which aims to create and sustain public places that build communities, has put forward 11 principles for successfully transforming public spaces into genuine community spaces. Since its founding in 1975, the PPS has worked in over 1,000 communities, and its method is always to make these changes through a community-based approach to planning. The principles below come from the organisation's book, *How to Turn a Place Around.*

6 Blackstock Mews, London N4 2BT, UK (rhino@dial.pipex.com), 2002, 300pp, ISBN 0 948826 59 2

Eleven principles for creating effective community spaces

1. The community is the expert: The most important point in developing a public space is to consult the community first. This not only results in an understanding of what is important to the local people, but also an awareness of their talents and assets; for example, people who can provide valuable insights into the way an area functions, or give an historical perspective.

2. Create a place, not a design: To make a place a vital space, a clever design is not enough. Physical elements, such as seating and landscaping, are crucial in making people feel comfortable in the area. The space should not be a separate domain, but have a relationship with surrounding shops and activities.

'Local partners are critical in terms of brainstorming ideas and future participation'

3. Look for partners: These could include museums, schools or local institutions, and are critical to the success of a public space improvement initiative, in terms of brainstorming ideas and future participation.

4. You can see a lot just by observing: Observing how people are using (or not using) public spaces can give a good indication of why a place is succeeding (or failing). Continuing observation will also enable managed evolvement of a community space over time.

5. Have a vision: Essential to a vision for a public space, which should emerge from the particular community, is what might go on in the space, how to make it comfortable and welcoming, how to give it a good image and how to make it important, and even a source of pride, to local people.

6. Start with the petunias – experiment!: Experimenting with short-term improvements can allow testing and refining of ideas over weeks, months and years. Many improvements can be added in a short space of time, such as murals, community gardens and seating.

'An outside stimulus links people and encourages them to converse'

7. Triangulate: Triangulation is the name of the process which occurs when an outside stimulus links people and prompts strangers to converse as if they know each other. Carefully positioned facilities can encourage triangulation: if a children's reading room in a library is put near a playground with a food outlet, then the accumulation of activities will increase.

8. They always say "It can't be done": The process of creating good public spaces inevitably involves overcoming obstacles. This is particularly the case with traffic engineers, urban planners and architects who often have a quite narrowly-defined task to complete which may not sit happily with the concept of creating a usable place. But it can be done.

9. Form supports function: Input from the community and partners, the results of experimentation and observation, and overcoming the obstacles helps provide the concept for the individual space. These elements reveal what 'form' is needed to accomplish a future vision for the space.

10. Money is not the issue: Once the basic infrastructure is in place, the cost of improvements is quite low, particularly if partners are involved in some of the activities and improvements. Also, if the space is successfully created, the community will be enthusiastic enough to view the costs as being outweighed by the benefits.

11. You are never finished: By their very nature, public spaces that serve the needs of their community are ever-changing and need attention. This refers not just to seats being worn out, but to adjusting to how a city or town changes over time.

• *These principles are excerpted from the book,* How to Turn a Place Around – a handbook for creating successful public spaces *(Project for Public Spaces, 2000, 125 pages, $30).*

• *To buy the book above, contact Project for Public Spaces, 153 Waverly Place, 4th floor, New York, NY 10014, USA (tel: +1 212 620 5660; fax: +1 212 620 3821; e-mail: pps@pps.org; web: www.pps.org).*

Urban Sanctuary Project – respite and help for today's urbanites

Paul Stevens

The Urban Sanctuary Project (USP) is an as yet unrealised idea based on a threefold approach, aiming to combat some of the problems arising from modern urban environments:

1) To introduce people to techniques and strategies that could help them to cope with modern, urban conditions that they can take into their everyday lives. These may relate to conflict resolution, to stress-relief and avoidance, or to ways in which they can improve their own living/working environments.

2) To promote more general ideas which relate to a 'culture of peace' and mutual respect.

6 Blackstock Mews, London N4 2BT, UK (rhino@dial.pipex.com), 2002, 300pp, ISBN 0 948826 59 2

3) To provide a micro-environment (both on an individual and a general level) that is beneficial in both physical and psychological senses, with the aim of promoting this as applicable to a macro-environment.

An important ethos of the project would be that information is presented in a practical, down-to-earth manner so that it is seen to be applicable to everyday life, and to people from all professions, social classes, abilities, ethnicities, orientations, sexes, genders and religions!

Example themes would include:

• Anger/Violence de-emphasis and control techniques
• Increasing self-esteem
• Strategies for coping with stress
• Respite from urban environment
• Techniques for improving personal/work environment

This would involve bringing in speakers for lectures and workshops that would be open to all (ideally free, but more realistically on a sliding scale related to income). Examples of subjects to be looked at would include:

• Conflict resolution in day-to-day life
• Anti-bullying strategies for educators
(ie techniques such as those used in the US 'Resolving Conflict Creatively' programme and UK 'Alternatives to Violence' projects)
• Surviving in a sick building
(eg lessening effects of VDU use, anti-RSI measures, relaxation techniques).
• Defining/Realising your 'purpose'
(similar to workshops such as 'Field of Dreams: Finding your Purpose', given by Julie Hotchkiss and Alison Boyle @ World Conference on Spirituality and Peace)
• Meditation for Busy People
(ie meditation techniques without ritualistic elements that are often found that can be applied in breaks during work, etc)
• Gardening workshops
(including window boxes and indoor plants – anything to enhance your living environment)

To start with, it is envisioned that the USP would simply involve occasional workshops and lectures in for hire public spaces in and around Edinburgh, UK.

Institute for Social Inventions, £15 subs, £17 from abroad by credit card, tel London 020 7359 8391

If this proved successful and funding was obtained, it could then be expanded to include more long-term aims such as outreach to schools, promoting classroom activities and creation of group-effort gardens (along the lines of Lantieri, L & Patti, J. 'Waging Peace in Our Schools').

'A permanent centre, the Urban Sanctuary, could be established'

Long term would be the acquisition of a permanent centre (the 'Urban Sanctuary': person- and eco-friendly, and mobile-phone-free) with a Peace Garden (centred around a World Peace Project 'peace pole'). This centre would then be a place where regular events could be held, as well as having space for community groups to stage their own events. It would also be a source of information as well as being a respite from the usual urban setting.

• *Paul Stevens (e-mail: paul@animistic.org.uk). Paul lives in Edinburgh, UK, and currently works as a researcher looking at bioelectromagnetics and parapsychology at Edinburgh University.*

Neighbourhood phone directories

Roger Knights

A telephone booklet containing the numbers of one's immediate neighbours would be a useful tool in many emergency situations such as power cuts, fuel shortages, wildfire, floods or suspicious noises at night. By making calls, individuals could both request for help, alert their neighbours and talk over possible strategies to deal with the problem in hand.

'We are rarely close friends with our neighbours, in fact, we often don't know their names'

We are rarely close friends with our close neighbours, in fact, we often don't know their last names, even though we occasionally speak to them. It is often impossible to call them when a community crisis arises. The solution would be for the government or local authorities to declare neighbourhood booklets as 'in the public interest' and to encourage phone companies to distribute them.

The many benefits of this scheme, including more potential for community organising and a support system would also throw a new perspective on how

6 Blackstock Mews, London N4 2BT, UK (rhino@dial.pipex.com), 2002, 300pp, ISBN 0 948826 59 2

to view citizens in need. Individuals could be empowered to help each other and themselves, rather than being viewed as isolated victims in need of public services. The only potential pitfall of the scheme is the problem of nuisance callers, but perhaps a system could be created that

• *Roger Knights is the Institute for Social Inventions' assistant editor in the USA.*

Local mule delivery service for ill and elderly

Summarised from an item, entitled 'Helping hooves', in Country Living magazine (January 2002 issue; www.countryliving.co.uk), monitored for the Global Ideas Bank by Yvonne Ackroyd.

A mule called Henry is providing a valuable service to the elderly residents of Ivybridge in Devon. Every Wednesday, Henry and his owner David Snelling pick up pre-ordered items from local shops and deliver them in special panniers around the village. The service is known locally as 'Henry's Hooves', and is free. Mr Snelling hopes to expand the service later in 2002 with a mule-drawn wagonette to transport people to the doctor, dentist or chiropodist. Rather than paying for the service, people are encouraged to donate to the Operation Henry Trust, a charity set up by Mr Snelling to give grants to cancer care and research charities.

• *Contact Operation Henry Trust, 17 Moor View Terrace, Plymouth PL4 7EB (tel: 01752 201222; fax: 01752 201220; e-mail: operation.henry@talk21.com; web: http://pilgrims.com/henry/index.htm).*

Neighbourhood childcare collectives

Kristie Reilly

Most American families, the 2000 US census says, are now made up of two income earners, and their kids are being taken care of during the day by someone else. What if every city block or neighbourhood got together to discover a person in their area who could take care of the kids every day?

It's very simple to do. Call a meeting for interested parents, and then put the call out for a volunteer in the neighbourhood, who could be anyone from a senior citizen to someone whose health problems prevent them from working, but not from being active. Parents' child care dollars would go to this person (who probably won't require as much as they're paying now), and he or she would take care of, say, 5-6 kids a day (more if they wanted and parents were comfortable) per several-block or -mile area.

Strict entry requirements (to avoid those whose interests in taking care of kids were not of the best sort) might not really be necessary, since, if neighbours are working together, more than likely they'll already have a good sense of who lives in their area and what those individuals are like, and will be able to share that knowledge with each other. Nevertheless, appropriate checks should be put in place, as for any people working with children. The only requirement would be that you live in the area, and if you qualified, you would have a ready-made income attached to the job. The process of choosing a child-care provider would allow residents in an area to get to know each other and potential providers better. The person chosen would, of course, have to be willing to be accountable to his or her neighbours for the care of their children, and demonstrate that. A sense of social responsibility and neighbourhood bonds in general are strengthened by everyone taking the care collective seriously, as they would need to in order to adequately care for the kids.

'Parents would feel safe knowing their kids were being cared for by someone local whom they trust'

This plan would make child care approachable and based around very small areas (in fact child care probably already operates informally in many areas just like this), and would give those in the neighbourhood who are traditionally cut off from involvement (the partially disabled, the elderly) a renewed chance for truly beneficial social involvement. Parents would feel safe knowing their kids were being cared for by someone who shares or supports their values (as is often the case in particular neighbourhoods, and would definitely be the case when parents deliberately choose the person they want to take care of their kids) and whom they can trust. Kids would be close to home, with people they know (making them feel safe) and have natural block-based friendship groups. The bonds of the area would be strengthened immeasurably by the process of choosing a particular person, and by this entire system of childcare in general.

Everyone is helped by this type of child care, because everyone gets a positive benefit: parents, kids, and neighbours. And the area would be a better, warmer, safer place for it. The best part of it is that anyone can do it anywhere, at any time: the principle would work the same no matter if the area were isolated, suburban, or urban.

• *Kristie Reilly (e-mail: kreilly@inthesetimes.com). Kristie is a writer in Chicago.*

6 Blackstock Mews, London N4 2BT, UK (rhino@dial.pipex.com), 2002, 300pp, ISBN 0 948826 59 2

Master-planned communities keep families together

Summarised from an article by Elizabeth Rhodes, entitled 'A family affair', in the Seattle Times (July 29th 2001), monitored for the Global Ideas Bank by Roger Knights.

The problem of how to keep the relatives close, but not *that* close, could be solved by a new type of 'master-planned' community springing up in the US. Though the original thinking behind the communities was to provide a range of different housing options in a secure, homely environment, many families have seen them as an opportunity to be closer to each other while still maintaining a necessary independence. Each community has a town centre, parks, a primary school, shops, restaurants and a variety of detached houses, smaller units and apartments. It is the combination of the different types of housing (a detached house for the family of four, an apartment for the grandparents etc) and the sense of neighbourliness and security that is attracting families to the new developments.

'It allows more family interaction, but only when wanted'

Many families are forced to take in an elderly relative, or try to house an in-law in an extension, but the master-planned community has the advantages of allowing families to live together without the loss of independence which so many elderly relatives, in particular, find difficult to deal with. It allows more family interaction, but only when wanted; more peace of mind, but not more responsibility; less isolation, but not less space to do things; more closeness, but not more dependency. As the communities are completely pre-planned, all residents are new and are keen to start afresh, making the towns very sociable places to live. One woman, who now has four generations of her family within three minutes walk of each other, says that her family have "made more friends here than we ever had [where we used to live]".

Cash-for-rats scheme to clean up Brazilian city

Summarised from an article, entitled 'City offers cash for dead rats', in the Seattle Times (October 11th 2001).

In an effort to defeat its rat problem once and for all, the Brazilian city of Nova Iguaçu has introduced a new cash-per-rat scheme. Residents are awarded two dollars for every two and a bit pounds of rat. The city, with a population of 750,000, has poor garbage and sewage services, which have resulted in rats outnumbering humans ten to one.

'Residents will be asked to report the locations of dead rodents'

The city's health department is placing rat poison in sewers, derelict buildings and other hot spots, and will be asking residents to report locations of dead rodents. It is not asking its inhabitants to kill the rats, or to touch the carcasses in any way, just to tell the authorities where the dead rats are. The co-ordinator of the plan, Uranis Assunção, said that he expects "to collect up to five tons of dead rats just in the first 20 days", making the cash incentive worthwhile. The only concern is that some more devious residents might establish rat farms to try and cash in on the city's offer, but the authorities believe they need a drastic solution to a drastic problem. Others, of course, might point out that improving the waste and public health services might have a more lasting effect.

Village shop owned by its community

Summarised from an article by John Vidal, entitled 'Village that shops together stays together', in the Guardian (June 10th 2002).

A small village in Wiltshire, UK, reacted to the possibility of its local shop closing by deciding to buy it themselves. The inhabitants of Maiden Bradley raised £21,000 from the government's countryside agency, and over 60 per cent of the village adults contributed sums of between £5 and £500 in return for shares in the shop. The shop's future has been assured, and the village now leases out the shop, with all proceeds going back into the community. More than preserving a local shop, though, this piece of direct action has strengthened the community as a whole. People have an interest in the shop, use it themselves, and it provides a centre for the residents of the village to chat or make contact each day.

'The local MP helped to paint the ceiling'

The village also refurbished the shop itself, with locals volunteering to strip, clean and repair the property. The local MP was seen painting the ceiling at one point. The strong reaction of the village came about because it had already lost its local school, doctor's surgery, dentist and police station, and has poor

6 Blackstock Mews, London N4 2BT, UK (rhino@dial.pipex.com), 2002, 300pp, ISBN 0 948826 59 2

transport links. At least in Maiden Bradley, the breakdown of another rural community has been halted, with the shop maintained as the social heart of the village.

'Any surplus profits go back into community projects and regeneration'

As the shop is answerable to the village itself, it provides a service for them, meaning that home-made bread, wine and luxury teas have been added to the shelves since the takeover. As the manager of the shop, Alan Secombe, puts it, "If anyone wants anything in particular, we will try to get it". The results prove the widsdom of this approach, with the shop making a profit every month. The shareholders benefit, with any excess going back into community projects and regeneration. It is here that it differs slightly from the original principles of the Co-operative movement, which worked on a distribution of surplus profits to its members based on the level of their transactions. In Maiden Bradley, their own brand of community co-operation works just as well, and could easily provide a model for other rural villages to follow.

• *A website devoted to Maiden Bradley can be found at www.btinternet.com/ ~JIM.DOWNES1/*

Volunteer neighbourhood mediators for dispute resolution

Summarised from an article by Chris Arnot, entitled 'Friendly persuasion', in the Guardian Society section (June 5th 2002).

Birmingham Council have given the go-ahead for eight volunteer mediators to help resolve disputes on their estates, and others near where they live. The idea is that people on the estates are more likely to listen to someone who lives nearby than to an official of the council's housing department. Rather than allowing tension between two parties to degenerate into screaming matches or lenghty legal battles, the volunteer mediators can be used to reduce ill-feeling and soothe troubled waters. Therefore, the council have sent eight volunteers on a conflict management course in preparation for full involvement.

Training up its own tenants as mediation workers might seem like something of a desperate act from a failing organisation, but the scheme does make a lot of sense. Contracting out mediation to independent businesses, or sending in someone from their own department is often met with the blunt, yet accurate sentiment of 'you don't live here, so you don't know what it's like'. The volunteer mediators can overcome this initial obstacle simply by saying 'I do live here, so I do know what it's like', and thus already have made more progress than an outsider might have. Vi Randle, one of those volunteering, has been doing this kind of informal diplomacy work for years, intervening amongst fighting teenagers or getting her husband to ask some illegal parkers to move. "Talk to teenagers like human beings and eventually they respond", is Vi's opinion, and that principle of reasoned discussion underlies the whole mediation scheme.

- *See www.birmingham.gov.uk for more details.*

6 Blackstock Mews, London N4 2BT, UK (rhino@dial.pipex.com), 2002, 300pp, ISBN 0 948826 59 2

ENVIRONMENT AND ECOLOGY

Legislating against light pollution

Summarised from an item, entitled 'Shining light on dark skies', in Green Futures magazine (May/June 2002 issue).

The Czech Republic recently introduced legislation to combat light pollution in the whole country. Starting in June 2002, light polluters can be fined up to £3,000 for offences. Lamp posts will have to be shielded from above with curved glass, and billboard lighting will have to face downwards from the top, rather than be uplit. The reduction in light pollution should help diminish some of the ecological consequences of drowning the night sky with artificial light. Light pollution at night is thought to impair human production of the hormone melatonin, to increase sight problems, to increase cases of insomnia and to damage the immune system. Bright lights on towers and skyscrapers also affect migrating birds, who rely on the stars to navigate. The birds either flutter about the light they are attracted to until they drop from exhaustion, or actually hit the object in question.

'The Czech Republic is the first country to take action on light pollution'

The legislation, led by the astronomer Jenik Hollan of the Copernicus Observatory, makes the Czech Republic the first country to take action on a concerted scale. Catalonia, in Spain, and Lombardy, in Italy, have *regional* initiatives, and the Czech law was modelled to an extent on the law in Lombardy which came about after 25,000 people signed a petition demanding action about light pollution. The law defines 'light pollution' as 'every form of illumination by artificial light which is dispersed outside the areas it is dedicated to, particularly if directed above the level of the horizon'. Under the law, Czech citizens and organizations are obligated to 'take measures to prevent the occurrence of light pollution of the air'.

'Astronomers are already claiming a spectacular improvement in the night sky'

Astronomers in Brno and other Czech cities are already claiming a spectacular improvement in the clarity of the night sky, and the Czech legislation could provide an example for other nations to copy. The International Dark-Sky Association hopes to encourage other governments around the world to follow suit.

• *For more information about the Czech campaign, see www.astro.cz/darksky or contact the International Dark-Sky Association, 3225 N. First Ave., Tucson AZ 85719, USA (tel: +1 520 293 3198; fax: +1 520 293 3192; e-mail: ida@darksky.org; web: www.darksky.org). The British Astronomical Association also have a Campaign for Dark Skies; see www.dark-skies.org*

• *For an item also related to the hazardous effects of night-time lighting, see 'Night-shift women workers at increased risk from breast cancer' on page 133.*

Logging underwater to reduce effects of deforestation

Summarised from an article by Fred Pearce, entitled 'The Logger of the Lake', in New Scientist (August 11th 2001; New Scientist subs £99 or $140, call 01444 475636 or e-mail ns.subs@qss-uk.com).

A new logging company has found a way of logging trees that are underwater, ensuring living trees elsewhere are not chopped down, and preventing the decomposition of dead trees emitting methane into the atmosphere. There are several forest areas in Brazil that were flooded in hydroelectricity projects, leaving up to one and a half million trees underwater. These trees are dead, but perfectly preserved in the oxygen-free water, so are fine for logging and exporting elsewhere, and each tree chopped down underwater saves one living one above ground. There is huge potential for underwater logging, the process of which has been accelerated by the invention of a robotic chainsaw barge, and environmentalists are fully endorsing the initiative.

'Removing the trees will improve the local water ecosystems'

As well as ensuring that living trees elsewhere are left intact, the underwater logging could have other positive environmental impacts. Firstly, the removal of wood that might otherwise rot away (albeit over centuries) and produce methane helps reduce the amount of greenhouse gas being released. Secondly, it is thought that removing the trees will be good for the ecosystems in the water, because trees contain natural chemicals to deter insects which leak into the water when the forest is flooded. Indeed, the system is so effective that it may soon be given approval by the Forest Stewardship Council, an organisation that issues certificates to timber operations which do not destroy forests.

• *For more information, see www.aquaticcellulose.com*

6 Blackstock Mews, London N4 2BT, UK (rhino@dial.pipex.com), 2002, 300pp, ISBN 0 948826 59 2

Goats used to reduce fire-risk vegetation

Summarised from an article by Patricia Leigh Brown, entitled 'California going to the goats – to help control fire risk', in the Seattle Times (October 14th 2002), monitored for the Global Ideas Bank by Roger Knights. This article originally appeared in the New York Times.

Goats are being used as a fire-prevention tool in California, and they are more economical and eco-friendly than traditional methods of human landscaping. The goats are brought in to eat at the undergrowth of flammable grasses and plants in areas of Berkeley and Oakland, which have often been devastated by forest fires. They are particularly effective at reducing the risk of fire because they focus on the grasses and lower branches, which diminishes the chances of a fire spreading upwards through foliage to the trees. (It is this movement, called 'laddering' by fire experts, which can turn a simple fire into an uncontrollable inferno.) The goats also have a particular fondness for manzanita, a volatile plant with a low point of ignition.

Residents in the area praise the use of goats for other reasons. One points out that they are better than something gas-powered, while others claim they bring an air of serenity to the area. They are also cheaper (by $300 an acre) than the equivalent human landscaping would be, and also work all day every day in contrast to their human counterparts. The demand for their services has been such that no less than four companies have sprung up in the area to supply goats, with Goats R Us now having a herd of 4,000 on its books. The goats are also now diversifying from simple fire fuel eradication to winter brush reduction and the removal of poison oak and star thistle where desired.

• *For more information, see www.goatsrus.com*

Betting against the governnment on carbon emissions reduction

Summarised from an item, entitled 'The Bet', in Positive News (Winter 2001; subs £12.50 by calling 01588 640022, e-mail office@positivenews.org.uk or see web: www.positivenews.org.uk), and from information on the Bet website (www.thebet.de).

Over 15,000 youth activists are betting their government that an eight per cent reduction in total carbon dioxide emissions can be achieved in eight months rather than eight years. The Kyoto agreement for the EU set eight per cent in eight years as the target to achieve, but those participating in 'The Bet' campaign are hoping to demonstrate that this can be achieved much more quickly. The participants in each country aim to live as sustainable a life as possible (taking public transport, regulating heating and water, using less packaging, etc) and note down their individual carbon dioxide savings. These are then amalgamated on a local and national level, using scientific formulae.

'Reductions can be achieved without expensive technology or complex trading schemes'

As well as bringing the possibilities of increasing the rate of carbon emissions reduction to the attention of their own government, the intention of the campaign is to show how this can be achieved without expensive technology or complex trading schemes. 'The Bet' also educates young people about climate change, and involves them in political action. Everyone can take part, including schools, universities, non-governmental organisations and individuals.

The Europe-wide campaign is based on a German scheme called 'Die Wette', in which an environmental group bet the German government it could save ten per cent of its carbon dioxide emissions. This was done in a seven-month period, proving the possibilities for swift action. Already, Switzerland, Denmark, Lithuania, the Netherlands, Romania, Bulgaria and Italy have won their national bets, with other countries nearing their own totals.

• *For more information, contact The Bet European Office,Rothenburgstraße 1612165, Berlin, Germany (tel: +49 30 79706610; fax: +49 30 79706620; e-mail: TheBet.office@gmx.net; web: www.thebet.de).*

• *See also http://www.canopusfund.org/bet.html*

Biodegradable cigarette filters

Brooke Meade

While observing the litter on our college campus I found that there are an abundance of cigarette butts. These cigarette filters are not biodegradable and will be there for years and years. I feel that with all of the new technologies that have been developed there should have been concerns for making a better environment. Sure, you could have an over abundance of ashtrays around campus but, would that be aesthetically pleasing? So what I am trying to say is that the cigarette companies should try to convert to biodegradable filters.

6 Blackstock Mews, London N4 2BT, UK (rhino@dial.pipex.com), 2002, 300pp, ISBN 0 948826 59 2

Smoking will never be good for people, or the environment, but cigarette manufacturers can reduce the ecological impact they have.

• *Brooke Meade is a student at Elon University (www.elon.edu) in North Carolina, USA.*

• *See also www.smalltrash.com, a website which, amongst other things, aims to see if there is enough political will to push for paper and/or biodegradable filters.*

Conservation certificates to protect hunted animals

Sam Hitt

My idea is to authorise states in the US to issue 'Conservation Certificates' that citizens could voluntarily purchase to protect large carnivores and their habitat. 'Conservation Certificates' would be the same price as hunting licences, but have the opposite effect. Funds generated could then be used to protect large preserves, provide biological corridors, manage prescribed fires and conduct environmental research. 'Conservation Certificates' would also provide an incentive to state game agencies to protect carnivores instead of hunt them, an issue which is becoming more and more important as time goes on.

This idea could obviously be extended to any country in the world where hunting and conservation come into conflict. It gives citizens the ability to proactively protect their own environments and local wildlife.

• *Sam Hitt (e-mail: sam@wildwatershed.org). Sam Hitt is a well-known conservationist in the Southwest US. He founded Forest Guardians and is currently the head of Wild Watershed based in Santa Fe, New Mexico.*

12 ways to save the world

Maurice Strong, chairman of the UN's Earth Council, outlined a 12-step plan to secure the world's future in the September/October 2001 issue of the Futurist (see www.wfs.org).

1 Promote the greening of the market system through such programmes as 'emissions trading'

2 Stop unnecessary and counterproductive subsidies for the water, transport, energy and agriculture sectors

3 Manage Earth and its resources as though it were a business

4 Accelerate the transition to environmentally sound energy

5 Close the knowledge gap between rich and poor countries and between science and policy makers

6 Move away from foreign aid and support homegrown economic development

7 Move to more flexible, incentive-based regulation

8 Provide more effective trusteeship over the global commons, such as the oceans, the Antarctic, the high atmosphere, and outer space

9 Prepare for natural disasters and extraterrestrial threats

10 Rejoice in human diversity and encourage it

11 Encourage lifestyles of 'sophisticated modesty'

12 Learn from the lifestyles and self-reliance of people in enclave groups, such as monastic communities

 • *For the full version of Maurice Strong's article, see the September issue of the Futurist; or see his book* Where on Earth are we going? *(Texere, 2001; ISBN 158799092 X).*

 • *Issues of the Futurist can be ordered online at http://www.wfs.org where the World Future Society's e-newsletter can also be subscribed to. Or contact the society at World Future Society, 7910 Woodmont Ave, Suite 450, Bethesda, MD 20814, USA (tel +1 800 989 8274; fax +1 301 951 0395; e-mail info@wfs.org).*

Seed balls for reforestation and revegetation of arid areas

Robert Alcock

All too often these days, the TV news shows footage of famine victims, refugee camps, desperate poverty and warfare. As much as the pathetic figures in the foreground, what has often had most impact on me is the backdrops against which these tragedies take place. The overwhelming impression is of desolate, arid hills, with little, if any, greenery in sight. There are many exceptions (Yugoslavia, Rwanda, Sri Lanka, Colombia, the Congo); but as a rule – whether it's Ethiopia, Algeria, Angola, Somalia, Palestine, Kuwait, Iraq, or, now, Afghanistan – most wars and disasters seem to take place in semi-deserts. It's a vicious circle, of course: deforestation and desertification mean famine and economic collapse, which lead to conflict, which in turn leads to further environmental degradation. Even disasters in humid areas (hurricanes, floods) often owe much of their devastating power to deforestation and degradation of the environment, as has been seen in Central America, for example.

Sometimes, as in Afghanistan, the situation on the ground is so desperate that even armies fear to tread. Dropping bombs hardly helps. Even dropping

6 Blackstock Mews, London N4 2BT, UK (rhino@dial.pipex.com), 2002, 300pp, ISBN 0 948826 59 2

food is, at best, a short-term solution. What hope is there, then, to break the vicious circle of environmental degradation and conflict?

Here is one idea that I have read about (at www.seedballs.com) and can't see the flaw in:

'A seed ball is essentially a mixture of different plant seeds suitable for the area and climate in question'

It's a method of revegetation for arid and semi-arid areas, using 'seed balls'. A seed ball is essentially a mixture of different plant seeds (generally at least 100 different species) suitable for the area and climate in question, in a matrix of compost, earth and clay so that when dry, they are hard and tough. They can also contain natural repellents such as chilli powder to prevent their being eaten by rodents. Once scattered, the balls lie dormant until it rains, whenever that may happen. The ball then disintegrates and the seeds have their own matrix of soil and fertilizer ready for them to grow; whatever plant is best suited to that particular place will thrive and spread.

The materials for making the seed balls are cheap and readily available. Locals and ecologists would be able to advise on the best seeds to use in the area in question, and where to get them. This would presumably be from less degraded areas nearby. The balls could be made and scattered locally, or, if necessary, dropped from the air. (Obviously for hilly areas the balls would have to be flattish, not round!)

'To revegetate a square kilometre would require ten million balls'

According to the website, seed balls weigh about 10–20g each and it is recommended to use ten per square metre of ground. Therefore, to revegetate a square kilometre would require ten million seed balls, weighing a few hundred tons. Dropping them from the air would therefore be a fairly expensive proposition; but small compared with the ongoing costs of war and poverty. Distribution on the ground with local labour, on the other hand, would not necessarily be expensive or difficult.

- *For more information, see www.seedballs.com*
- *Robert Alcock (e-mail: robal@iname.com). Robert Alcock is a freelance writer, translator and ecologist. His idea for a 'Smart urban transport website' was featured in last year's annual compendium published by the Institute for Social Inventions,* Cornucopia of Ideas *(ISI, 2001).*

Incentives for toilet-recycling

Summarised from an article by Christine Clarridge, entitled 'Toilet-recycling event is flush with crowds', in the Seattle Times (August 19th 2001), monitored for the Global Ideas Bank by Roger Knights.

'The Great Toilet Round-up' is the brainchild of the Seattle Public Utilities department, who have run two of the toilet-recycling events in recent months. The event invited citizens to trade their older toilets in for new ones. Each toilet turned in, along with a proof of purchase, got a $40 rebate towards a new water-saving toilet.

'A new toilet can reduce water usage by 9,000 gallons a year'

Old toilets are the biggest wasters of water in the home, and a new model can reduce water usage by 9,000 gallons a year and the water bill by 20 per cent. The event resulted in 5,000 toilets being traded in, which the organisers estimate will save almost 40 million gallons each year. The old toilets had any wood and plastic parts removed, and were then taken away in dump trucks. They will be crushed and used in road manufacture in the future.

• *See http://www.cityofseattle.net/util/ for more information*

Online environmental education prevents ecotourism damage

Garry Fletcher

In ecologically sensitive areas we can use new technology to educate and promote conservation without risking the impact of ecotourists consuming the fragility of the environment. Such was the idea behind the racerocks.com project in Southern British Columbia in Canada. The website www.racerocks.com has been made possible by the combined efforts of volunteers and partners. It provides continuous images and information from this ecologically sensitive location using live 'QuickTime' streaming technology, and web-based readings from underwater environmental sensors.

As well as reducing the direct physical impact of eco-tourists at the site, the use of new technology in this way also reduces numbers of people travelling to the area by car or plane. The environmental benefits are, therefore, twofold.

• *See www.racerocks.com for more information, or contact Garry Fletcher (e-mail: gfletcher@pearson-college.uwc.ca), a faculty member in Biology and Environmental Systems at Lester B. Pearson College in Victoria, B.C., Canada.*

6 Blackstock Mews, London N4 2BT, UK (rhino@dial.pipex.com), 2002, 300pp, ISBN 0 948826 59 2

Encouraging the use of clotheslines not dryers

Submitted to the Global Ideas Bank by Alexander Lee. Alexander works at the Public Utility Commission of New Hampshire, USA, and is the volunteer executive director of Project Laundry List.

Project Laundry List was set up to encourage people to use clotheslines instead of clothes dryers to reduce energy consumption, since six to ten per cent of residential energy use in the US is attributable to the dryer. This is roughly equivalent to the total amount of energy an average African household uses annually. The project organises National Hanging Out Day on April 19th every year to promote the benefits of clotheslines, and to lobby against communities that ban washing lines for aesthetic reasons.

'The average household can save up to £65 annually on its energy bill'

As well as saving the average household up to $100 (£65) each year, and helping reduce the environmental impact of daily living, using a clothesline can have other benefits. The act itself can be therapeutic, giving a chance to slow down, take in the fresh air and think about other things. It is also said that clothes last longer and, depending on where you live, smell nicer. As well as the National Hanging Out Day, the project campaigns against communities which have banned clotheslines: several US states have recently introduced so-called 'Right to Dry' legislation. It also promotes the scheme through distributing clothes peg badges (or 'clothespins') for people to wear.

• *Project Laundry List, 27 Holly St., Concord, NH 03301, USA (tel: +1 603 226-3098; fax: +1 509 472 4553; e-mail: info@laundrylist.org; web: www.laundrylist.org).*

Encouraging thermal underwear to reduce fuel consumption

Greg Wright

A systematic campaign to promote the use of thermal underwear in winter climes could vastly reduce the use of (mostly fossil-fuelled) home heating. An environmental group or organisation could team up with a manufacturer of thermal underwear to encourage greater use of the clothing and the corresponding decreased use of home heating by fuel, oil and coal-fired electricity. There could even be discounts on thermal clothing on joining environmental organisations.

I polled the people I visited during the holiday season as to how many were using thermal clothing to fend off the cold temperatures, and found a very low usage rate indeed. This was despite a large number of complaints about the cold weather, and a number of people falling ill with cold-related illnesses. The campaign could also be extended to include the donation of thermal clothing to the people with the smallest environmental footprint of all: the homeless.

• *Greg Wright (wright@sunutility.com) is the founder of Wright Thinking, and the winner of an Social Inventions award for his idea for a Global Suggestion Box, which became the Global Ideas Bank*

Green Letters – children discussing environmental issues by post

Justin T. O'Conor Sloane.

In an effort to create a foundation for, and a legacy of, productive communication and dialogue among the young and future generations concerning our global environment, children all over the world could write letters to one another discussing environmental issues. These letters, which could be called

6 Blackstock Mews, London N4 2BT, UK (rhino@dial.pipex.com), 2002, 300pp, ISBN 0 948826 59 2

'Green Letters', would detail their concerns, ideas, fears and optimism about the environmental problems confronting humanity and what they think can be done in addressing and resolving them.

Teachers and school administrators could greatly facilitate and encourage this process of communication by establishing 'sister school' relationships in which the students at schools in different countries write to one another regularly during the school year, year after year, with each grade level corresponding with their respective peer group. Students would write 'Green Letters' several times throughout the school year. Letters would be read aloud in class and occasionally letters could be read to the whole school at assembly.

'It could also promote language learning'

The need to translate the 'Green Letters' could be kept to a minimum if they were to be written primarily in English; or the scheme could be used to help promote the learning of new languages. Schools in countries sharing a common language may choose to write to one another, which is perfectly wonderful, but an important aspect of the 'Green Letters' idea is that children from geographically, ethnically and culturally diverse backgrounds should participate together in a productive dialogue about the environmental problems and issues that unite them in such a fundamental and profound way.

To eliminate paper and postage costs associated with the letters they could be written as e-mails and sent via the internet where possible. An e-mail listserv would allow for conveniently sending the letters to any number of schools. A website could be created to post up 'Green Letters' for everyone to read. Batches of the letters could be sent to elected officials to read. Teachers could incorporate the letters into their environmental education, geography, science, social studies or civics curriculums.

'Establishing international dialogue on issues of global importance'

The children of today writing 'Green Letters' will grow to be the adults of tomorrow who, as a result of a simple exercise in international communication, will hopefully possess a deeper understanding of the shared, unifying dimension of the environmental problems facing all of humanity. Perhaps they will better recognize the importance and necessity of actively working together to establish improved international dialogue on protection of our global environment and the need for responsibility, agreement and partnership in protecting it.

- *Justin O'Conor Sloane (e-mail: KingOConor@yahoo.com). Justin is an AmeriCorps Volunteer and president of the National Association for Political Participation in the US.*

Littermovement – a public solution to litter around us

Tuula-Maria Ahonen

The idea of the Littermovement is a simple one: that a member of the movement picks up daily at least one piece of litter, and invites at least one new member to join and do the same. Littermovement started in Finland in April 2000, and has now spread to many countries. The members are people of all ages, from the oldest grandparent to the younget child. Even some dogs in Finland have been taught to pick up litter, as part of a general enlisting of all who can help tidy up their street or town.

• *The Littermovement homepage, translated into 16 languages, is at www.kolumbus.fi/japelto/littermovement.htm*
• *Tuula-Maria Ahonen (e-mail: tma@kolumbus.fi) is a journalist and the founder of the Littermovement.*

A global citizenship and sustainable development education programme

Summarised from an item, entitled 'Global Footprints', in Human Scale Education News (Summer 2001 issue; www.hse.org.uk).

A new educational project aims to empower children in taking steps towards a sustainable future, by giving them access to information about lifestyle alternatives, citizenship skills and, in particular, the ecological and social impact of the way they live. In this sense, the project aims to extend the concept of the 'ecological footprint' into children's lives, and in the context of their school. By exploring methods of measuring environmental impacts on a human level, the Global Footprints scheme hopes to encourage and enable those taking part to be come involved in local environmental issues and the way their schools and homes are run.

'Providing chidren with an understanding of the impact of consumption'

Global Footprints also aims to provide children with an understanding of the links between countries, and the impact of consumption on distant places in the developing world. The footprint is, again, the key to introducing the

6 Blackstock Mews, London N4 2BT, UK (rhino@dial.pipex.com), 2002, 300pp, ISBN 0 948826 59 2

concept of each local action having a global impact, even if cumulatively or collectively. The children are then shown how steps can be taken to reduce footprints on the path to sustainable development. The programme is being implemented with the co-operation of eight Development Education Centres around the UK.

• *For more information, contact Andrew Ball, Global Footprints (tel: 020 7364 6405; fax: 020 7364 6422; e-mail: globalfootprints@gn.apc.org; web: www.globalfootprints.org).*

• *To calculate your own ecological footprint, see http://www.esb.utexas.edu/ drnrm/EcoFtPrnt/Calculate.htm*

• *See also 'Reducing Western nations' ecological footprints' in* Creative Speculations *(ISI, 1996).*

Planting trees to stimulate the brain and speed convalescence

Summarised from an article by Mike Hewitt, entitled 'Can Trees Cut Pain', in the Times (September 4th 2001).

'A healthy tree population makes for a healthier human population'

The medicinal effects of trees are well-known, but many experts now maintain that being in the presence of trees can itself produce measurable health benefits. In response to this, 'Trees for London' (www.treesforlondon.org.uk) and other so-called 'urban forestry' units advocate major planting initiatives in town centres and inner cities. They claim that a healthy tree population makes for a healthier human population.

Studies carried out in a suburban Pennsylvania hospital between May and October when the trees were in full foliage, showed that within five minutes of being viewed, certain nature scenes can foster more positive feelings and promote beneficial changes such as lower blood pressure and faster recovery times. Professor Robert Ulrich, Professor of Architecture and Landscape at Texas A&M University who studied this phenomenon has also published studies that indicate that tree-lined roads can make drivers calmer and more alert. And Terry Hartig of Uppsala University, Sweden has conducted studies demonstrating that subjects who have been exposed to woodland areas perform significantly better in concentration tests than those who haven't.

The authors of 'Growing Greener Cities', Gary Moll and Stanley Young, report that in 12 months a tree can provide about £150 of material benefits.

The canopy reduces harmful radiation by up to 90 per cent; leaves and branches can reduce wind speeds by up to 80 per cent and noise levels by around 40 per cent. Of particular importance is the tree's function as a natural filter, absorbing such pollutants as sulphur dioxide, carbon monoxide, nitrogen dioxide and ozone.

'The leaves help to filter out pollutants from the road'

Some initiatives are being taken as a result of these studies. Last year, residents of Poplar, East London, helped the environmental charity 'Trees for London' to plant a woodland belt beside the busy A102 road. The charity believes that when the trees are fully grown the noise from the road will be much reduced, and furthermore the leaves will also help to filter pollutants such as carbon monoxide, and trap fine diesel particles, known as PM10s, which have been shown to aggravate asthma and bronchitis.

Further Benefits

Sheila Hogan, head of the Casey Tree Foundation in Washington D.C., has stated that, with the help of trees, "Obesity can even be reduced. People can get out and walk in shaded comfort."

Meanwhile, Frances Kuo and William Sullivan who run the Human-Environment Research Lab at University of Illinois at Urbana-Campaign, relate tree cover to public safety. Their findings have shown them that "greener spaces are used more often which means people are around which, we think, discourages perpetrators." So trees reduce crime as well: there would appear to be no end to their talents.

A 'plastax' on single-use shopping bags to reduce usage and waste

Summarised from an article, entitled 'As Ireland goes green and imposes a tax on plastic shopping bags, should Britain follow suit?', in the Independent (March 5th 2002).

Ireland has introduced a tax of nine pence on single-use plastic shopping bags, payable by the shopper not the shop. The imposition of the tax is aimed at reducing the use of the bags in order to cut down litter and waste in the environment. The Irish government expects to raise £100 million annually

6 Blackstock Mews, London N4 2BT, UK (rhino@dial.pipex.com), 2002, 300pp, ISBN 0 948826 59 2

from the tax, all of which will be put into environmental projects in the country. It also hopes that the tax will encourage many more shoppers to buy re-usable bags than is presently the case.

'Plastic bags constitute a third of all plastic waste in the UK'

To say that plastic bags are a problem is something of an understatement. In Britain, for example, shoppers use eight billion carrier bags a year (134 per person) and plastic bags constitute a third of all plastic waste. Plastic bags are thought to take between 20 and 1,000 years to degrade in the environment, and hundreds of thousands of birds and other animals are killed by plastic rubbish every year. Furthermore, landfill sites are filling up rapidly and the other two options are incineration (which is unpopular and polluting) and recycling (but only 0.5 per cent of plastic bags are recycled at present). The Irish government hopes that the tax will encourage many more shoppers to buy re-usable bags, be they linen, strong plastic or paper.

Other European countries have taken different approaches, with Belgian supermarkets offering points on loyalty cards for those re-using bags, German stores charging up to 30p for plastic bags, and Dutch bag incineration programmes being used to heat hospitals. Yet the problem remains huge, and it could be that a tax is the only way to have a larger effect, hitting the consumer where it hurts most: in the wallet, not the conscience.

Go M.A.D! – 365 daily ways to save the planet

A review of Go M.A.D.! – 365 Daily Ways to Save the Planet *(published by Think/The Ecologist, 2001, ISBN: 0954135306, 178 pages, £3.99). Reviewed by Kate Weinberg.*

Go M.A.D. (Go Make A Difference) is a small but ambitious book with '365 daily ways to save the planet', divided not, as it may be imagined, into days of the year but into themes that range from 'Birth' and 'Community' to 'Compost'.

It's hard not to feel a bit weary picking up a book with this title, which seems like it will be an equivalent to being invited into a headmaster's office for a stern talk and a consequent reduction of privileges. But although the book does from time to time slip into a 'preachy' tone, the emphasis on humour (with the comic illustrations and lively style of the writing) and the accessibility (each idea is presented in bite-size chunks) makes for a light, enjoyable and, most importantly, edifying read.

Institute for Social Inventions, £15 subs, £17 from abroad by credit card, tel London 020 7359 8391

'Individuals don't need to adopt monk-like existences to help save the world'

This is no mean feat. Books written in such a commercial format rarely have such worthy intentions. But then again, rarely are they compiled by non-profit making magazines such as *The Ecologist*. In the introduction, the editor of the organisation, Zac Goldsmith, makes the point that individuals don't need to 'adopt monk-like existences' to collectively save the world. For the main part, the following pages bear this out – suggestions for living a greener lifestyle tend to be modest and manageable, from fitting aluminium foil behind your radiators (to maximise and heat and waste less energy) to leaving extra packaging at shops rather than taking it home with you. Neither is it all dull prosaic stuff. Imaginative suggestions for recycling can be found on most pages for example using colourful old clothing to make fun, rag toys for kids rather than buying into cubic metres of the newest plastic toys.

On the other hand, there are definite moments when the tone can slip into a less forgiving 'we're all human after all' mode, and some of the suggestions veer towards a 'hippy fascism' that seem to take quite a lot of the fun out of life. One example was 'Don't use the freebie mini soaps and shampoos' at hotels – which, we are told encourages the use of unnecessary packaging and wastes resources. Or even more ascetically, the tip for cutting down on toilet paper is 'to only use two sheets at a time'.

Moments like these lose the spirit of humour and goodwill the book for the most part upholds and fly in the face somewhat of Goldsmith's claim that we don't need to be 'monks' to do our part in contributing to a greener world.

'Nudging the younger generation into adopting greener attitudes'

On balance though, *Go M.A.D.* is a great idea, and packaged in a way that can appeal to children too. Some of the tips are prefaced by 'Kids...', followed by a suggestion that will provoke them into more environmentally conscious and nature-loving people and directing them away from the all too-present temptations of the material and commercial world. Ideas are as simple as growing watercress in boxes and baking biscuits. These are the moments when I felt the book to be at it's best, and most realistic. Rather than trying to turn us all into saints, it nudges the youngest generation into adopting newer, greener attitudes that can also be fun.

6 Blackstock Mews, London N4 2BT, UK (rhino@dial.pipex.com), 2002, 300pp, ISBN 0 948826 59 2

Green gyms – exercising the body for the environment

Summarised from an article by Sam Murphy, entitled 'Back to Nature', in the Guardian Weekend magazine (September 22nd 2001), and from the Green Gym website (www.greengym.org.uk). Additional information from Green Futures magazine (May/June 2002 issue), and from an article by Jill Papworth, entitled 'Why they're happy to lean to the green', in the Guardian Money section (June 8th 2002).

The 'green gym' is a conservation project that aims to benefit the participant in two ways: through outdoor physical exercise and through benefiting the environment in their community. At each site, members of the gym do work such as hedgelaying, tree planting and repairing fences, in between sessions to warm-up and cool down. A recent comparison between the work in the 'green gym' and an aerobics class revealed that those working outdoors burned off 86 more calories over an hour, and burned them off with a purpose.

'Exercising outdoors tends to be more varied, challenging the brain as well as the body'

There is increasing evidence that being outdoors is good for us, including research finding higher outdoor levels of serotonin and negative ions (both of which have a positive effect on the brain). As well as improving mood and reducing stress, exercising outdoors tends also to be more varied and more challenging: the brain is used as much as the body when responding to different terrains or doing different tasks. This is something that does not happen in a standard indoor gym. Nor can an indoor gym offer the benefits of exercising in the cold, in which the body has to work harder and therefore burns off still more calories. At the 'green gym', not only can a person help themselves get fit, help their local environment prosper and reduce their stress levels, but they can do all this in the beautiful outdoors, rather than facing a row of treadmills and TV screens.

The schemes have also been boosted by the new trend for exercise referral by GP's, keen to see their patients exercising in any way possible. As the exercise tends to improve psychological health as well, referred patients benefit doubly from the prescribed treatment. Some councils have gone further still, with Stockport Borough Council encouraging its GP's to prescribe walks in parks and woods to depression sufferers, and Glasgow incorporating greenspace in its newly-designed 'homeopathic hospital'.

Conservation holidays

In addition to the 'green gyms' outlined above, many environmental charities are now offering conservation holidays, in which people go and work as a paid volunteer on a particular project. These combine an inexpensive break from the daily routine, outdoor exercise every day, and the rewards of helping a charitable project. There are several organisations which run the holidays in the UK, and several more that do similar projects abroad; the latter is increasingly frowned upon, though, as the environmental impact of the flight out to the Amazon or Borneo may nullify any positive work they may do when they arrive.

> • *For more information on Green Gyms in the UK, contact the Oxford Centre for Health Care Research and Development at Oxford Brookes University (tel: 01865 485 293; web: www.greengym.org.uk), or see www.bctv.org/greengym*

> • *Also see www.outdoorfitness.com for tips on exercise outdoors.*

> • *For environmental holidays, contact BTCV (tel: 01491 821600; web: www.btcv.org) or the National Trust (tel: 0870 429 2429; web: www.nationaltrust.org.uk/volunteers).*

Recycling elephant dung to make paper

Summarised from an item reported by Reuters, entitled 'Elephant Park Recycles Dung to Make Paper' (July 24th 2001). Additional information from TNT magazine (www.tntmagazine.com), monitored for the Global Ideas Bank by Yvonne Ackroyd.

An elephant park in Ayutthaya, Thailand has been recycling elephant dung to make paper. Keepers at the park extract parts of the dung which are fibrous and dry them out to make paper. Everything else that remains is used for fertilizer. Not only does the scheme ensure there is no waste of the waste, but sales of the unusual paper raise money to be invested back into the running of the park. In this way, the elephants help ensure and protect their own environment simply by doing what comes naturally to them.

'The dung is liquidised, strained and dried in the sun'

The director of the park, Sompast Meepan, calls the elephant a 'paper factory', and explains that "to produce a higher quality paper, we liquidize the pulp in a blender. (Then) we strain the paper onto a fine sieve and leave it to dry in the sun to create the final product". The park's resident vet expresses the scheme's benefits more simply: "We call it golden dung".

Thailand is also looking at using the excrement of its prison population to create biogas. The country has been particularly successful in recycling pig dung into biogas as an alternative fuel, and now intends to put its criminals' waste to similar use.

Eliminating 'widows' from webpage printouts

Greg Wright

No doubt this has been decried and then explored, but I wonder what, if any, solutions have been advanced for the vast waste of paper that is occasioned by those last pages of minimal content that so often occur when printing out a webpage?

It seems to me that some kind of widely distributed application could be propounded that would automatically not print the last part of any webpage when that content would appear on an additional piece of paper and when the amount of that content is under a certain amount of vertical space, or if the content is a footer. Alternately, the techno-fix might be to automatically compress the last amount of content so that it is squeezed onto the bottom of the previous and now-the-last-page.

'A defined amount of expendable material'

The amount of material that would be defined as expendable, or compressible, would be defined by a default value, which users could redefine to include more material (eco-minded users) or less material (forest-destroying persnickety types who don't want to miss a single letter or piece of punctuation).

A more fundamental solution might be to include some kind of 'universal page break' indicator into webpage-authoring software that would allow website designers and webmasters to assure up-front that printouts of their sites' webpages will produce no or minimal numbers of these 'widow pages.'

Meanwhile, here's my low-tech proposed solution:

The bottom line of every webpage on environmentally-minded websites would be a small but boldfaced strong suggestion to 'REUSE OR RECYCLE THIS LAST PAGE IF IT DOESN'T ADD ANYTHING IMPORTANT TO THE PRINTOUT!' or some such statement.

• *Greg Wright (wright@sunutility.com) is the founder of Wright Thinking, and the winner of a Social Inventions award for his idea for a Global Suggestion Box, which became the Global Ideas Bank.*

Environmentally friendly wedding lists

Summarised from an item in the 'Seeds of Change' column in Green Events magazine (June 2001; subs £8 from Green Events, 2nd Floor, 97-99 Seven Sisters Road, London N7 1QP), and from information on the Centre for Alternative Technology website (www.cat.org.uk).

The Centre for Alternative Technology (CAT) is launching a wedding list with a difference that will make a difference. Couples can choose from CAT's range of environmentally friendly products, and start married life in a socially responsible way. The concept is that couples need feel no guilt about being extravagant on their wedding day, because every present they receive will be produced ethically and be designed to help people live more sustainable lives. The list includes organic bed linen, organic paints and recycled glasses, all of which are ideal for the eco-homemaker. CAT even suggests 'a romantic weekend' away for newlyweds learning about alternative sustainable lifestlyes, although this may not be everyone's idea of romance.

'Planning ahead for yourself should include planning ahead for the planet'

Julie Blower and her husband Toby used the Centre's list for their wedding and said that "in the special time around your wedding it feels more important than ever to do business with people like CAT", because planning ahead should also include planning ahead for the planet. It may not be long before brides have to have something old, something new, something recycled and something green.

• *For a copy of the 'Buy Green By Mail' catalogue, contact Sabrina Wise, Centre for Alternative Technology, Machynlleth, Powys, SY20 9AZ (tel: 01654 705959; fax: 01654 705999; e-mail: mail.order@cat.org.uk).*

Spiders' webs monitor pollution

Summarised from an article by Rachel Nowak, entitled 'Saved by spiders', in New Scientist (June 8th 2002; New Scientist subs £99 or $140, call 01444 475636 or e-mail ns.subs@qss-uk.com).

The webs of particular species of spiders are so effective at trapping airborne particles that they make excellent detectors for pollutants. This was the discovery made by an eco-toxicologist in New South Wales, Australia. While examining spiders' webs in the Blue Mountains, it was found that the webs

6 Blackstock Mews, London N4 2BT, UK (rhino@dial.pipex.com), 2002, 300pp, ISBN 0 948826 59 2

near roads had levels of lead and zinc up to ten times higher than those in other caves. The scientists believe that this is due to the particular group of spiders called cribellates, whose webs consist of matted fibres that entangle their prey. It is this matted structure, as opposed to the more common wheel-like webs, which makes the webs particularly effective at trapping particles of pollution.

'Particular webs could be used as low-tech biosensors'

This finding has a negative and a positive result. The negative one is that the spider population may be in danger in the area, because spiders groom themselves regularly and therefore may be ingesting some of the pollutant material on their web. Reducing traffic in the area is now a priority for those concerned with the welfare of the cribellated spiders, as they attempt to cut pollution. The positive side is that the scientist who made the finding, Grant Hose, believes that these particular webs could be used as biosensors to detect and monitor levels of pollution. The low-tech approach to monitoring pollution would not only be significantly cheaper than current methods, but could also allow scientists to look at readings across a large area, including houses, roads, caves, trees and anywhere else spiders make webs. They would then be able to pinpoint areas where pollution is thought to be high and move in with more sophisticated equipment and techniques.

Seven simple (environmental) wonders of the world

Summarised from an item, entitled '7 Wonders', in YES! A Journal of Positive Futures (Fall 2001 issue; subscriptions $24 + postage from Positive Futures Network, P.O. Box 10818, Bainbridge Island, WA 98110-0818, USA; tel: +1 206 842-0216; fax: +1 206 842-5208; web: www.yesmagazine.org).

In a book called *Seven Wonders: Everyday Things for a Healthier Planet*, John Ryan draws our attention to the simpler things that have come to be taken for granted in our lives. They are things, six of them human innovations, which meet people's needs and help the world run more smoothly and harmoniously.

Ryan's seven wonders are:

• **The Bicycle** – the most efficient form of transportation created, a bicycle is the most energy-saving, affordable, health-giving, peaceful mode of getting around

- **The Condom** – the benefits of the condom are only really understandable when a world without it is imagined, both in terms of the number of unwanted pregnancies and in terms of the unchecked spread of sexual disease
- **The Ceiling Fan** – ceiling fans use the same amount of power as a light bulb, but reduce temperature by up to ten degrees Fahrenheit; unfortunately, air conditioners are now responsible for a sixth of all electricity used in America

'Using a clothesline can reduce a family's annual carbon emissions by a ton'

- **The Clothesline** – exchanging a tumble dryer for a clothesline (or horse) can reduce a single family's carbon emissions by a ton, and save them hundreds of dollars over the years
- **Pad Thai** – these Thai noodles are low in fat, of high nutritional quality, and are produced with a relatively low environmental impact
- **The Public Library** – the library is still one of the great educational tools of the age; open to all, and providing a gateway to every subject known to man, they also help keep paper levels down by encouraging readers to loan not buy
- **The Ladybug** – one of nature's inventions, the ladybug is one of the most effective pest-controllers on the planet, eating 5,000 crop-destroying insects in its lifetime; the ladybug, and its brethren, do four times the work of pesticides around the globe

- Seven Wonders: Everyday Things for a Healthier Planet *by John C. Ryan (University of California, 1999; 128 pages, $12.95, ISBN 1578050383).*

Coffee as an eco-friendly slug and snail treatment

Summarised from an article by Mark Henderson, entitled 'Just one more cup of coffee before you go', in the Times (June 27th 2002).

If a neighbour is spotted brewing a pot of coffee before spraying it all over their garden, people may worry about their sanity; but they may simply be employing a new treatment for killing slugs. New research by the US Department of Agriculture has found that slugs (and snails) are repelled by caffeine, even at low concentrations. This could mean cups of coffee being a replacement for highly toxic slug pellets, which are a danger to animal and plant life.

6 Blackstock Mews, London N4 2BT, UK (rhino@dial.pipex.com), 2002, 300pp, ISBN 0 948826 59 2

'The dregs of filter or cafetiere coffee may be more successful'

Coffee is also less likely to harm insects or plantlife, although it may cause the leaves of some ferns and lettuces to yellow. The scientists found that even a weak concentration of caffeine worked as a repellent, but those who have filter or cafetiere coffee may find their dregs to be even more successful. As caffeine is a natural product, and is recognised as a safe compound, it has huge potential as an environmentally acceptable alternative solution to the enduring problem of slugs in the garden.

SCIENCE, TECHNOLOGY AND ENERGY

Pedal-power for computers and office electricity

Summarised from a letter from Christopher Harris, entitled 'Wind-up to a healthier lifestyle', in the New Scientist (September 22nd 2001; New Scientist subs £99 or $140, call 01444 475636 or e-mail ns.subs@qss-uk.com).

Christopher Harris suggests that a bicycle-powered computer could be a hugely important invention for the 21st century. As more and more people are seated around the world in front of computers, so less and less are having any form of exercise through their profession. A simple pedal-dynamo system beneath the desk could enable employees to power their computers, desk lamps and even printers and photocopiers. In bigger offices, there could be a central hub where all power generated is collated, before being distributed around the office where needed. The benefits would be threefold: exercise for sedentary workers, a reduction in pollution (through a reduction in power use from fossil fuels) and a cut in costs for the company.

'Gyms could also be self-powered, utilising the work done by people exercising'

Many other people have also suggested to the Global Ideas Bank that gyms should be hooked up in a similar fashion, utilising the work done by people on exercise bikes and the like. The energy produced could help power the electrical features of some machines, the air conditioning system, or the rows of televisions which are often an inevitable feature of such places. The amount of electricity that could be generated in this way, given the number of gyms in the country and the number of people who use them on a daily basis, is potentially huge, and would seem to indicate that further examination of the idea could be worthwhile.

6 Blackstock Mews, London N4 2BT, UK (rhino@dial.pipex.com), 2002, 300pp, ISBN 0 948826 59 2

Making the UN building a beacon of solar power

Greg Wright

Perhaps solar-photovoltaic tiles could be applied to one of the large flat and windowless sides of the United Nations building in New York. As well as supplying solar power for the landmark building, such an undertaking would also serve as a highly visible model for solar energy and its diverse usefulness. I believe that one of the sides of the building faces more or less south along New York's East River, making it suitable for solar power.

'Tiles could be contributed by organisations and individuals'

Furthermore, the tiles could be individually contributed, or in blocks, by companies, organisations, nations, groups, individuals, and other UN or solar-energy supporters across the world. Each tile could then be credited on a map of the wall in the building's lobby, as well as an interactive map on a website which links to the supporters' individual sites.

I would further suggest that the tiles be arranged to create a suitable mural or pattern, such as a dove against a New York sky, the United Nations flag or something similar. A competition could be held to come up with a suitable design if necessary. Being the international landmark that it is, regularly appearing on news broadcasts across the world and being visited by international leaders and politicians, the UN building would be a wonderful place to signal the world community's commitment to sustainable technology and environmental issues.

• *Greg Wright (wright@sunutility.com) is the founder of Wright Thinking, and the winner of an Social Inventions award for his idea for a Global Suggestion Box, which became the Global Ideas Bank*

Rating system of experts vs. generalists to distinguish them

Dr. Karl H. Wolf

With experts (specialists) and generalists in any profession (or discipline or knowledge domain) the question often arises as to the contribution each can make; should our education system emphasise one or the other and when (eg in secondary school already or in which year in university); does a corporation or government rely on the opinions of only experts; and so forth. I claim that we need bot and that we need a rating system to distinguish them for different situations.

Experts are the ones correctly ascertaining to be able to exclusively do the best-possible job in any social setting, whether in science, technology, medicine, engineering, industry, business, administration, finance, investment, public or civil service, politics, etc. No argument here: admittedly, there is no progress without experts in any field of endeavour where research, innovation, and development are undertaken.

'There are situations where a synergetic approach is the key to advancement'

However, there are unequivocal situations where advancement, or the discovery of alternatives as well as the prevention of disasters, is only possible or likely through the involvement of generalists, in particular where an holistic (or integrative, or systems analytical, or synergetic, if one wishes a near-synonym) approach is used. It is the generalist then who can offer broader or even global viewpoints, perspectives, and contexts.

'A generalist's abilities may encompass numerous specific disciplines'

Questions may arise as to how one can more precisely define and describe an 'expert (E)' and a 'generalist (G)' because most individuals or institutions are exclusively neither one or the other. Experience and abilities of an expert often cover in various degrees several knowledge domains beyond their particular speciality; and a generalist's abilities may encompass numerous specific disciplines, again in varies degrees, all of which ought to be identified and described.

How to describe these many possible combinations? Two suggestions-cum-questions for consideration follow: (a) Find a more precise working definition of these two words for each profession-cum-discipline in order to be able to set (even if initially roughly only) a boundary between them along a continuum or spectrum. This continuum can then be divided numerically to assist in describing a person's abilities. (b) Find a semi-quantitative measure of one person's or institution's E-G mix. It ought to be possible to eventually (after trial/error experimenting) classify both the E and G according to a 1-to-10 scale. [Also, a ratio of either E/G or G/E might be useful in some instances.]

For example, a 'pure' generalist's experience or abilities can be expressed as: science (4) writing/editing (3) philosophy (3) history of science/technology (2); and a 'narrowly trained' expert's as: science (9) economics (2) writing

6 Blackstock Mews, London N4 2BT, UK (rhino@dial.pipex.com), 2002, 300pp, ISBN 0 948826 59 2

ability (-1). [For 'science', one can use any other disciplines; and -1 means 'inadequate ability and thus requires training'.] Any person can apply this sort of reasoning to obtain a semi-quantitative self-analysis for personal and professional use. (a) and (b) can be used separately or in combination.

The use of the 1-to-10 scale has already been used in many situations other than the above described one. For instance, any health practitioner may ask a patient: 'How much pain do you have on a scale from 1 to 10?' There are numerous other theoretical and applied examples.

Further explanatory comments

Re: Experts vs. Generalists. (a) About rating. Inasmuch as this idea is, I believe, rather new, there are several aspects one should consider. The 'rating' has to be done on the 'self-analysis' (or 'auto-analysis') basis as well as by, say, an interviewer during a job, promotion, or research-fund application. Total honesty has to be assumed, of course, not to exaggerate ones abilities or not to downgrade them. If a very important situation arises where the 'classification' of one's 'expert' and 'generalist' experience and abilities are involved (eg if someone is destined to become Director of Research Institute), then an 'independent body' should do the rating after an interview and discussion. (b) Important to repeat is that the idea ought to be tested by one or more professional bodies and associations. Also, sociologists and psychologists should engage in research to develop, test, and retest the ideas I propose above.

'A continuum between expert and generalist knowledge'

(c) I think 'continuum' is probably a better term than 'spectrum'. The Oxford Dictionary definition of 'continuum' is: 'a continuous (uninterrupted) series of elements passing into each other'. The 'colour spectrum' would be one example of a 'continuum'. In our present context, we use 'continuum' only. Well, if we have a 'continuum between expert and generalist knowledge, experience, and ability' we could imagine the '100 per cent expert ability together with 0 per cent of generalist ability' at one end of a line and '0 per cent expert ability together with 100 per cent generalist ability' at the other end. Any specific person would fall somewhere in between. Wouldn't *that* offer a bit of information for discussion and result in formulating meaningful questioning? Of course, this 'continuum' could be accompanied or even replaced by the 1-to-10 scale (this scale being, of course, a type of continuum), where the degree of expertise is expressed by a number (10 indicating 'fully-experienced expert'). Using this scale idea would only indirectly imply the 'degree of generalist ability'.

I almost think that one could adhere to the 1-to-10 scale concept – and perhaps forget about the 'continuum' idea! But it ought to be kept continually in mind that the scale indeed is a continuum – at least implicitly.

To be more specific in regard to 'knowledge domains', the words 'expert' and 'generalist' will have to be replaced by specific disciplines or better sub-disciplines. Take a chemist's experience, for example, several of these continuum-lines may be needed. One line would be for his or her ability in organic chemistry, the second for industrial experience, the third for applied mathematics, the fourth for Philosophy of Science (Methodology), and so forth. The respective points, pointing to the 'degree of experience' along the four lines would be, for example: at 90 per cent, 70 per cent, 40 per cent, and 50 per cent. Or use the 1-to-10 scale instead.

* *Dr Karl Wolf (e-mail: wolfwisdom@bigpond.com).*

Solar-cell sun visors powering a car's internal electrics

Kelly Peters

I know that ideas on solar powered cars have been developed, however, I had an idea about having solar powered sun visors in your car. And these solar powered sun visors could power the lights in your car, or power the windows, etc; I also felt that this idea could apply for solar powered sun roof covers. You could put a solar shield within the roof cover of the sunroof, and it could also power internal car electrics.

Solar-powered air conditioning

Brandon Dent suggested a similar idea, in which solar power would be used to maintain an air conditioning system to prevent dogs suffocating in cars (and also to keep it cool for when the driver returns).

'Any excess power from the solar panels could be channelled to pwer the car itself'

Any excess power from these solar panels on the car could then be channelled to help power the car itself, improving fuel consumption and reducing emissions.

* *. Kelly Peters and Brandon Dent are students at Elon University (www.elon.edu) in North Carolina, USA.*

6 Blackstock Mews, London N4 2BT, UK (rhino@dial.pipex.com), 2002, 300pp, ISBN 0 948826 59 2

Micro-hydro turbines in drains to generate electricity

Sami Grover

Turbines could be installed in urban drainage systems to generate electricity for domestic use, or alternatively to power street lights, traffic lights, or other communal electrical items.

'All major cities have a drainage system that is an untapped energy resource'

All major cities have at least a rudimentary form of drainage system and the constant flow of large amounts of water is an untapped resource that could be used to reduce the need for non-renewable sources of power. The rate of flow of water would obviously be a factor in determining where this process would be applicable, as would a relatively regular flow.

This form of electricity generation would provide a cheap and renewable source of electricity with the additional advantage of being situated extremely near to where electricity is most needed i.e the city. In addition to this, the amount of work needed to install such systems would be relatively small compared to other micro-hydro power installations, as the channelling of water etc would already be completed.

• *Sami Grover (e-mail: sami_grover@hotmail.com). Sami lives in Bristol and works for a publishing company specialising in academic literature on languages, multi-culturalism, education and sustainable development.*

Baby strikes to prevent nuclear plant construction

Summarised from an article, entitled 'The Finnish Line', on the Planet Ark website (www.planetark.org; April 5th 2002), monitored for the Global Ideas Bank by Tom Atlee of The Co-Intelligence Institute, P.O. Box 493, Eugene, Oregon 97440, USA (e-mail: cii@igc.org; web: www.co-intelligence.org).

In an effort to persuade the Finnish government not to build a fifth nuclear reactor, hundreds of Finnish women have declared that they will not bear children for four years unless the plan is scrapped. A similar protest was undertaken in 1986 after the Chernobyl disaster, and the Finnish government eventually backed down. The protesting women, who have all signed a petition confirming their declaration, hope that this protest will have the same effect.

'The form of protest is logical because this doesn't just concern our generation'

It is another example of innovative direct action, and one which also has some logic to it; as Elina Venesmaki, one of the strike organisers, points out, "this form of protest is logical because this issue doesn't concern just our generation". The government believes that nuclear power is the only way for them to meet electricity demands and enable cuts in greenhouse gas emissions, but this is fiercely opposed by the protesters, who say the risks are too high and that the problems of disposal have never been satisfactorily explained. By protesting with their wombs, the women are making not only a point of protest, but a point about long-term environmental thinking: decisions taken now affect later generations.

- *For more information, see www.valvomo.org/lakko*

Predictions for the next century

Summarised from an article by Raymond Kurzweil and Arthur C. Clarke, entitled 'Arthur C. Clarke Offers his Vision of the Future', on the KurzweilAI website (www.kurzweilai.net). This item was noted in the Arlington Institute's FUTUREdition e-newsletter (December 13th 2001; subscribe at http://www.arlingtoninstitute.org/products_services/futuredition.html).

In December 2001, the legendary science fiction author and futurist Arthur C. Clarke gave his predictions for changes to our society in the next century. While some may seem fanciful or over-optimistic, particularly those which would run up against the interests of big business, they nevertheless offer an interesting, and at times frightening, insight into what one of the world's most visionary thinkers foresees in our future. What is particularly interesting is his view of the future as one that will involve progression to new technological vistas but also a regression to the past in certain areas; public space travel will sit alongside the recreation of hunter-gatherer societies.

Arthur C. Clarke's predictions for the next century

2002: Clean low-power fuel based on a new energy source emerges (possibly based on cold fusion)

2003: The car industry is given five years to replace its dependence on fossil fuels and their derivatives

6 Blackstock Mews, London N4 2BT, UK (rhino@dial.pipex.com), 2002, 300pp, ISBN 0 948826 59 2

2004: The first publicly admitted human clone
2006: The last coal mine is closed
2009: A city in a third-world country is decimated by an atomic bomb
2009: All nuclear weapons are destroyed
2010: A new form of space-based energy is taken up
2010: Most crime is eliminated by an ubiquitous monitoring system
2011: Space flights become available to the public
2013: Prince Harry goes on a space flight
2015: Complete control of matter at the atomic level is achieved
2016: A universal currency based on the 'megawatt hour' is adopted
2017: Arthur C. Clarke, on his hundredth birthday, is a guest on the space orbiter
2019: A meteorite hits Earth
2021: The first man walks on Mars: there is an unpleasant surprise
2023: A dinosaur zoo filled with dinosaurs cloned from DNA opens in Florida
2025: Brain research leads to an understanding of the five senses. Full immersion virtual reality becomes available, with the helmet-wearing user able to enter 'new universes'
2040: A nanotechnological replicator can create any object from food to jewels. The only thing that now has any value is information
2040: The whole concept of human 'work' is phased out
2061: Hunter-gatherer societies are recreated
2061: Halley's comet is visited by humans on its return
2090: Large scale fossil fuel burning is resumed in order to replace carbon dioxide
2095: A true 'space drive' is developed; the first humans are sent out to nearby star systems already visited by robots
2100: History begins
   • *To comment on Arthur C. Clarke's predictions, or view countless other stimulating articles on what the technological future may hold, go to www.kurzweilai.net*

TRANSPORT

Passengers pack with airline-supplied suitcases at the airport

Cindy Maslanka

Airline security needs to be strengthened. One way to do this is to monitor who and what goes onto the airplane. Luggage can easily contain harmful substances. To solve this problem the airline would supply the suitcases for passengers. The passengers would then pack the suitcase under the watchful eye of videocameras and security personnel. Passengers might even pre-order their luggage with whatever they would like in the suitcase. The luggage would be directly shipped to destination. This would control what and how much was brought on board of the airplane, thus reducing the risk of hazardous weapons or bomb making materials being on the airplane.

Pre-packed suitcases

Summarised from a submission by Ellen Briggs, Ashley Conway and Tyler Ramey. They are all students at Elon University in North Carolina, USA.

'You could order your suitcase when you purchase your ticket'

In reference to the events of September 11th, we were given an assignment to creatively think of a new way for airport safety that we had not heard of before. We came up with the idea of pre-packed suitcases. There is a lot of questioning at present about luggage and safety. With our idea, you could order your pre-packed suitcase when purchasing your ticket. There could be a catalogue for everyone, inexpensive to more expensive, all the way from Walmart to Gucci, depending upon what the person wants. As well as clothes, the catalogue would cover toiletries, razors, adaptors and other necessary items. These suitcases are then packaged by airport staff, and given to you upon your arrival at your destination. There could even be a rental scheme for some items, whereby they could be used by different passengers a number of times.

• *Cindy Maslanka is a sophomore at Elon University (www.elon.edu) in North Carolina, USA.*

6 Blackstock Mews, London N4 2BT, UK (rhino@dial.pipex.com), 2002, 300pp, ISBN 0 948826 59 2

Improving the environment in underground stations with music

Summarised from a proposal sent to the Global Ideas Bank by Michael Mudoy, entitled 'Improving the environment at the London's Underground stations'.

Michael Mudoy's proposal for improving the atmosphere at underground stations is to have specific, targeted music played over the speaker system. To combat the stress and hectic nature of commuting on the Tube, sounds of nature could be played to transport passengers to an imagined oasis of calm; and, to reflect the diversity of the city that uses the system (London, in this proposal), different forms of world music could be played, such as traditional African music, or Tibetan monks chanting.

'Focuses attention on the psychological needs of commuters'

The idea is that the music should be trialled at one station, then along the whole of one line and then, finally, implemented on the whole underground system. It rightly focuses attention on the psychological needs of the underground's customers, something which is often overlooked amongst the talk of functional improvements in signalling, train renovation and ticket-pricing.

Interestingly, London Underground have tried out some new musical projects in recent months, primarily by changing the present rules on busking. Under the trial initiative, performers who were successful at auditions are permitted to entertain passengers at stations. In a parallel with Mr Mudoy's suggestion, this trial also aims to have different types of music playing at different stations across the network.

• *Michael Mudoy, 107c Chapter Road, London NW2 5LH (tel: 020 8451 5295; e-mail: michaelmudoy@hotmail.com)*

Car insurance by the mile for greater fairness

Summarised from an item, entitled 'Coverage by the mile', in Newsweek (March 11th 2002), monitored for the Global Ideas Bank by Roger Knights.

The integral unfairness of the car insurance system, in which the occasional driver is charged as much as the daily commuter travelling hundreds of miles, could finally be changing with the introduction of insurance charging by mile. Three states in America have now allowed 'by-the-mile' insurance, although some companies may wait for improved global positioning systems that can track mileage accurately. Otherwise the system would be open to abuse in the same way as happens with second-hand cars having their mileometers tampered with. Nevertheless, calculating insurance premiums with annual mileage, as well as gender and age, should lead to a fairer system, particularly for those who use their cars sparingly.

Aeroplane food used to make fuel

Summarised from an article by Sarah C. Greene, entitled 'At last, a good use for airplane food', in Discover magazine (October 2001 issue), monitored for the Global Ideas Bank by Roger Knights.

Los Angeles International Airport has teamed up with the city's Public Works department to introduce a scheme in which uneaten air passenger's food is transformed into fuel. The leftover meals are pulverised, mixed with water and heated; bacteria then break down the food, releasing methane gas to be piped to a nearby power plant. The airport dumps over 8,000 tons of leftover scraps every year, so the potential use of them for renewable energy is substantial, as is the potential for doing the same around the world. It also makes a change for the airline business to be doing something positive for the environment, rather than polluting it.

A cycle-bus for energy efficiency and exercise

Alastair McGowan

This idea is for a lightweight bus no bigger than a car, that takes about eight people, or bigger versions with many more people, who provide cycle power for the bus. It would also have solar cells on the roof. The bus would be aimed at more energetic people who find cycling too dangerous, but who want to get around town cheaply and with concern for the environment. An efficient use of road space, it would be likely to be cheap because there is no gas involved and the electric motor would be used only part of the time.

6 Blackstock Mews, London N4 2BT, UK (rhino@dial.pipex.com), 2002, 300pp, ISBN 0 948826 59 2

'Pedalling hard would earn a person some of their fare back'

A passenger would buy a card for a small amount of money which on entering the bus they would put in a vacant slot. They would then take the corresponding seat and pedal. A monitor on their handlebars connected to a computer would tell them how much energy they are putting in compared to their journey length. If they pedal hard then they will earn back some of their fare. If they don't pedal then it gets deducted from their card, if their card gets used up they pay the driver to recredit it. If they pedal really hard then they might actually earn some money. For some people that last option might offer a way to get some extra cash and feel that they are contributing to society and the environment.

If people are pedalling harder than the bus needs then this power could be diverted to a generator which charges the batteries along with the solar charger. When there are fewer passengers then this power would be used, or if the driver needs to accelerate quickly, the motor kicks in. The deceleration and braking of the bus also feeds kinetic energy into the generator. If it's sunny and lots of people have just used it, the batteries would be fully charged, and so no-one needs to pedal.

'The bus would also have solar cells on the roof, and have a chargable battery'

Such a bus would have solar cells on the roof, batteries and a charger. It would also have an electric motor. It could be lightweight because it won't go too fast, allowing ease of control for the bus driver. Adaptions to the cycle input could be made so that a wheelchair type input would allow wheelchair users to contribute power. The sides would be open in warm climates, in colder climates lightweight panels could be attached. Because it doesn't go very fast it need only be constructed as strongly as a bicycle, but would be a lot safer because the people would be enclosed.

• *Alastair McGowan (e-mail:mcgowanam@cardiff.ac.uk). Alastair is a human-factors graduate at Cardiff University in Wales.*

Fight terrorism: fly naked

Tim Caudill

Obviously, airport security is insufficient in these times of shoe-bombers and highly trained terrorists cells. Terrorists are quite intelligent and highly adaptable to their surroundings; hiding explosives in their shoes or box cutters in their clothing are just two examples of their cunning ability to allude detection. To end the possibility of a terrorist smuggling any type of explosive or weaponry on to an airplane I suggest that everyone flies in the nude.

In the nude a terrorist is rendered harmless without any of the weapons that they would use to take over the plane as the terrorist did on September 11th.

'Would you rather be naked in public or be on a plane with a terrorist?'

Some societies frown on public nudity (including the US and Great Britain). Would you rather be naked in public for a few hours or a captive of an insane terrorist? In the modest countries passengers could travel in disposable hospital examination gowns that would be issued to them at the airport. It is time to drop our ideals or morality and think as one world united to defend itself.

• *Tim Caudill (e-mail: mtcaudill@yahoo.com). Tim is a freelance web designer, fiction writer, and former US Marine. He lives in the United States.*

6 Blackstock Mews, London N4 2BT, UK (rhino@dial.pipex.com), 2002, 300pp, ISBN 0 948826 59 2

Maps for walking short-cuts around cities

Submitted to the Global Ideas Bank by Myron Edwards, who is an entrepreneur looking to develop this scheme not only in the UK but in other countries. He is 48 years old and lives in Essex, England.

In an effort to encourage the oldest form of transport in the world, a website has been set up which gives details of walking short-cuts around London. It demonstrates how to beat the rush hour hassles on tubes and buses in the city by using a taxi-driver's type of knowledge, but for walking. Many people who travel one or two stops on the tube, or change buses every five minutes, may be amazed to discover that it would have been quicker, easier, and healthier to walk to their destination. Walking in London, and other cities, can also lead to unknown parts of the city, hidden parks and green spaces or quieter areas away from the hustle and bustle of the traffic. Maps with walk duration times are available as part of the service, and are becoming available in other languages for tourists. They could prove particularly useful for the latter who tend to move from central attraction to central attraction, often in a stressed and haphazard manner.

• *For more information see www.tubewalking.co.uk or e-mail myron@tubewalking.co.uk*

Online database of unwanted cars so parts can be salvaged

Phil Spencer

My suggestion is for an online database into which people can enter details of their unwanted vehicles, so other people can salvage spare parts for their own vehicle. This would help to alleviate the increasing numbers of abandoned cars, and reduce the wastage of serviceable parts when the vehicles are crushed. Eventually, this could lead to a reduction in levels of new part production, meaning less materials are wasted unnecessarily.

• *Phil Spencer (e-mail: phil@pjspencer.swinternet.co.uk). Phil is a new media developer from Leeds, UK.*

Driving tips of the week in local papers to reduce errors and irritation

Sax Jones

With all the frustration of today's roads getting nothing but worse as the amount of traffic spirals upwards out of control. There's nothing more irritating than your fellow driver not interpreting the road, roundabout, or junction etc just the way you do. Especially as so many times our local road designers stray away from the standard examples given in the Highway Code. Therefore, I propose that, at very little extra cost local newspapers, ragmags or flyers could print a kind of 'junction of the week' or 'round-about tip for today' etc. Each time, in diagrammatic form, it could be explained how a local interchange, junction or roundabout is best tackled. Hopefully with this in place, the majority of local drivers will be on the same wavelength at the Give Way sign.

• *Sax Jones (e-mail: sax206@aol.com). Sax is a non pilot aircrew living in North Scotland.*

Cheap fares for kids going to school to encourage use of public transport

Raj Curry

I am not an incontinent give-everything-free-to-everyone type person, but in this case we could have a win/win option.

'Children should be allowed to board any train or bus for a nominal fare'

Children attending school should be allowed to board any train or bus for a nominal fare, say 10p, to encourage their protective mothers to allow them to get to and from school by public transport, thereby avoiding the school rush hour jam. Although costing something to the local authorities, if it works this measure would pre-empt heavy capital expenditure on improving the transport system, as well as cutting down on unnecessary car traffic.

6 Blackstock Mews, London N4 2BT, UK (rhino@dial.pipex.com), 2002, 300pp, ISBN 0 948826 59 2

[Additionally but separately, fares for adults in general should be calculated purely on the hour in which the ticket was purchased, and have nothing to do with the distance travelled or zone, because as the trains run throughout the day anyway, they may as well be fuller during the slack hours, and less full during rush hours.]

• *Raj Curry (e-mail: TangorePress@onetel.net.uk). Raj lives in Richmond, London.*

Compulsory swift lie-detecting at airports

Summarised from an article on the Cosmiverse website (http://www.cosmiverse.com), entitled 'New Liar Test Could Become Standard at Airports' (January 3rd 2002), originally noted in the Heads Up e-newsletter (subscribe at http://gocreate.com).

Lie-detection has been considered for improving security at airports for some time, but it was always considered too time-consuming and too impractical for processing large numbers of people. In the wake of September 11th, though, people have been looking at the idea again, and there is now a new lie-detection technique which could make it workable. The improvements to security could be significant, and help to alleviate the huge pressure on the personnel responsible for vetting passengers.

'The new technique picks up minute hot flushes around a person's eyes'

The new technique uses a high-definition thermal imaging camera to scan a person's face, and it picks up minute 'hot flushes' around the eyes when a person lies. In tests, the technique correctly identified three quarters of the 'guilty' people (those who had been asked to stab a dummy, rob it and then lie) and 90 per cent of the 'innocent' individuals (who had no knowledge of the 'crime'). If the system was to become practicably workable, its possible uses are almost infinite: everywhere there is a security check-in, there could be a test, from customs points to governmental buildings.

White night cabs to regulate minicabs and bring prices down

Summarised from a letter to the Times from Daniel Dennis, entitled 'Affordable night cabs', on the letters page (November 17th 2001).

To solve the problem of providing safe, regulated taxis at night, Daniel Dennis suggests licensing a whole new section of cab drivers who would only be able to work between the hours of 8pm and 8am. Their prices would be set at the same level as daytime cabs, and they would be painted a different colour to differentiate them – in London, this could be white instead of black. The effect of such an introduction of new taxis would be twofold: people would be able to afford a cab at night without resorting to unlicensed minicabs, and the unlicensed drivers might be encouraged to become the driver of a 'white' cab, therefore becoming legitimate and able to be regulated.

'People would not have to resort to drivers with no training or background checks'

There have been several instances of rape and assault in unlicensed minicabs in recent months in London and other UK cities, and this idea could help prevent people resorting to trusting people who have had no background checks or training for the job. The idea could also apply to other major cities around the world where taxi prices at night are extortionate: New York could have green versions at night instead of yellow, and so on.

Ring and ride buses revitalise rural transport links

Summarised from an article, entitled 'Transports of delight?', in Green Futures magazine (August 2001).

Rural transport has long been a problem in the UK, with fixed bus services either needing to be subsidised or pared down to a minimum to survive and provide a necessary service. To get round this problem, a number of different innovative projects have sprung up in rural areas around the country. These include 'ring and ride' buses, taxi-bus services and per-mile buses.

In Devon, there are several 'ring and ride' schemes, in which users book a place on the bus the day before and are returned to their home on the day in question. In the Honiton area, for example, the bus caters for a different rural parish each day of the week, ensuring that everyone has a chance to get mobile,

6 Blackstock Mews, London N4 2BT, UK (rhino@dial.pipex.com), 2002, 300pp, ISBN 0 948826 59 2

particularly the more frail and elderly members of the community. The single vehicle is subsidised not by the council or by government but by being used to take children to and from school, and through letting itself out for private hire in the evenings. That covers a third of the organisers' annual costs.

'The bus wiggles off-route to pick up passengers'

In Wiltshire, meanwhile, they have what is known as a 'wigglybus', so-called because there are no strictly defined bus routes, so the bus 'wiggles' off to pick people up. The bus then drops people at home on request, and all for the fraction of the cost of a taxi: £1.20 per journey or, for those paying a £20 annual subscription, just 40p. As well as being used by the elderly, the council claims that a fifth of users are drivers choosing to leave their cars parked in the garage.

Finally, the PlusBus in Cumbria works by charging fares on a mile-by-mile basis, with a minimum charge of 10 pence. Again, pensioners are the primary users (with one comparing the effect of the service to being released from prison), but the co-ordinators have again been surprised by the amount of young people using the service. As with the Wiltshire 'wigglybus', a significant number of those were also car-drivers leaving their vehicle at home.

• *For more information, see http://www.local-transport.dft.gov.uk/ruralbuses/*

COMMUNICATIONS AND THE INTERNET

The power of the internet for social good

A review of The Internet Galaxy *by Manuel Castells (published by Oxford University Press, 2001, ISBN: 0199241538, 292 pages, £14.99). Reviewed by Nick Temple.*

New technology has always had the power to change the way we live our lives, from the telephone to the automobile, and this continued apace in the latter years of the twentieth century. In the 1990s, the main catalyst for change was the advent of the internet and its increased take-up, and this is the subject of Manuel Castells' new book, *The Internet Galaxy*: the ways in which the internet is affecting all parts of society, be it politics, business, community or the environment, and how it might continue to do so in the future. It is Castells' conjecture that we have "entered a new world of communication: the internet galaxy", by which term he means to infer both the pervasiveness of the new form of global communication in all areas of society and the extent to which it is an unknown quantity, a realm of some mystery and power over us. More than just an immense technological innovation, the internet is a social innovation that has given rise to innumerable projects and ways of improving society, and this has made it one of the most interesting areas of creative imagination and experimentation in the world today.

Origins of co-operative creativity

The book starts with a fascinating look at the way in which the internet came about, as Castells traces its origins in the American military, the networks of computer programmers at universities across the US, and the individual innovators across the world. The key lesson from the history of the internet is that is was built on consensus, freedom of information and innovation: despite its ties to the US government and its defense department, there was a large amount of leeway given to the early internet pioneers, meaning that free thinking and creativity was not stifled in any way. This was partly due to the military's limited understanding the true potential of the technology, and partly because it was desperate (from the 60s through to the 90s) to be ahead of the Soviet Union in every possible area. Thus, the academics who provided crucial parts of the internet's structure, be it Paul Baran (ARPANET), Robert

6 Blackstock Mews, London N4 2BT, UK (rhino@dial.pipex.com), 2002, 300pp, ISBN 0 948826 59 2

Kahn and Vint Cerf (TCP/IP) or Tim Berners-Lee (http, html and url), were unfettered by the constraints of big business and government funding, and were able to build the internet by consensus, co-operation and international communication.

'Open source software allowed swift collaborative improvements'

The concept of 'open source' software, in which all information, codes and programming was made available to all, allowed swift collaborative improvements to be made on applications, and the simultaneous involvement of programmers and computer scientists across the globe. It is noticeable that this consensus-building meritocracy has remained at the heart of the internet's workings, with non-governmental institutions overseeing both the distribution of domain names and also the protocols and development of the web. Though commercialisation has inevitably occurred, most significantly by Microsoft, other applications remain committed to the ideals of open source, unbounded communication and co-operation. For the origins of the internet show how a co-operative creative system of innovation can have massive effects, and work in a much more effective way than restrained, closely-monitored and narrowly-funded research.

The internet and community

One of the areas in which the internet is having a transformative impact is community, and what that word means in the twenty-first century. It is Castells' contention that we are now living in a 'network society', a society in which, rather than place-based relationships, we have individual, or me-centred, networks of ties to people. The breakdown of communities in the modern age, particularly in the urbanized western world, has been well-documented, and the ways in which the internet can diminish (or increase) this trend has been a topic of interest for researchers since its inception. What the internet has done is accelerated the growth of interest-based communities, through chat rooms, bulletin boards and web sites linking fans of a particular band or television programme. These communities are 'virtual', in that they exist online, but many later translate into face-to-face interaction

'Users of the internet have larger social networks than non-users'

Other communities are built around a subject of interest, such as sufferers of a particular disease, or their partners, who can find information and a network of support where they could not previously (if there is no local

Alzheimers' support group, or even any sufferers in an area, the internet is able to fill this gap). There is evidence, too, that e-mail and mailing lists are enabling a greater and more consistent level of contact between families and friends in an increasingly dispersed and mobile world. Indeed, a survey in 2000 found that users of the internet tend to have larger social networks than non-users, primarily because of e-mail. This finding goes against a widespread belief that those who use the internet regularly are isolated, and lose contact with the outside world. This image of computer geeks tapping away at their keyboards in a darkened room is, however, now not only obsolete but disproved by most research. The closest Castells comes to giving any credence to this idea is when, in analysing such a study, he writes that there may exist "a threshold of Internet use beyond which on-line interaction takes a toll on off-line sociability". Obsessiveness in one area of life takes its toll on the other: hardly a new discovery.

What others argue is that the internet is the most incredible tool of communication yet invented, and that it has added an extra method of connecting individuals to one another. These connections also frequently do lead to face-to-face interaction, the lack of which is a common complaint of the internet critics. This was the concept behind, for example, the Institute for Social Inventions' participatory events website, www.DoBe.org, which aims to provide the means by which people can find events they can participate in and find like-minded people in every city of the world: essentially retribalising the cities. As with other media and technology, the internet will have the effects *we* want it to, and there is no reason, at least as far as communities are concerned, that they should not be positive.

Information-sharing and a new politics

As well as sharing interests and conversations, Castells also draws attention to the power of the internet as a tool of democracy: of information sharing and dissemination. There has simply never been a more effective tool for political activism and direct interaction in democracy. The anti-globalisation movement is one such example of a global network sharing information and organising protests and co-operation over the internet. But there are potentially more interesting political uses of the internet. Direct democracy, be it through online voting or e-mailing individual representatives, could potentially reverse the modern plague of apathy. Imagine an election in which everyone can read each party's manifesto (in summary, or detailed form) just minutes before voting; or imagine the increased power of a community (or interest group) that can discuss its issues, solutions and actions via an e-mail list or a bulletin board. As Castells writes, "the Internet brings people into contact in a public agora, to voice their concerns and share their hopes": it is

6 Blackstock Mews, London N4 2BT, UK (rhino@dial.pipex.com), 2002, 300pp, ISBN 0 948826 59 2

the largest forum for debate the world has ever known, and this is one reason why it is crucial to keep it as much as is possible under the people's control.

The digital divide - bridging the gap

Yet all of this positivity and optimism has a downside. The internet not only raises problems of privacy, fraud and control, but has also created a new form of disenfranchisement: lack of access and lack of (computer) skills. It is these two aspects of what has been termed 'the digital divide', as Castells acknowledges, that will determine the future of the internet. They are the keys to unlocking the internet for millions of people in the poorest countries, and for millions who lack the necessary skills to use access. If it is agreed that the internet is invaluable as a knowledge resource, a method of communication and a means of co-operating successfully, then access to it should be available to all at the lowest possible course, otherwise the advantage the rich have over the poor will be compounded. This is something that has to be dealt with by every government in every country in the world. The internet will not replace water, food, and housing, but it can provide weather information, details of schemes about other projects, how to build your own house, irrigation methods, ways of selling produce, and ways to collaborate with other local people for co-operative benefit. And all for a relatively small cost.

'The emphasis will shift from learning to 'learning-to-learn' '

The digital divide is also a knowledge divide, though. There are countless people who have the opportunities of access, but not the skills to use them, particularly in the older generations who did not grow up with computers and the internet. Castells is particularly illuminating on this subject, with his differentiation of learning and 'learning-to-learn'. The emphasis of computer education will shift from learning information and knowledge to learning how to learn, that is how to search, how to retrieve, how to process and how to utilise the information the internet makes available. This is a new type of learning that aims to develop the capacity 'to transform information into knowledge and knowledge into action'. Internet access without attendant computer skills is like having the telephone but not having the ability to speak.

Conclusion

This book is a well-researched, well-structured study of the world that has the internet increasingly intermingled with it at every level. Covering business, community, politics, inequality, culture and activism, Castells discusses each area dispassionately and lucidly. He is clearly a great believer in the internet's transformative power, but equally aware of the great challenges it will pose face in the future: challenges of freedom, privacy, equality of access, environmental impacts and, perhaps most crucially of all in the way it affects all the others, the challenge of maintaining the internet's founding ethos: creativity, innovation, co-operation and accessibility to all. It is our responsibility to ensure the internet galaxy remains, and becomes, what we want it to be.

A mass network forum for interactive public communication

Summarised from information available on the Common Forum website (www.common-forum.org) and from the Common Forum Project Plan, as put together by Jason Diceman.

The Common Forum, to quote directly from its website, is a 'centralized mass collaborative forum democratically organized through public links, yet individually sorted by complex queries'. Its creators believe it will be an ideal system for a more direct and interactive democracy, being, as it would be, a universal technological tool for public communication. The system is intended to go beyond the limits of such online facilities as bulletin boards and mailing lists by allowing a whole variety of interfaces and options for personalisation. The overall intention is to make the web freer, more interactive and more egalitarian, because anyone will be able to contribute, as if in a virtual town hall. It also aims to solve the problem of the fragmentation of public discourse on the web, that two people can be talking about similar issues and topics, but not always to each other.

'Complex queries will give more specific, high-quality results'

In this way, the Common Forum is intended to be a step on from the web, particularly in its use of new, smarter linking systems. Authors of documents will be able to set up links signifying relationships between articles: A describes B, A is the opposite of B, A is an example of B and so on. In this way, a complex network of relationships between documents builds up, one that allows more specific searching. A person could ask for articles that answer the question 'what are the important issues in London today?', but also ask for ones that have been highly recommended by certain other Common Forum users. When looking for an article with a particular point of view, this system would bring up articles arguing the opposite point of view, or related articles, or other

6 Blackstock Mews, London N4 2BT, UK (rhino@dial.pipex.com), 2002, 300pp, ISBN 0 948826 59 2

contextual information. And, as more and more people add personalised links and reviews, complex queries that use author reputations, article popularity, and user reviews will give more specific, high-quality results that are 'fully contextualised through links'.

'It could provide the first steps to a system of mass deliberative democracy'

This plan is, perhaps inevitably, quite complex itself. Essentially, the Common Forum's aim is to be a version of the web that adds many more features of interaction and discourse. Perhaps the most revolutionary aspect would be the way that documents would become rated. Rather than a webpage being judged solely on how many other pages link to it or on how many people visit it, the Common Forum would also allow it to be judged on its relevance to particular queries, and also by *any* member of the public who wishes to add a review. The theory would be that anyone abusing this system (ie posting abusive and unsubstantiated reviews about particular pages) would gradually become discredited by the other users becoming wise to it. Nevertheless, the forum remains a wifully anarchic idea, with all the associated freedoms and risks that implies. Its most immediate impact could yet be as a sort of smart search engine, giving results that are both relevant and contextualised to any particular query. Its major long-term contribution, if successful, could be a much greater one, though: providing the first steps to a genuinely interactive system of mass deliberative democracy.

- *For more information contact staff@common-forum.org or go to www.common-forum.org where a version of the full project plan can be downloaded.*

Internet van teaches farmers the potential benefits of new technology

Summarised from an item on the United Nations Integrated Regional Information Networks e-newsletter (February 15th 2002; www.irinnews.org), monitored for the Global Ideas Bank by Michael Norton.

A project in Pakistan has been launched which aims to introduce farmers to the internet, to educate them in how to use it, and to make them aware of how the technology can be turned to their advantage. A van containing computer equipment is being driven around many rural villages, showing farmers how to log on and browse, and encouraging them to continue their internet use in local cafés or elsewhere. The farmers can then download weather reports, information on seeds, fertilisers and pesticides, read the latest on crop diseases and find out how to procure loans to help them expand.

'Networks of support and knowledge can help improve connections between farmers'

The use of the internet (and e-mail) can also help farmers communicate with each other, leading to unofficial information exchanges. Networks of support and knowledge can help improve connections between farmers, and encourage sharing of help and information. The organisers of the project are looking to expand it with more vans to reach more of the rural population: 70 per cent of the Pakistani population live in rural areas, and there is still a very low usage of the internet, which is mostly due to education rather than opportunity. This innovative van project could help farmers and their families exploit the potential of the new technology.

• *See www.Pakissan.com for more information*

Self-organising groups better than experts at problem-solving

Summarised from an article by Gary H. Anthes, entitled 'Symbiotic Intelligence', in ComputerWorld magazine (October 22nd 2001), monitored for the Global Ideas Bank by Roger Knights.

The internet and other technological advances are aiding the formation of symbiotic networks of information and help. These informal groups of people, some experts have suggested, are better at solving complex problems than experts. This is because today's main problems, such as fighting terrorism or managing (or resisting) global capitalism, are complex and distributed and therefore less able to be solved by experts bestowing answers from above. Informal groups of people, connected by the internet and computer networks, facilitate the flow of information and help create a kind of collective knowledge. This knowledge can then be utilised by the same people.

'70 per cent of the information needed comes from informal sources'

This is what Norman Johnson, a physicist at Los Alamos National Laboratory in New Mexico, calls 'symbiotic intelligence', and he claims that this symbiotic system of computers and humans is the key to solving complex

6 Blackstock Mews, London N4 2BT, UK (rhino@dial.pipex.com), 2002, 300pp, ISBN 0 948826 59 2

problems. This theory could change the way we organise corporations, educational courses and the introduction of new technology. A recent survey in America of employees at large companies revealed that 70 per cent of the information they need to do their job comes from informal sources (ie not from training courses, manuals or instructions from a superior). If this informal information can be more easily and effectively supplied to people, along these symbiotic networks, then productivity and job satisfaction should increase proportionally.

Johnson suggests that managers looking to improve productivity should encourage the use of the internet, especially e-mail, and encourage risk-taking and individual approaches, rather than defined training courses. According to his research, diversity of people and approaches is the key to creating symbiotic intelligence in organisations. Similarly, work environments that promote interaction on an informal level can help foster these social connections. The theory can equally be applied to charities or activist groups, for whom collaboration and cooperation can increase their effectiveness significantly.

Solar powered internet connections in Cambodian village

Summarised from an article by Rajiv Chandrasekaran, entitled 'Life in Cambodian village transformed by Internet', in the Seattle Times (June 17th 2001), monitored for the Global Ideas Bank by Roger Knights. This item originally appeared in the Washington Post.

Two computers, a satellite dish and a set of solar panels has revolutionised life in the village of Rovieng in Cambodia. As is the case with many small villages in the country, there is no telephone service and no electricity in Rovieng, and the people are further disconnected by mountains and jungle. Now the village has been transformed, with silk scarves made in the village being sold over the web and profits being put into a pig farm. It is hoped that profits from the farm and the scarves will go on to fund medical care for the village.

'Small amounts of computer hardware can have a significant impact'

The project, set up by the American Assistance for Cambodia charity, aims to demonstrate how simple (and small) amounts of hardware can have a significant difference in developing countries. And as the costs of computer equipment continue to fall, the possibilities for improving access to new technologies for poorer countries increase. The only expensive hindrance with this project was the satellite connection, which the charity got a company to pay for, and any state funding for such projects would have to weigh up the pros and cons of spending large amounts of money on new technology. Mit Mien, the chief of Rovieng has no doubts, though: "I don't really know what the internet is or how it works, but it is changing our lives". As long as the change is for the better, there could be a proliferation of such projects around the globe aiming to bridge what has become known as the 'digital divide'.

• *To buy silk scarves from the village, and learn more about the project, go to www.villageleap.com*

Ten commandments of internet searching

Summarised from Intelligence Weekly, a free newsletter from Washington Researchers (www.washingtonresearchers.com)

The key tool for effective use of the internet is the search engine. There would be no use in having billions of pages of information (of varying quality and accuracy) if there was no way to chart a path through them. As with all methodologies, though, there are right and wrong ways to search the internet. Users should be aware that they are not searching the whole internet, nor that the most relevant items to their search will always come at the top. Similarly, there are simple steps that can be taken to ensure time-saving and effective internet searches. The following are ten commandments distilled by Washington Researchers, a firm specialising in business and competitive intelligence:

1. Know your search engine, and choose it carefully. Only a portion of all the websites are indexed by the best search engines
2. Use multiple search engines, or metacrawlers which combine the results of several individual search engines

'No searches are completely anonymous'

3. No searches are completely anonymous: be aware of 'cookies' (enable or disable with your internet browser as wished)
4. Search for sources of information, not necessarily the information itself; people and organisations you can contact may get you there quicker
5. Don't believe everything you read: just because something is down in print does not make it true. Information can also be easily typed incorrectly or copied mistakenly from another source. Cross-reference as much as possible

6 Blackstock Mews, London N4 2BT, UK (rhino@dial.pipex.com), 2002, 300pp, ISBN 0 948826 59 2

6. Don't be afraid of paying for access to some information: it may well have a cost because it is of high quality and usefulness

7. Before going online, ask if the information you are looking for is actually likely to be findable on the internet

8. Decide if you are searching or surfing: one has a definite end point, the other does not, so the methods should be different

9. Don't be afraid of typing words in: often the more words inputted, the more relevant the outcome will be. Also use exact wording and phrasing within inverted commas

10. Buy a timer, or set a desktop alarm, to limit the time spent searching. Otherwise, you could end up surfing.....

The Global Ideas Bank recommends:

www.google.com (obviously)
www.wisenut.com (less obviously)
www.northernlight.com (especially for US info)
www.ixquick.com (good metacrawler)
www.alltheweb.com (more pages logged than Google)

• *Subscribe to the Washington Researchers Intelligence Weekly newsletter at www.washingtonresearchers.com/public/intelli.html*

A database of common sense

Summarised from an article by Lamont Wood, entitled 'The World in a Box', on the Scientific American website (January 15th 2002; www.sciam.com) and from the Cycorp website (www.cyc.com).

Doug Lenat has been amassing a database of human common sense for over 18 years now, in an attempt to give computers the ability to understand language in the way that humans do. His vision is that applications that incorporate common sense will be less likely to fail in the real world. So, over one and a half million facts about the everyday world have been put into Cyc's (short for encyclopaedia) memory banks. This means that it knows that a glass is held with the open-side up, that people stop buying things when they die, and that trees are generally found outdoors. This common sense, or 'consensus knowledge', as Lenat's company prefers to call it, enables the computer to reason as a human would using applications and documents. This could eliminate one of the few things left that differentiates humans from computers.

'The search engine will not ask 'Would you like to buy a Guatemala?' '

As an example of what Cyc can presently do, it is being used to improve the quality of retrievals for the Lycos search engine. Thus, when a term such as 'Guatemala' is entered, the search engine will not immediately pop up with several 'would you like to buy a Guatemala?' or 'where can I get free Guatemala online?' offers. In the same way, but on a more positive note, if a term such as 'dime' is entered, the engine will offer Franklin D. Roosevelt as a topic, because it knows his picture is on that coin. Common sense ensures a greater relevancy and accuracy.

Lenat believes that all software will eventually incorporate common sense, although it is taking him a lot longer than originally thought to amass the facts needed. This is mostly due to the computer not only needing to be fed facts, but also the context for those facts, without which some of them can be misleading, ambiguous or just plain wrong. The potential uses for such a database are massive, though. Imagine an internal security system that takes account of disaffected ex-employees, or a spreadsheet that notices hourly and monthly figures being mistakenly added together. Imagine, ultimately, a computer with common sense.

• *For more information, contact Cycorp Inc, 3721 Executive Center Drive, Suite 100, Austin, TX 78731, USA (tel: +1 512 342 4000; fax: +1 512 342 4040; e-mail: info@cyc.com; web: www.cyc.com).*

An internet bus to help first-timers overcome fears

Summarised from an article on the internet entitled 'Netti-Nysse is I.T. Bus' (http://www.tampere.fi/kirjasto/nettinysse/english.htm).

In Tampere, Finland, the local authorities and schools have transformed a local bus into a computer consultation area, in an attempt to introduce different parts of the community to the internet in an original way. Furnished with 11 computers and a mobile connection to the internet, as well as a show-room and study area, the bus travels the streets of Tampere inviting a range of people from housewives to immigrants and the unemployed to come aboard and learn about the internet.

On board, small groups of customers are helped by tutors whose main aim is to make computer jargon accessible to everyone, as well as helping them understand what the internet can offer them

6 Blackstock Mews, London N4 2BT, UK (rhino@dial.pipex.com), 2002, 300pp, ISBN 0 948826 59 2

'As a hidden curriculum we also hope to create and support the feeling of a community'

The bus will act as a social space to bring diverse parts of the community together, and hopes to be able to cross the boundaries between people's relationships with each other as well as their participation in a new inclusive 'information society'. The organisers of the project hope that the bus will also help to create and foster support links in the community: the town itself built the bus, owns it and provides the staff to run it.

A solar-powered net bus has also been travelling round Australia in an effort to survey how the public there are participating in the new e-conomy, and what is stopping those who are not. It was undertaken by George Bray, a roving ambassador for the Internet Industry Association's Digital Bridge taskforce. The bus, or 'mobile internet application showcase', used all the latest wireless communication and video publishing technologies, and finished its 'tech trek' earlier this year.

• *For more information on the Netti-Nysse, see http://www.tampere.fi/kirjasto/nettinysse/*

• *To read the Tech Trek's report, and to check out the Digital Bridge taskforce, go to www.techtrek.tv*

Peer-to-peer program to combat life-threatening diseases

Summarised from the Intel website (www.intel.com/cure). Originally monitored for the Global Ideas Bank by Michael Norton.

A new project links up hundreds of thousands of computers, using peer-to-peer technology, in order to use their unused resources to process data for medical research. Anyone who has a PC and an internet connection can join in the venture, simply by downloading a program onto their computer. The program runs by using that individual's computer resources to process a small parcel of data, before sending the results back to a server. It then requests a new parcel of data to process and so on (the sending and receiving of data is only done when the individual is connected to the internet). The program does not affect the computer's performance, because it only uses processing power that is not being used. In this way, hundreds of thousands of computer owners can contribute to the fight against illness and disease, simply by using their computer and the internet.

'The more people that are connected, the bigger the computer's power and reach'

Peer-to-peer technology is best known for being the basis for the music-swapping website Napster, but it simply refers to the sharing of resources (such as hard drives and processing cycles) among computers and other intelligent devices. In essence, the technology creates a huge virtual super computer by virtue of connecting lots of smaller ones together, and the more people that are connected, the bigger the computer's power and reach. There are those who have concerns about privacy, security and other issues with regard to peer-to-peer technology, but it has massive potential for doing good as well, as this project makes clear. Such projects could promote a whole new era of what might be termed 'techno-philanthropy': there are already other peer-to-peer initatives fighting aids, researching nuclear waste disposal, looking for extra-terrestrial life and 'folding' proteins (which could impact on Alzheimer's research).

More on peer-to-peer technology

As well as philanthropic projects, peer-to-peer could have powerful positive effects in the business workplace as well. The technology's ability to facilitate fast communication and collective power makes it suitable for large businesses to use for distributing information. Rather than having to have a large central server on their premises, the business can set up a system whereby an employee's PC simply downloads the file from the nearest computer that has the file. This speeds up the process and reduces the need for costly servers.

While much is written about the security dangers of peer-to-peer, with its potential for unregulated, anonymous distribution of information, it is also worth noting that the technology could be used to improve computer security. It may not be long before anti-virus updates and 'patches' to mend problems with software are distributed in this way, ensuring a far quicker tightening of loopholes for viruses and hackers. The possibilities for collaboration, instant messaging, document distribution and anonymous storage are also massive, and could lead to a complete computing revolution in the forthcoming decade.

- *For more information, see the Peer-to-Peer Working Group's website at www.p2pwg.org; the group exists to facilitate and accelerate the advancement of infrastructure best-known practices for peer-to-peer computing; the group is concerned that issues of interoperability, security, performance, management and privacy may stifle the growth of innovation in this area. See also www.openp2p.com*
- *To download the program for your PC, go to www.intel.com/cure*
- *For other peer-to-peer projects, see www.aspenleaf.com/distributed/distrib-*

6 Blackstock Mews, London N4 2BT, UK (rhino@dial.pipex.com), 2002, 300pp, ISBN 0 948826 59 2

*projects.html , www.fightaidsathome.org and http://setiathome.ssl.berkeley.edu
The latter SETI@home project had its half-billionth download in June this year,
and has 3.6 million users, after originally aiming for 50,000.*
    • *For previous Institute articles on similar technology, see 'Freenet – rewiring
the internet' in* The Book of Inspirations, *p.246 (ISI, 2000).*

The tipping point: how to start a social epidemic

A review of The Tipping Point *by Malcolm Gladwell (published by Abacus,
2002, ISBN: 0349113467, 285 pages, £7.99). The book was suggested for review
by Roger Knights, the Institute's Assistant Editor. Reviewed by Nick Temple.*

The Tipping Point is a book about change, and particularly about attempting to understand how changes can come about quickly and unexpectedly.
Malcolm Gladwell endeavours to explain how these 'social epidemics' take
hold: how an unknown book becomes a bestseller, how viral marketing works,
how word of mouth has such power. The phrase 'tipping point' has its origins
in epidemiology, the study of illness epidemics. It is the point at which
epidemiologists label a virus as having reached critical mass: the moment when
numbers begin to increase very rapidly. Gladwell's argument, essentially, is
that there is a tipping point in all walks of life, be it television, selling shoes or
teenage smoking, and that ideas, behaviours and products "move through a
population very much like a disease does". The theory has immense potential
for all sorts of people, be they charities working on a limited budget or
educators trying to reach a great number of students.

'A small change can be the difference between obscurity and ubiquity'

An interesting aspect to Gladwell's theory is that it can be a very small
adjustment that can mean the difference between obscurity and ubiquity. As
an example he recounts a tale from the creators of a kids TV show called *Blue's
Clues* putting clues together for children to solve. The answer to the question
was penguin, and the producers had stipulated three clues to be given in order:
ice, waddle, then black and white. In a test on 17 children, four guessed it after
the first clue, six after the second and four after all three. But when a teacher
put the clues to nine children in her class in the order black and white, ice, then
waddle, the results were very different. No children got it right after the first
clue, one after the second and six more after the third clue. Simply by changing
the order of the clues, the teacher had kept suspense to the guessing game, and

had also allowed the children to think more broadly after earlier clues: black and white led to guesses of pandas, cows and dogs, while ice led to polar bears and cougars. This small change led to *Blue's Clues* being a hugely successful educational television programme that children loved.

'Groups can magnify the epidemic potential of an idea'

Gladwell also has interesting things to say about the effectiveness of groups at magnifying the "epidemic potential of a message or idea". He uses the examples of book-groups to show how this can occur, but also goes on to talk about the rule of 150. This rule suggests that groups with greater numbers than 150 lose the community ethos, and can become divided and alienated, which prevents the spreading of an idea or method or message by the groups. Gladwell focuses, in particular, on the example of the Gore Associates company (who make the Gore-Tex fabric), who have limited all their plants to 150 employees. This has led to bonds between workers being strong, informal relationships being effective, and no need for middle management. The size also helps encourage peer pressure for those groups to be successful, meaning that the Gore ideal, of remaining innovative and driven and focused like a smaller company, actually becomes reality. And because each of the 150 knows everyone personally, they know their strengths, weaknesses, ways of working, and how best people interact; and they also know that information and ideas can filter much more swiftly among them – the size enables the tipping point to take effect more easily.

'Mavens are accumulators of knowledge who then share their understanding'

The above demonstrates one of three rules that the book claims is crucial to reaching tipping point: 'the power of context' (environment is important). The other two rules are 'the law of the few' (that it only take a small number of people to make a big change) and 'stickiness' (as illustrated by the clues on the TV programme). In addition to these rules, Gladwell also identifies three main personality types who are crucial to the spreading of a social epidemic: 'connectors', 'maven' and 'salesmen'. Connectors are the people who know lots of people, the people with the fullest address books. Mavens are the accumulators of knowledge (on particular topics) who then share this understanding with others. Salesmen are those who convince that this information is valuable, relevant or important. All three play a key role in tipping an epidemic.

The value of this book, aside from the fact that it is accessible, well-written and entertaining, is in its potential balancing of the inequalities of life.

6 Blackstock Mews, London N4 2BT, UK (rhino@dial.pipex.com), 2002, 300pp, ISBN 0 948826 59 2

Charities with small budgets can have a bigger impact than all the marketing might of a major corporation; ideas can be spread like a virus throughout a country, or even the world; powerful change can occur with a minimum of initial effort. Essentially, what Malcolm Gladwell has done is take a scientific theory and transferred it to make it relevant to our lives. In doing so, he has shown why the public should no longer be surprised at unforeseen runaway successes, or word-of-mouth bestsellers. In addition, more tellingly, he has demonstrated how people might attempt to start their own 'positive' epidemics for social good.

ARTS, LEISURE AND LIFESTYLE

Concession card for those on low incomes

Rachel Gomme

Many people in London don't qualify for concessions to arts events etc because they're not students or on benefit, but are still on very low incomes, and so can't afford to profit from a lot of what's on offer. If there was a scheme for concession cards for people on low incomes (which could be classified, for example, as those who are employed but don't pay any tax, or in some other way), many people could enjoy events and organisers and venues could probably gain more income, as more people would be attending. There might have to be a nominal charge for the card to cover administration (say £5 per year), and anyone who applied would need to send some proof of their low income.

  • *Rachel Gomme (e-mail: rachelgomme@hotmail.com). Rachel Gomme is a performer and dancer based in London, and is interested in improving quality of life and strengthening community in the city.*

Tube carriage as art gallery

Summarised from information in Arts and the City magazine, distributed by London Arts (Issue 6; Spring 2002), and from an article on the BBC website, entitled 'Tube passengers to catch mobile gallery' (www.bbc.co.uk; November 1st 2001).

For the month of November 2001, a Piccadilly line underground train in London was transformed into an art gallery. 42 artists submitted two pieces of work to fill all six carriages of the train with art where the adverts would usually be. The artists featured included Yoko Ono, Damien Hirst and Vivienne Westwood, and included paintings, photographs and fashion items. The project extends other innovative exhibitions on the Underground, including the 'Platform Art' project and the world-famous 'Poems on the Underground' scheme.

The 'Art-Tube' was the brainchild of the Canadian artist Gordon McHarg, who had exhibited his own drawings on Vancouver's bus system some years back. That experience inspired him to curate the exhibition for London Underground, which reached a substantially larger audience. Each carriage

6 Blackstock Mews, London N4 2BT, UK (rhino@dial.pipex.com), 2002, 300pp, ISBN 0 948826 59 2

travels 45 miles through London on each journey along the line, and there are 52 stations on the Piccadilly line. At peak times, there are 76 trains on the line, giving the passengers a one and a third per cent chance of catching an art carriage each day. Mr McHarg pointed out the benefits of the scheme, saying, "It will liven up people's journeys, and I'm sure that thousands of people who would never normally go anywhere near an art gallery will benefit from it". Art-Tube 2002 is already in the pipeline, and is planned to tour the underground train systems of the world in the coming months.

* *For more information, and to see some of the featured panels, see www.art-tube.com*
* *This idea was also one that emerged from the Internet-Free Day 'brainstorm walk', held by www.DoBe.org in January 2001, as a way to improve London (and other cities).*

Picture the Globe – a democratic photography project

Adam Morgan

This idea consists of distributing sturdy one-time use cameras randomly to hundreds of people around the globe. The intention of this is to encourage people to think of the world as an interconnected place, and also help to make people aware of the conditions and lives led by people elsewhere. In this way, the photographs would help foster a belief in a global community or village, as well as providing an interesting insight into other worlds.

The cameras should have a small set of instructions printed on them saying the following:

'Please take one photo of anything you like and pass the camera on to a stranger. If you take the last photo please put the camera in any mailbox to be sent back for processing. When you have taken your photo please logon to this website xxx.xxxxx.xxx, enter the code number on this camera along with your name, city and state.'

Then when the cameras are returned and developed , there could be either a book published entitled 'Picture the Globe' or a website or other type of media. This would enable further publicisation and furthering of the project's aims.

* *Adam Morgan (e-mail: morganad@bc.edu). Adam is a 23 year old graduate student of chemistry in Boston, Massachusetts.*

Dust protects antique books

Summarised from an article by Simon de Bruxelles, entitled 'A better class of dust falls on National Trust', in the Times (March 4th 2002).

National Trust staff have been ordered not to dust the shelves in half of its stately homes for three years, because it is believed the cleaning process may harm the books more than the dust. Although dust can be corrosive to the books, the dusting is also a form of erosion, with fragile spines and bindings being damaged by being moved from shelves. Research is now under way in several of the Trust's homes to determine the best balance of cleaning and preserving the half a million books it looks after.

'Finer particles remain and form a concrete layer of dust over time'

It may be that books on shelves between waist and shoulder level need more regular cleaning than those higher up, because it is at this level that the majority of dust (from visitors) settles. It would also seem that larger pieces of dust do fall to the floor, but that finer particles remain and can form a concrete layer over time; it is this layer which can be difficult to remove without damaging the book underneath.

The National Trust are keen to ensure that the right balance is achieved between allowing the books to remain undisturbed and keeping the stately homes looking spick and span. Up until the new dust research, every single book in the Trust's possession was taken down once a year and cleaned with a shaving brush. One feels that the Trust's staff may be hoping the change is made a permanent one.

• *Peter Brimblecombe, who is conducting the research, can be contacted at the University of East Anglia in the Environmental Sciences Department. The website of the National Trust is www.nationaltrust.org.uk*

Itemised printouts of household TV watching

Stefanie Sovak

TV cable companies could send a printout of each month's activity by listing what shows were watched (and when), along with that month's bill. With this sort of useful information, parents would be able to see what interests their children and find times that their kids are most likely to watch TV, and substitute those times with other activities.

6 Blackstock Mews, London N4 2BT, UK (rhino@dial.pipex.com), 2002, 300pp, ISBN 0 948826 59 2

'The printout would act as an itemised phone bill does'

The printout would act as an itemised phone bill does, letting the parent (or TV owner) know how long the TV is on for at a time, what programmes are being watched, and give daily and monthly totals of hours spent watching TV.

It is a question of providing the information – if they're not aware there is a problem, they can't solve it. With this information at their fingertips, the parent or guardian can decide if they need to change their kids' TV habits (or their own!).

• *Stefanie Sovak is a student at Elon University (www.elon.edu) in North Carolina, USA.*

Camping at the zoo for an urban adventure

Summarised from an article by Michael Kernan, entitled 'Camping at the Zoo', in the Smithsonian magazine (August 2001), monitored for the Global Ideas Bank by Roger Knights.

The Smithsonian's National Zoo in Washington D.C. has introduced a novel scheme to encourage more people to come to the zoo. The 'Snore and Roar' programme allows people to spend the night at the zoo in a tent, as well as having a nocturnal tour of certain areas of the park. It was introduced for a number of reasons: to increase the amount of people that come to the zoo, to enable people to see the animals' behaviour at night, to earn the zoo more money to maintain its existence, and to provide an exciting night for adults and children alike. In cities and towns, where it is not always easy to take a camping trip in the wild, the zoo scheme provides an interesting alternative, with roaring lions in place of alarm clocks.

The visitors are taken on a night-time tour of the ape house, the elephant enclosure and others, and it also aims to highlight the lesser known nocturnal species, such as macaques, maras and caracals. Then everyone returns to their tents on Lion Tiger Hill to sleep, with periodic interruptions from gibbons and lions. The only problem the zoo has now is the project's success: all of the places for 2002 are sold out, and there is now a waiting list for night-time visits in the coming years.

• *For more information, contact Smithsonian National Zoological Park, 3001 Connecticut Avenue, NW, Washington, D.C. 20008, USA (web: http:// natzoo.si.edu; e-mail: nationalzoo@nzp.si.edu).*

The future of culture

Brian Eno

This article originally appeared in Resurgence magazine (September/October 2001 issue; to subscribe, call 01208 841824 or e-mail: subs.resurge@virgin.net).

What makes for a great carnival? I've pondered this question as I've watched, year by year, the Notting Hill Carnival in London expanding to become the world's second largest (after Rio).

'Carnival is good when it dignifies and rewards all sorts of abilities'

My conclusions? Carnival is good when the number of participants isn't grossly outweighed by the number of spectators. Carnival is good when many of the 'spectators' are actually also joining in – dancing and singing along. Carnival is good when the participants exhibit a range of skills from the absolutely minimal to the absolutely astonishing. Carnival is good when people of all ages, sexes, races, shapes, sizes, beauties, inclinations and professions are involved. Carnival is good when there's too much to look at and everything's mixed up and you have to sort it out for yourself. Carnival is good when it dignifies and rewards all sorts of abilities – singing, jumping, laughing infectiously, dressing weirdly, writing the hit song of the carnival, wiggling your backside, standing on a soapbox praising Jesus or the local hardware store, inventing symphonic arrangements for steel bands, designing and building fabulously impossible things. Carnival is good when people try to outdo each other and then applaud with delight those who in turn outdo them. Carnival is good when it gives people an alibi to become someone different. Carnival is good when it lets people present the best part of themselves and be, for a little while, as they'd like to be all the time. Carnival is good when it gives people the feeling that they're lucky to be alive right here and now. Carnival is good when it leaves people with the feeling that life in all its bizarre manifestations is unbeatably lovely and touching and funny and worthwhile.

Now substitute 'culture' for 'carnival'. There's a vision for the future of culture.

• *Brian Eno is a musician, author and innovator, and patron of the Institute for Social Inventions.*

• *For further information on how carnival and the carnivalesque can be used as a frame for looking at the world and society, see:*

Rabelais and His World *by Mikhail Bakhtin (1940) and*

'The Frames of Comic 'Freedom', by Umberto Eco in Carnival!, *ed. T.Seebok (1984).*

6 Blackstock Mews, London N4 2BT, UK (rhino@dial.pipex.com), 2002, 300pp, ISBN 0 948826 59 2

Upgradable (recyclable) shoe sale system

Matthew A. Beadnell

As everyone knows, people, and especially kids, often want the newest and most recent shoes that can be found. People will spend countless amounts of money in order to buy the best of the best. And once they have those shoes, they are outdated within weeks, maybe days. Then after the money is found to buy the newest shoes again, what becomes of the others? Sometimes they are left in the dust because they are outdated, and the newest of the new are preferred.

'A customer plan for upgrading to the newest shoe'

My thought on the situation is to sell a plan of sorts for the customers to get when they purchase a shoe. This plan will enable them to turn in their shoes and maybe pay the difference, if there is one, in shoe costs, and get the newer pair of shoes.

If the shoes are returned for another pair within a specific number of days, lets say, then they could be touched up, and resold to those who have yet to buy that style. But the ones that are returned after the time limit, after so much usage, would be sent to other countries, or given to foundations to benefit those without the luxury of shoes to begin with.

• *Matthew Beadnell is a student at Elon University (www.elon.edu) in North Carolina, USA.*

A reading challenge for the whole community

Summarised from an article by Lisa Pemberton-Butler, entitled '10 million minutes of reading? No problem', in the Seattle Times (June 11th 2001), monitored for the Global Ideas Bank by Roger Knights.

The community of Enumclaw in Washington State found a novel way to encourage reading and promote literacy amongst its inhabitants: it challenged them to read 10 million minutes in six months. The school authorities and business leaders came up with the idea, hoping that it would benefit children who, as well as being encouraged to read, would also see their parents and other adults reading. Progress in the challenge was monitored by giant thermometers at various locations in the area, and on the School District's website; people simply filled out slips with their name and the number of minutes they'd managed this week and put it in special boxes. After three months, the inhabitants of Enumclaw had already achieved 8 million minutes reading time, and they went on to smash the target by a significant margin.

'The school bus had special seat covers designed to hold books'

The challenge originated as part of the region's schools literacy campaign, which has also included a school bus with special seat covers that hold books, a summer-literacy camp and a scheme in which a new book is given to every child born at the local hospital; and the reading standards in the area have improved substantially over the past few years. Yet the challenge has had wider effects, reigniting people's love of books and leading to the formation of new book clubs, book swapping evenings and much more discussion between people in the community over a common passion. In the schools, teachers were delighted (and amazed) to see that children were sitting and reading even when it was not a designated reading time or class. One school set up a bookclub to discuss books, poetry and plays at lunchtimes. Even the mayor got involved, reading, appropriately enough, a book called *Principle-centred leadership*. This year the challenge has been stepped up a notch: the target is 25 million minutes.

• *For more details of the scheme see http://www.enumclaw.wednet.edu/ FAQ.htm*

The Floating Library – limitless book-sharing for all

Jane Inkle

Self-appointed 'floating librarians' (no qualifications necessary) will select books which they have enjoyed or books that they believe others will enjoy and donate them to the library. A short text is written in the front of the book explaining that it is property of the 'Floating Library' and that anyone wishing to borrow it may do so, but must either pass it on to someone they know once they have finished with it, or leave it in a public place for someone to find. The text should also make clear that new donations are always welcome. The book is then left somewhere for people to find (phone box, loo, cafe, bus, train, in the middle of the woods, wherever...). The 'Floating Library' has no buildings, employees or library cards. This kind of library has featured for some time

6 Blackstock Mews, London N4 2BT, UK (rhino@dial.pipex.com), 2002, 300pp, ISBN 0 948826 59 2

in various hotel rooms around the world, but extending it out to trains, shops and other public places could help share the joy of reading.

[In Norway there is an actual 'Floating Library' on a boat which visits small villages and communities living amongst the difficult-to-access fjords.]

• *Jane Inkle works at the Hitchcocks Vegetarian Restaurant in Hull, UK.*

Privatising national parks to save them

Summarised from an article by John Pomfret, entitled 'Privatizing China's Parks', on the Washington Post website (July 5th 2001), and from an item in Liberty by Fred Smith, monitored for the Global Ideas Bank by Roger Knights.

China has taken a radical approach to ensuring some of its most beautiful national parks are maintained and tended for. In the city of Huangshan, the national scenic area is 60 square miles, and it is managed by the Huangshan Tourism Development Company, who are listed on the Chinese stock exchange. It has come to this because the state simply has no money to maintain all of the national treasures and scenic areas in the condition they should be. So they effectively auction them off to the highest bidder, with the winner owning a majority stake in the park or other attraction. The argument behind the idea is that privatisation is the only way in a country with no money for nature.

'The park did have 6,000 tons of rubbish; it now has 525 rubbish collectors'

In Huangshuan's national park, for example, the effect of privatisation has been huge. In 1986, it was reported that the park had 6,000 tons of rubbish lining its 44 miles of pathways, that the streams were polluted and that trees were being felled at a huge rate. That was when it was run under the state, with its confusing mix of bureaucracy and competing ministries. Today, the park is completely clean, with 525 rubbish collectors, outside contracting for laundry to avoid water pollution and an increase in forest cover of 60 per cent compared to the 1980s. Since the park was privatised, it has attracted 300,000 more visitors per year, and is regarded as a model for other schemes.

The Chinese, despite being an ostensibly socialist (even communist) country, are embracing this radical free-marketeering, with private firms running temples, parks and even terracotta warrior exhibits. Even sections of the Great Wall itself are owned by a private company. There are a number of concerning factors about the scheme, not least of which is the conflict of interest between people who are both government bureaucrats in control of these areas and also directors of the firms bidding to take them over. Similarly, environmentalists point to an increase in developments on various sites and the negative aspects of commercialising historical artefacts. The counter-argument is simpler still: without the money, what would happen to these places?

Free lollipops to people leaving night clubs to keep the noise down

Summarised from an item in Wyre Reporter, reported in the Guardian Society section; (August 10th 2001).

Police in Blackpool have been issuing free lollipops to those leaving nightclubs to reduce noise levels for surrounding residents. The hope is that the grown-up gobstoppers will keep the decibel level of the high-spirited members of the clubbing scene down to an acceptable minimum.

Dance music soundtracks encourage reading amongst young people

Summarised from an article, entitled 'DJ gives classics the spin on radio', in the Guardian (February 26th 2002).

A company called Urban Soundtracks has put together classic stories read by well-known figures with a contemporary musical soundtrack. The aim is to make books more accessible to youngsters in a world dominated by video games and television. The business was co-founded by the well-known dance music DJ Paul Oakenfold, who himself suffered from dyslexia in his child-hood. This experience inspired him to use what he does best (make music) to make reading not only more accessible, but also more credible. Reading a classic book (titles include Pinocchio, Cleopatra and Jack the Ripper) on the way to school might get you mocked by friends, but listening to Paul Oakenfold through your headphones certainly won't.

At the moment, the Urban Soundtracks have only been broadcast on the radio (by commercial stations including Galaxy and Kiss FM), but plans are

6 Blackstock Mews, London N4 2BT, UK (rhino@dial.pipex.com), 2002, 300pp, ISBN 0 948826 59 2

afoot for cassette and compact disc versions. Next time the personal stereo on the train is nagging away at you, it could be a classic tale being listened to, even if there is a drum beat to back it up.

Hotel service for plants whose owners go on holiday

Summarised from an item, entitled 'Bedding plants', in the Guardian Society section (July 6th 2001).

Crowfoot Nurseries, a garden centre in Norfolk, has started a scheme in which people going on holiday can leave their plants there to be looked after. The plant 'hotel' charges 50p per night to care for the plants, and keep them watered, fed and happy.

Watching TV improves your social life (or perception of it)

Summarised from an item, entitled 'My imaginary friends', in New Scientist (May 2002 issue; New Scientist subs £99 or $140, call 01444 475636 or e-mail ns.subs@qss-uk.com).

New research has concluded that people who watch more television feel like they have more friends compared to those less glued to the small screen. Satoshi Kanazawa, an evolutionary psychologist at Indiana University, has put forward the theory that the human brain counts every person it sees as an actual friend, whether this is on television or not. This acknowledgement of faces as friends leads to the brain then making the person feel satisfied with their social lives, as satisfied as someone with an active (and actual) social life.

The second part of Kanazawa's thesis, which he drew from studying data in the annual US General Social Survey, is that women and men have this response of satisfaction to different types of programmes. His slightly shaky theory is that, because women are more likely to have kin amongst their close friends, they get the feelings of a good social life from watching sitcoms and dramas (which are more concerned with the familial and domestic arenas). Men, meanwhile, have more co-workers among their close friends, meaning that they get the feelings of satisfaction through watching news and issue-based programmes (which relate more closely to these arenas).

'Seeing familiar environments on television leads to feelings of social satisfaction'

Despite this theory being debatable in a number of areas (women having friends at work, sitcoms set in work environments etc), Kanazawa maintains that it is backed up by the evidence from the Social Survey. So, seeing familiar 'friendship environments' on television leads a person to believe (unconsciously) that they are part of that environment, leading in turn to feelings of social satisfaction. It could also be that television has replaced community participation in a way not previously acknowledged, by creating a virtual group that the viewer 'takes part' in. And yet this participation is a virtual and, even, an unconscious one: and no replacement for the real thing.

6 Blackstock Mews, London N4 2BT, UK (rhino@dial.pipex.com), 2002, 300pp, ISBN 0 948826 59 2

National Slacker Day – raising awareness of the importance of relaxation

Summarised from the Oncus website (www.oncus.com). The item was first noted in the Heads Up e-newsletter (subscriber at http://gocreate.com). Additional material from an article by Kathleen Melynuka, entitled 'Preaching Slack', in ComputerWorld (July 2nd 2001), monitored for the Global Ideas Bank by Roger Knights.

The second National Slacker Day took place in the UK on February 22nd 2002 in an effort to raise awareness of the need for relaxation in an increasingly hectic and stressful world. The campaign, run by the small creative company Oncus, included targeting DIY stores to ask them to close and lobbying television channels to put on well-known films for the day. Though doing so in a tongue-in-cheek manner, the organisers were making a serious point, as the UK has the longest working hours in Europe and has one of the shortest average life expectancies in the Western world. The work ethic, something which has long been a cause of national pride, has mutated into a 'work comes first' culture, and this is something that National Slacker Day hopes to draw attention to and counteract.

'Slacking is about an ethos of re-framing things'

Dr Jason Rutter, a research fellow in Innovation and Competition at Manchester University, supports the campaign, pointing out that "relaxing at home...can help recharge your batteries, develop new skills and leave you with a better perspective on your working life. Slacking isn't just about doing nothing but an ethos of re-framing things so you can enjoy what you do".

'We need to be a little less efficient in order to be more agile'

Tom DeMarco, an expert on efficiency and effectiveness in business, also articulates the importance of 'slack'. His theory is that we "need to be a little less efficient in order to be more agile". That is to say that being too efficient can also mean being too busy, too tense, too scared and being unable to look long-term because there is total focus on the present. He rails against overtime as a cause of burnout, mental fatigue and people quitting their jobs for feeling used. Slack, in DeMarco's opinion, means "the time and freedom to go about a job in a way that satisfies you and allows you some personal growth". This need not mean taking half a day off every week, but simply not being driven by the clock, by taking time out to think, consider and plan, as well as work.

• *For more information, see www.oncus.com/slackerday/index.php*
• Slack: Getting Past Burnout, Busywork and the Myth of Total Efficiency *by Tom DeMarco (Broadway Books, 2002; 224 pages, $14, ISBN 0767907698).*

• *For more on this topic, see 'Laziness – the key to longer life', in* Cornucopia of Ideas, *p.107 (ISI, 2001).*

Citywide reading builds community feeling

Summarised from an article by Marc Ramirez, entitled 'On the same page?', in the Seattle Times (March 24th 2002), and from an article by John Patterson, entitled 'A novelist for my town', in the Guardian (February 22nd 2002). The former item was monitored for the Global Ideas Bank by Roger Knights.

An idea which originated in Seattle's public library has spread throughout America and beyond in the past few months. The concept is simple: help to build a sense of commonality in a city by getting everyone to read the same book at the same time. As well as encouraging reading as a pursuit to be enjoyed by all, the scheme allows strangers to interact by discussing the book on the tube or the bus on the way home, as well as promoting reading as an experience to be shared in families and schools. The idea came from Seattle librarian Nancy Pearl who launched the 'If All of Seattle Read the Same Book' project in December 1998 with Russell Banks' *The Sweet Hereafter*. Her original program used author visits, study guides and book discussion croups to bring people together with a book, but the idea has since expanded hugely to many other American cities, and even to Hong Kong and Trinidad and Tobago.

'Copies of the chosen book were loaned out 7,000 times from the library'

In Chicago, the mayor went on national television to announce the choice of Harper Lee's *To Kill a Mockingbird* as the first book in their 'One Book, One Chicago' program. Copies were distributed to public libraries, readings were funded and an advertising campaign undertaken, with the result that the book shot back up the bestseller lists and copies of the book were loaned out over 7,000 times over seven weeks. Reading clubs and neighbourhood groups have now sprung up around the city, and the book for spring, *Night* by Elie

6 Blackstock Mews, London N4 2BT, UK (rhino@dial.pipex.com), 2002, 300pp, ISBN 0 948826 59 2

Wiesel, is attracting a similar amount of attention. Across the country, from Kentucky (*The Bean Trees* by Barbara Kingsolver) to Milwaukee (*Snow Falling on Cedars*, by David Guterson), stories emerged of parents and children reading to each other at night, of waitresses sitting down to join in discussions, and of strangers chatting away on the bus about plot, character and theme.

'It works best in medium-sized cities where a sense of unity can be achieved'

The only problems arose in New York which could not decide on one book to represent its huge diverse population. The literati of the city then descended into bickering and infighting over whether the scheme was worth getting involved in and whether this or that book was inappropriate, before finally settling on *Native Speaker* by Chang-rae Lee, a novel speaking to the near-universal New York experience of immigration and being uprooted. This divisive arguing may show that the idea works best in medium-sized cities or large towns, where a greater sense of unity can be achieved. Or it may show that New York rather missed the point, putting all its energy and passion into the choice of the book rather than the discussion about whichever book was chosen. Ultimately, as Nancy Pearl points out, the level of success is not measured by how many people read a book, or by how many copies are sold, but by how many are enriched by the process, have had issues raised by a book that they would never have come across otherwise, or have spoken to someone they would not otherwise have shared a single word with. It is not a political issue, but a simple case of sitting down and turning the page.

Examples of novels chosen in US cities

Seattle: *The Sweet Hereafter* by Russell Banks
Buffalo: *A Lesson Before Dying*, by Ernest Gaines
Chicago: *To Kill a Mockingbird* by Harper Lee
Gainesville: *The Diary of Anne Frank*
Orlando: *Charlotte's Web* by E.B. White
Los Angeles: *Fahrenheit 451* by Ray Bradbury

and suggested novels for elsewhere.....(as suggested in an Oliver Burkeman article in the Guardian; February 27th 2002):

Edinburgh: *Trainspotting* by Irvine Welsh
Birmingham: anything by David Lodge
Dublin: *Ulysses* by James Joyce
London: *Money* or *London Fields* by Martin Amis

Telephone storytelling service for busy parents

Summarised from an idea submitted to the website www.idea-a-day.com by Rupert Kaye (August 25th 2001).

Rupert Kaye's suggestion is for a low-cost telephone service in which parents could pay for a story to be read to their children. The service could prove useful for busy parents, but also for those with reading difficulties, or for those desperate to entice their children away from the television. It could provide another way of introducing books and literature into children's lives, but in a way that is more familiar to them than radio or cassettes. Rupert Kaye goes on to suggest that the service could run a bookmark system so that longer books could be spread out as desired. And his suggested name for the scheme: the 'Phone Book', of course.

- *To receive an idea every day by e-mail, subscribe at www.idea-a-day.com*

Big Brother programme with 12 different religious or academic participants

Submitted to the Global Ideas Bank by G, who is a university student that resides in Australia.

One of the television phenomenons of recent years has been the rise of the reality TV programme 'Big Brother'. The general notion is that a group of 12 people spend three months locked in a house with no contact with the outside world and they are given tasks and goals to complete. Each week, the group nominate two of their number for eviction, who the public then decides between. The programme has been criticised for its banality, its voyeurism and for encouraging the rise of fame for fame's sake.

My suggestion is to change the selection criteria for the householders. I have two different suggestions:

'Ethical quandaries to tackle as well as physical tasks'

- to have 12 religious leaders or representatives (eg Catholic priest, Buddhist monk, Presbyterian minister, Jehovah's Witness, Hindu, Muslim, pagan etc) put together in the house, and give them ethical or spiritual

6 Blackstock Mews, London N4 2BT, UK (rhino@dial.pipex.com), 2002, 300pp, ISBN 0 948826 59 2

quandaries to solve as well as physical tasks. I think this would be more interesting than the present programme tends to be

• to have 12 academics in the house; perhaps a counsellor, a genetic engineer (or some such), a historian, a sociologist, a lawyer, a medical doctor, a psychologist, bioethicist, a theologian etc and give them similar quandaries to solve as well as physical tasks

I think it would be a very interesting concept, not only to see what manner of ethical and spiritual leaps and bounds can be made from group discussion but also to see how representatives from different membership groups can act together to accomplish physical goals through team work. The main obstacle would be persuading such people to take part in being locked up together for three months.

• 'G' (e-mail: gshorrock@medscape.com)

<u>INTERNATIONAL AND</u>
<u>DEVELOPING WORLD</u>

Mechanisms of hope: a local global project

A new wide-reaching project in Johannesburg intends to set up a number of 'initiatives of hope' to inspire, celebrate and demonstrate the real possibilities for sustainable communities around the world. Based around Joubert Park, the intention of the organisers is to create 'centres of hope', which can serve as a model for what can be achieved in the future, and as an example to other groups and nations around the world. The scheme is being led by Colin Hudson, who organised the successful Village of Hope project in Barbados in 1994 (see the Institute compendium, *DIY Futures*), in an attempt to extend the impact of such initiatives of hope. Interactive 'centres of hope' can work as inverted museums, helping people interact with and look at the future, not the past.

The project is designed to coincide with the World Summit on Sustainable Development, which takes place in Johannesburg, South Africa and runs from August 26th to September 4th 2002. What follows is an overview of the project, written by Dr Hudson, detailing the theories and principles that lie behind it, and the actual concrete steps to be taken in September 2002.

Concerns and necessary changes

Consumption has been advertised as the route to happiness; apparently the advertisements were misleading. Bigger and bigger organizations and projects in the globalisation process leave individuals bewildered and daunted. Prices may be lowered but costs increase and poverty of spirit compounds poverty of livelihood. Many wish to tread more lightly, but only the tools of heavier tread are easily available. In every way, relationships, of man to nature, man to man, present to future, are breaking down.

A paradigm shift is needed towards these better relationships, with happiness and sparkling innovation as its hallmarks.

Paradigm shifts require a heart change and a head change.

Heart change. We must renew our awe for the laws of nature, and regain our sense of connection to the earth and its wonder. It is our only home.

6 Blackstock Mews, London N4 2BT, UK (rhino@dial.pipex.com), 2002, 300pp, ISBN 0 948826 59 2

Intelligence is synonymous with 'living in harmony with nature' (perhaps still the best definition of sustainability). Our first purpose therefore is to help to effect heart change by understanding and acknowledging the wonder of our home with celebration.

'Enabling 6.1 billion people to tread more lightly on our home, whilst simultaneously improving the quality of their lives'

Head change. Heart change must be matched by intelligent technical response to the million problems which have to be solved in moving from an unsustainable paradigm. So our second purpose is to help introduce the means to share 'best practice' which helps individuals to develop and adopt mechanisms to enable 6.1 billion people to tread more lightly on our home whilst simultaneously improving the quality (happiness) of their lives – from the richest to the poorest. In other words, inspiration.

This combination of celebration and inspiration = **HOPE**

Purpose of the project
- To leave legacies to inspire change, especially at the individual level
- A long-lasting contribution to happiness through improved relationships
- To innovate and implement mechanisms of hope.
- To inspire problem-solving which leads to better relationships
- To show that better relationships, fairness and justice result in a happier life for man and his colleague species
- To empower people to tread more lightly and live more richly

Principles of the project
- By the people, for the people, with the people
- Enough structure to ensure orderliness
- Enough chaos to maximise creativity
- Fun at all levels and at all times
- Pervasive celebration
- Competency and transparency
- Interaction rather than instruction
- High return on footprint use
- Compassion toward nature and each other
- Mutual boosting

Precedents proving this is practical, not just idealistic

A Village of Hope accompanied the 1994 UN Global Conference in Barbados on Sustainable Development of Islands. It was largely successful in providing (1) an important addition to the Conference and (2) in stimulating subsequent action, including the creation of a permanent Centre of Hope (The Barbados Future Centre). Gus Speth, Director of UNDP (the United Nations Development Programme) wrote in the guest book that "The Village of Hope is our Hope".

Other centres of hope such as the Earth Centre, the Centre for Appropriate Technology, Die Kleine Erde, Gaviotas Village, Rocky Mountain Institute, Wuppertal Institute and Findhorn are all wielding increasing influence and in most cases are also now financially sustainable. And, although they are not as comprehensive as the previous examples, there are already centres of hope in South Africa. For example Wildrocke Farm and Valley Trust for Permaculture, and Orange Farm and the GreenHouse Project for community building [the GreenHouse project is an environmental and community centre which demonstrates workable living alternatives].

'A parallel world of museums exploring the future rather than the past'

Furthermore, people love interactive centres – Disney World, Epcot, Woburn Park, LegoLand and countless museums have all proven this. So why not envision a parallel world network of centres of hope — interactive 'upside-down museums', exploring the future rather than the past?

Specific proposals

• The creation of a 'Village of Hope' in Joubert Park, which will include:
– a 'celebratory centre', a travelling 'caravan of hope', and a global component created by the UK Earth Centre
• Linking with, and boosting, permanent local centres of hope both within and without Johannesburg, including:
- 'flagship' project in Soweto (Mountain of Hope), the Greenhouse project etc, and others around the world, such as Gaviotas and the Future Centre in Barbados
• An exhibition entitled 'the Cosmology of Hope', and further educational initiatives, run by GrassRoots Education
• So-called 'windows of hope' to inform everyone about all the on-going initiatives
• A 'Virtual Village' in the form of a Web of Hope, Book of Hope, Posters of Hope etc

6 Blackstock Mews, London N4 2BT, UK (rhino@dial.pipex.com), 2002, 300pp, ISBN 0 948826 59 2

'Every component is designed with its own legacy of social transformation'

Every component is designed with its own 'legacy' in mind. Even though temporary, the village in Joubert Park will leave legacies of social transformation and buildings and exhibits for the GreenHouse Project. The park is intended to be the centre for exhibitors and musicians, as well as being sustainable itself, with LETS schemes, green electricity, composting toilets etc

The South African government, business and international organisations (including the UN and Ashoka) are behind the idea. The Development Bank in South Africa has also pledged involvement and contributions. Literally hundreds of other individuals in South Africa in various walks of life, especially educators and community leaders, and of widely differing interests have become intrigued by, and supportive of, the ideas. With one exception, we have not yet had a negative comment. The exception is whether ingenuity and resources are adequate to change Joubert Park's reputation as a dangerous area to being the safest area in South Africa as part of the Village of Hope's mission. This may be the greatest challenge the project faces.

Hoped-for outcomes

In South Africa:

• Everyone associated with the Summit as residents, participants, observers, or visitors saying on September 12th, 2002, "that was an inspiration!"

• A chain of permanent centres of hope, of which one (Chiawelo in Soweto) has been started already. These would extend and reinforce the initiatives already in place by health specialists, permaculturists, educators, community builders, and conservationists. They would likewise extend and reinforce initiatives such as IUCN, SEED, the Natural Step Movement, and so on. Above all they act as rallying points for the increasing number of innovative and passionate individuals who care but aren't sure what is happening

• A permanent National Centre of Hope in Johannesburg

• A tremendous boost to the development of the GreenHouse Project in Joubert Park. An even bigger boost to everyone if the creation of the Village of Hope becomes associated with the Park known as the safest place in Africa

• An ongoing 'Initiative of Hope' in the informal settlements

'100,000 small and meaningful changes in the way things are done'

• 100,000 small and meaningful changes in the way things are done by the 100,000 people who will be touched by these initiatives during September 2002

- An opportunity for the media to discover and share success stories by personal interaction with exhibits and exhibitors of which they are probably unaware
  - Reinforcing community spirit and feeling

Globally:
- Reinforcing/encouraging/informing/providing-a-rallying-point-for the passionate and effective leaders and groups who are pioneering sustainability – often in quite lonely or discouraging situations – all around the world
- An opportunity to show and share good practice for those who may not be aware of the multitudes of hopes already in place. Especially we find that decision makers are often discouraged by the many larger-scale failures and greatly helped by carefully articulated, practical and effective experience at a lower level
- Millions of people enjoying celebration and inspiration via media coverage and reports
- A deepened understanding of basic relationships, particularly those between humans and nature and humans and each other
- The adoption of ideas by the serendipitous connection of entrepreneurs with innovation.
- Popularizing books, journals, magazines, radio and TV programmes, and web sites of best practice

'The adoption of centres of hope as rallying points for citizens to effect change'

- The wider adoption of other Earth Centres, Future Centres, Inspiration Exchanges, and Eco-villages as permanent rallying points for citizens to effect change towards sustainability

Governing the mechanisms of hope

Ultimately the people and entities whose lives will be changed must govern the process. In the Barbados circumstances it was found that if the right structure was in place, wise, effective and trustworthy people appeared and volunteers and paid helpers rallied willingly to these leaders. 'Governance' became, de facto, these leaders with 'orderliness' being limited to maintaining an environment in which they could communicate and work effectively, each in his or her own way.

- *Colin Hudson runs the Future Centre in Barbados (e-mail: treadlight@sunbeach.net).*

6 Blackstock Mews, London N4 2BT, UK (rhino@dial.pipex.com), 2002, 300pp, ISBN 0 948826 59 2

Goodwill stamps to raise money for charity

Adriana Fels

I have always thought that in order to raise funds it is better to ask frequently many people for a small contribution than to use the opposite strategy (asking fewer wealthy people to make greater contributions less frequently).

Let us imagine we were able to create a little 'Goodwill Stamp' with a minimum value (1 to 5 cents) to be optionally stuck to ordinary mail in order to finance social development projects to meet social problems and the challenges of global poverty. It would be a way of establishing a kind of voluntary universal contribution system. Together with persuasive advertising I think our goal can be achieved.

'The potential funds to be raised are in proportion to the amount of mail in the world'

If we take into account the enormous amount of letters and postal deliveries that occur worldwide per year (some 440 billion, according to the Universal Postal Union, a United Nations Agency) we may well infer that the funds to be raised are potentially huge.

If the question raised were who could set into motion and manage such a programme, I would say the United Nations and all its agencies are furnished with the sufficient institutional structure to take on said responsibility on a global scale. So far, they have been solely dependant on the economic support provided by the richest nations which for some reason or other have always cut it down. This would be a way to attain the United Nations budget autonomy and further develop its potential.

The Universal Postal Union is the most qualified body to resolve technicalities to be confronted, and the other agencies (UNICEF, UNESCO, UNHCR, PNUD, WORLD BANK, International Monetary Fund, etc) are provided with the most capable professionals to start the job. I say starting the job to be done, because it will be necessary to appeal to all the available human resources: national civil services, international agencies, as well as the growing social sector. There are many things to be done and many hands will be needed.

I may well understand this proposal could be considered utopian. But in times like these, it would be very appropriate to create a generous movement whose ideology were only prudence and goodwill. In a present world which has been plunged into a hopeless and futureless race of speculation, we should

Institute for Social Inventions, £15 subs, £17 from abroad by credit card, tel London 020 7359 8391

think to globalize solidarity, just as John Paul II called for not very long ago. Perhaps the present paradox shall be that without any utopia, reality will no longer be sustainable.

Charity stamps sold at post-offices
Kate Weinberg

Giving money to your favourite charity is often considered a one-off act or something to do in your spare time. A scheme in which charities devise their own colourful picture stamps to sell at post-offices for a fraction above the normal rate could make this an easy and everyday initiative. In this way, someone sending a letter by mail could contribute regularly and gradually to their favourite charity by buying the stamp of their choice, and mailing it to a friend. This practice could also appeal to stamp-collectors by producing 'limited edition' stamps from each charity before changing the design.

> 'Letter writing, which has been all but eclipsed by e-mail, could become a new, more worthwhile practice with this scheme'

Letter writing, which has become all but eclipsed by e-mail and text messaging, could become a new, more worthwhile practice with this scheme. By simply paying a penny or two above the cost price people who don't usually see themselves as donors might be encouraged to contribute to diverse charities.
* *Adriana Fels is a busy housewife in Argentina (e-mail: felsita@fibertel.com.ar)*

Reality tourism: overtly political and educational holidays

Summarised from an article by Margot Roosevelt, entitled 'Greetings from Zapatista Land', in Time magazine (September 3rd 2001), monitored for the Global Ideas Bank by Roger Knights.

As sun, sea and sand holidays become blander and more predictable, people are starting to look for more interesting alternatives. Eco-tourism has been one controversial genre to spring up, but another is 'reality tourism'. The idea is that holidays are taken in places where holidaymakers can learn about the repression or political situation of that country or region. Examples include travelling in Laos to meet landmine victims and learning how the CIA were

6 Blackstock Mews, London N4 2BT, UK (rhino@dial.pipex.com), 2002, 300pp, ISBN 0 948826 59 2

involved in the region, meeting Zapatista rebels in southern Mexico, or spending a week in Guatemala learning about the history of political violence there.

'A new kind of internationalism on the ground'

The reality tours are proving a success for activist organisations, hoping to spread their message and raise funds, and with the public, who are looking to find a more personal understanding of the stories in the newspaper headlines. One enthusiast, who has followed up a visit to Palestine (where he met Israeli settlers and members of Hamas) with a trip to Mexico, says that the thrill is in "finding out about their lives...it's history in the making". The organisers claim they are building a new kind of internationalism with people on the ground, although sceptics will have a different opinion of making a spectacle or holiday attraction of people who are often fighting for their lives. Nevertheless, be it political voyeurism or a genuine wish to help and understand that motivates the reality tourists, the number of tours is increasing all the time; and the memories may not slip away so easily.

- *For details of some reality tours, see www.cloudforest-mexico.org and www.globalexchange.org*

Simultaneous global policy making for a new world

A review of The Simultaneous Policy *by John Bunzl (published by New European Publications, 2001, ISBN: 1872410200, 202 pages, £9.95). Reviewed by Nick Temple.*

Introduction

While some concentrate on small-scale incremental solutions to the problems that face them every day, others focus on the big picture, the global canvas that determines how lives are led in so many ways. John Bunzl is one of those who is looking at a global solution, and this book outlines the theory behind his idea and the practicalities of the idea itself. The Simultaneous Policy is an attempt to find a way of replacing the global system of competition and 'free' trade with a framework for international co-operation, and the innovative concept behind it is that every nation in the world would implement the measures needed for the new framework at the same time.

Now an instant response to this idea, the details of which are looked at below, is to state that it is simply too ambitious to ever succeed. Certainly getting all of the countries to agree on replacing the current system from which many of them benefit in terms of power and influence seems hugely idealistic. What incentive is there to give up a system reliant on competition if you are the strongest competitor and always win? Why give up substantial profits and a high standard of living so that other people can benefit? I put forward these questions and issues at the start, because it seems to me that, as much as a change of policy, John Bunzl's idea requires a change of attitude from many of the most powerful people in the world. Bunzl's response to charges of idealism is robust and hard-headed. He quotes from M. Scott Peck's book, *The Different Drum* as defence:

'It is the idealists whose thinking is more in accord with the reality of human nature'

'I would define the idealist as one who believes in the capacity for transformation of human nature. For whatever the other characteristics of human nature, it is precisely this capacity for transformation that is responsible for the evolution and survival of the human species. It is the...so-called realists who are out of touch with the essence of what it means to be human, the idealist[s]...whose thinking is more in accord with the reality of human nature. It is the idealists who are the realistic ones.'

This is powerful stuff, and an unapologetic idealism could be crucial for changing all our futures: it is, after all, nothing to be ashamed of. And, to paraphrase Brian Eno's words from his foreword to last year's compendium, human beings do one thing better than any other species on Earth: they imagine how things could be better. With that ringing in our ears, we can approach grand ideas like the Simultaneous Policy with open minds.

Theory

The theory behind the Simultaneous Policy is a simple one. The rich are getting richer, and the poor poorer. Global competition is benefiting the few rather than the many, and more and more people are pressing for change as a result. Tax initiatives, corporation regulation, strict environmental laws and wealth redistribution are just a handful that spring to mind. But, while these might work on a small-scale in a particular country or area, unilateral agreement is needed across the globe. Bunzl's argument is that, for any truly global agreement to be brought into place, this will have to be done simultaneously.

The aim of the policy, 'the transformation of the international economy such that it operates in harmony with the global natural environment and with the needs of human nature', can only be achieved if this happens at the same

6 Blackstock Mews, London N4 2BT, UK (rhino@dial.pipex.com), 2002, 300pp, ISBN 0 948826 59 2

time everywhere. This simultaneous implementation, Bunzl argues, eliminates mistrust, fear and competition because all nations are in the same boat. In the same way, the euro was introduced simultaneously to avoid discrepancies, loopholes or the possibility of exploitation of the change. The theory is for a future in which there is a community spirit in the world, with nations co-operating to improve matters for all. Businesses and governments, whose primary fear is being disadvantaged or weakened by regulations and laws, would have nothing to fear, because everyone would be making the same step.

Practical Steps

Quite aside from what the policy would involve, and Bunzl makes clear that this would be for the countries to decide, the main barrier to its implementation is to get all countries to agree to it. Bunzl's idea to overcome this is to introduce a preliminary stage, whereby a country can say that it has 'adopted' the policy and is waiting for the rest of the world to join them before implementing it. As more and more countries adopt, so the pressure will build on those who are yet to adopt, until everyone has agreed. Or so the theory goes. Thus the simultaneity of the policy is two-fold: the policy will eventually be implemented simultaneously by all countries, but, in the meantime, countries will simultaneously continue with the present competitive economic system whilst having adopted the, contradictory, co-operative system as a future policy they are committed to.

'Countries will increasingly look for alternatives to the present system'

At the stage before that lies the question 'How will countries be persuaded to adopt?' Here Bunzl believes that a concerted lobbying campaign could be the key. He imagines scenarios whereby enough individuals have adopted the idea to make them an important force in domestic politics: a by-election where the result hinges on those in favour of the policy could result in a candidate adopting it to ensure victory. Or he looks at the possibilities of a 'third party' in a country being persuaded to adopt the policy in order to gain its credibility on the national stage.

He also believes that the lack of control a domestic government has over its own affairs will become a bigger and bigger issue as the years go past. Already major countries are hindered from introducing policies by the wealth and power of transnational corporations, and this is a trend which is set to continue and grow. As a result, more and more countries, perhaps the smaller developed ones, will look for major alternatives to the present system. They will be looking for a system that increases the quality of democracy, rather than the quantity of it, around the world.

Institute for Social Inventions, £15 subs, £17 from abroad by credit card, tel London 020 7359 8391

Assuming that countries did adopt the policy, Bunzl envisions the developed countries leading the way and being the most important to persuade. With them on board, many of the smaller, less powerful developing nations will follow, due to their dominance of the world's economic and military power. This will be an inevitably gradual process, possibly lasting for a quarter or half a century, but one with a far more longer-lasting results.

Measures of the policy

Bunzl foresees the measures of the policy coming in three stages, stabilisation, access and change. The stabilisation stage would include a 'Tobin' tax on currency transactions, dismantling and banning of nuclear weapons, and third world debt being cancelled. The access stage would be intended to include measures to allow access to the boardrooms of major institutions and corporations, with, for example, the government holding a percentage of shares in all companies in their country. The change stage could include more ambitious changes, such as taxing corporations to provide funds for the developing world, and improving intellectual and property rights legislation. Bunzl is keen to point out, though, that these are just his suggestions, and the measures and timescale would be fluid and flexible depending on agreement of all those taking part. The stages above are intended to show what the policy could achieve if implemented, not to be definitive measures set in stone.

Conclusions and problems

Bunzl's idea is a well-thought out, ambitious proposal and one that deserves to be taken seriously. It lays out a practical framework for achieving changes that many people want to see, and, in that sense, his book is an enthralling read. One becomes excited by the possibilities he outlines, and the vision of a new world opens out before your eyes. It is a grand, top-down solution, but one that relies on individual take-up and mass democratic participation for success. It is also impressive that he includes the need for competition (internally) as a driver of improvements: the idea of competition is not rejected out of hand, just that it should be subordinate to co-operation rather than the other way round. There are, however, problems that emerge when reading the book and its proposals.

'There has been a marked trend of isolationism and divisiveness since September 11th'

Firstly, the book opens with a reference to the developed world's comfortable dominance and the 'physical security enjoyed by their citizens'; further, it refers to the concept of mass loss of life being 'unthinkable' in those

6 Blackstock Mews, London N4 2BT, UK (rhino@dial.pipex.com), 2002, 300pp, ISBN 0 948826 59 2

countries. Unfair as it might be to criticise a book written before that date, things are different after the events of September 11th, and this needs to be acknowledged, as I'm sure it will be in future editions of this book. The citizens of the strongest developed countries no longer have that physical security: there may be no wars between major nations, but there is the so-called asymmetrical 'war on terrorism'. And the response of the developed nations, in particularly America, has not been to look at co-operating with the countries where such opposition has been fostered. It has been to use its military and economic superiority to try and crush individuals and organisations. The change of attitude referred to above, or what Bunzl calls the 'universal vantage point of rationality', seems more distant than ever. Rather than a greater community feeling, there has been a marked trend of isolationism and divisiveness, as with George W. Bush's comment that 'you are either with us or against us'.

Secondly, and this is related to the first, we must consider the role of rogue nations in this theory. Bunzl does refer to those non-democratic nations that might require some 'further coercion' to encourage them to implement, such as economic sanctions. Yet these measures have failed in the past: will Iraq ever be coerced into accepting the principles that lie behind the Simultaneous Policy? Or will the 'force of argument and goodwill' really suffice in Burma or North Korea? And if there are countries that wilfully exempt themselves from the policy, will this hold up implementation or will they be ignored allowing major loopholes for businesses and others to exploit? Given the choice between being based in Iraq making huge profits and compromising global ethical principles, how many businesses will demur? These are questions I feel need to be dealt with more fully.

Finally, this very issue of businesses and the way they look at the world needs to be addressed. Whilst discussing the benefits of the policy for business, Bunzl writes that the 'general alleviation of intense competitive pressures should come as some welcome relief to business people who are at the sharp end of competition', and that this will allow them to 're-deploy their talents in more creative and imaginative ways that put people before profits and excessive executive salaries'. This seems optimistic to say the least; many businessmen thrive on the competitive edge of business, even if that makes them stressed. Similarly, the thought that businesses will gladly accept massive corporation taxes, government interference and strict environmental guidelines seems off the mark. (Will lobbying for the Simultaneous Policy not be overpowered by the lobbying power of big business?) Again, a massive change in the way people view the world and society is the only way this could ever happen, and this seems many years off: rarely has such a gigantic change been seen before.

It is also worth noting that the policy has been criticised for, essentially, missing the point about modern realities. Those who favour a human-scale approach, with smaller, sustainable living at its core, point out that size is the problem and that, rather than confronting the problem with a solution of equal global size, that the problem should be dealt with by returning to smaller-scale communities and nations. Bunzl's defence to this seems to be that the policy can not get anywhere without massive grass roots support, and that, if put in place, it could help bring about many of those sustainable, environmental initiatives people are campaigning for.

'A rallying point for the myriad anti-globalisation organisations'

These points should not detract, however, from the main core of the idea, and this book: that there is an alternative to the way the world currently operates, and there is a method here, for implementing that change successfully. There are numerous steps that need to be taken before the policy could possibly be implemented, and this may even take hundreds of years, but that is no reason to not contemplate the possibilities. John Bunzl's proposal is a creative and imaginative one which deserves widespread circulation, and it could provide a central rallying point for the myriad of movements and organisations who agree with anti-globalisation principles. The more people that learn about the idea, the more likely it is to succeed.

It is also worth noting, as a postscript, that John Bunzl has put his money where his mouth is and runs the International Simultaneous Policy Organisation, which is the lobbying group that he believes is necessary to encourage countries to adopt the policy. This idea is not purely theoretical: it is being promoted in the real world by a real organisation, and deserves support.

• *To join the International Simultaneous Policy Organisation, or to buy copies of* The Simultaneous Policy, *contact ISPO, PO Box 26547, London SE3 7YT (fax: 020 8460 2035; e-mail: info@simpol.org; web: www.simpol.org).*

Globally integrated humanitarian farming

Ben Malone

As seen with United States food drops during military actions in Afghanistan, humanitarian efforts have become increasingly integrated with military campaigns. This centres around the fact that social unrest tends to go hand in hand with drought, famine, and economic collapse. The problem is compounded by inadequate relief efforts that are limited in scope and resources.

6 Blackstock Mews, London N4 2BT, UK (rhino@dial.pipex.com), 2002, 300pp, ISBN 0 948826 59 2

'Farming establishments could be set up for a specific country's aid needs'

An innovative way to solve these problems could be the following: farming establishments could be established here in the USA. (which has plenty of fertile land) that would produce food, a large majority of which would be used for humanitarian distribution in other countries. Under this system, a network of farms would be established for a specific country in need of aid. Then, several thousand (or as many as is appropriate and practical) citizens from the nation in need of food could be given transport to the United States as guests and help to farm the crops. These people from the country in need could be given temporary passports to come to the United States for a period of several months, during which time they would be paid for their labour, would be exempt from taxes, and would receive educational courses and training for other jobs if they so desired. The money these people make, along with any education and job skills they learn while here, will return home with them at the end of their stay, along with the much needed food they harvest. Since the economies of countries in need of humanitarian aid are almost always suffering, the money, job skills, and education earned by the farmers would provide a much needed boost, and may even promote more long term stability.

'Contributors to the programme could write it off as a tax break'

The portion of food products not allotted for humanitarian consumption (between 10 per cent and 25 per cent as a rough estimate) could be specially labelled as a product of humanitarian farming efforts and sold across the nation in order to help offset the costs of the programme. Americans who contributed money to the programme would be able to write it off as a tax deduction, and a small tax could be enacted to help pay for the program costs as well.

Shops, cultural centres and museums that deal with the history and culture of a particular nation could be located both on its farming combines and in major cities, where schools and the general public could pay admission (which of course would go to help pay for the project) to learn more about the nation. In order to reinforce the effectiveness of the programme and increase international awareness, students would be required to visit at least two or three different museums or cultural centres during their high school careers.

Shops on a countries' farm network could sell traditional crafts, goods, art, and other things made in that country here in the United States. Money generated for these sales could be both sent back to the needy country to help its economy, or be used to help fund the farming programme here in the

United States. All of these aspects of the program could be partially staffed by citizens of the country in need on the same temporary visa programme with the same benefits as the farmers.

'It would allow the nation in need to help itself more effectively'

This entire system of integrated humanitarian farming could be of huge benefit to numerous nations around the world, and could be enacted in other wealthy nations as well as the United States. Not only would this programme go a long way towards eliminating hunger and economic hardship, but it would allow the people of nations in need to really help themselves and their fellow citizens instead of just taking the help we give them. Also, it could go a long way towards creating peace and reducing the animosity of nations like Afghanistan. With Americans working alongside people of other nations both here and abroad to help alleviate some of the underlying causes of terrorism, terrorists would have less of a motive to act, as well as less backing in their countries of operation. Many experts talk about the inevitable globalization and integration of industrial and consumer economies, so why not globally integrate the humanitarian aid process as well.

• *Ben Malone is a student at Elon University (www.elon.edu) in North Carolina, USA.*

Voluntary exchange of citizenship

Axel Boldt

I submit that the countries of the World ought to let any two people voluntarily exchange their citizenship. If this scheme were adopted, citizenships would become a tradeable commodity. Poor people from rich countries could trade their citizenship with well-off people from poor countries for a monetary payment. Both parties freely enter into this trade and therefore benefit from it. Furthermore, the rich country benefits in that it gains an enterprising new citizen; the poor country benefits in that the person who left will presumably continue to support his or her relatives and friends from abroad.

Some retirees from rich countries may prefer to live out their final years in inexpensive and sun-rich countries; they can easily do so by exchanging their citizenships, thereby giving a young person an opportunity in a strong economy. These retirees could either sell their citizenships, or they could opt

6 Blackstock Mews, London N4 2BT, UK (rhino@dial.pipex.com), 2002, 300pp, ISBN 0 948826 59 2

for a more charitable approach, for instance offering their citizenship as a reward to promising students. In this scenario, poor countries benefit enormously from the spending power and experience of the retirees.

To ensure that the citizenship trade always occurs on a strict one-to-one basis, one rule has to be added: a citizen who gained his or her status by trade loses the right to claim citizenship for his or her immediate family.

• *Axel Boldt (e-mail: axel@uni-paderborn.de). Axel Boldt, originally from Germany, is a professor of mathematics at Metropolitan State University in Saint Paul, Minnesota, USA.*

Reduced-rate and free subscriptions for libraries in developing countries

Sami Grover

Publishers could grade their subscription rates according to a country's ability to pay. This is already being done by some companies, but not enough at the moment. Obviously an objective means of deciding on which countries qualify is necessary, the Human Development Resource Index being one of the most obvious. Thus, libraries and institutions in those countries could receive important journals and publications for free or at a low cost, ensuring there is not a parallel inequality of infomation as well as of wealth.

• *Sami Grover works at Multilingual Matters Ltd, who provide a service similar to the one outlined above (info@multilingual-matters.co.uk).*

WAR AND PEACE

A conflict barometer to predict nations approaching civil war

Summarised from an article by Robert Adler, entitled 'Countdown to crisis', in the New Scientist (October 27th 2001; New Scientist subs £99 or $140, call 01444 475636 or e-mail ns.subs@qss-uk.com).

A research team in America have developed a 'conflict barometer' which could provide early warnings of countries approaching civil war. Using a computer system that analyses news stories and categorises them, the inventors claim that they can predict when regimes and governments are nearing a fall. This could enable other nations of the world to monitor those situations ahead of when they might otherwise do so, and hopefully allow for some peaceful (or other) intervention to avert an internal war. It is also thought that it could be used to forecast the collapse of threatened currencies, as the factors that lead to civil war are also substantially similar to those that lead to economic collapse (indeed, the two often go hand in hand).

'An equation gives the result: a nation's conflict carrying capacity'

The computer is fed with thousands of Reuters news stories, which it then separates into approximately 200 categories. From that point, Craig Jenkins and Doug Bond, of Ohio State and Harvard universities, calculate how many events involve civil protests, how many involve government repression and how many involve violent outbreaks. These three factors are then put into an equation which gives a result which they call a nation's 'conflict carrying capacity' (CCC). A CCC of 100 equals complete stability, while a CCC of zero equals complete chaos. If the figure is kept below 85 per cent for a number of months, there could well be a crisis in gestation.

'The barometer would have predicted civil war in Algeria months in advance'

Although the barometer is yet to be proven by any recent events, the researchers have gone back and looked at ten years worth of CCC levels for a number of countries. They found that their barometer would have predicted civil wars in Algeria and Sri Lanka more than six months ahead of them taking place. Equally, the system can chart a country's return to stability from civil

6 Blackstock Mews, London N4 2BT, UK (rhino@dial.pipex.com), 2002, 300pp, ISBN 0 948826 59 2

strife. The Swiss Peace Foundation, meanwhile, use the measuring system as a way of identifying countries whose currencies are at risk, demonstrating its usefulness in a number of areas. Although it is essentially a form of very close observation of events, the conflict barometer speeds up the process (no human could process news stories as the computer does) and provides a figure that can be traced and tracked over a number of months and years.

• *See http://www.acs.ohio-state.edu/researchnews/archive/earlwarn.htm for more on the system, plus graphs illustrating how it works.*

• *See also www.hiik.de/en/ for a different conflict barometer based at the Heidelberg Institute of International Conflict Research in Germany.*

• *The Italy-based Non-Governmental Peace Startegies Project also produces an online World Peace Index, which also analyses news to give an overall world stability rating: see www.ngpsp.org*

Co-sovereignty in areas of conflict

Deborah Reich

A new alternative for reconciliation of intractable national or ethnic conflicts, co-sovereignty (modelled on co-parenting or joint custody, from family law) would be a great experimental option. Instead of either winner-take-all or grudgingly dividing up the pie, both sides rule – simultaneously – and learn to be functional partners, as co-parents with joint custody of children do.

• *Deborah Reich (e-mail: debmail@netvision.net.il). Deborah is a writer, editor, translator, and freethinker active in Jewish-Palestinian reconciliation in Israel.*

A commission for conflict resolution

Summarised from an editorial by Satish Kumar, entitled 'A nonviolent response to terrorism', in Resurgence magazine (November/Decemer 2001 issue; to subscribe, call 01208 841824 or e-mail: subs.resurge@virgin.net).

Satish Kumar's suggestion, in the wake of September 11th, is for a Commission for Confict Resolution under the auspices of the United Nations. The main tenet behind the idea is that violence is rarely the answer: Vietnam and Northern Ireland are testaments to the fact that negotiation works better and with more lasting effects. So the UNCCR (as it would be called) should hold a conference with all the globally aggrieved parties (Saddam Hussein, Osama Bin Laden, Hamas etc) using terrorist methods being able to have face-to-face discussions with the major governments of the world.

'Working towards peaceful solutions to the root causes of terrorism'

It may well be inconceivable for some time to have Saddam Hussein or Bin Laden round a table with a delegation from the G8 countries, but certainly there is opportunity for progress in the Middle East and surrounding countries. The UNCCR, headed by a respected, impartial statesman (such as Mikhail Gorbachev), would work towards peaceful solutions to all the root causes of terrorism. The Commission would need to be completely impartial to have any effect, and to maintain any moral authority, but it could be a step to negotiation or discussion in trouble zones around the world. As with any disease, prevention is always better than cure, and is the only true long-term solution.

A World Tolerance Park as a memorial to World Trade Center
Kara Fultz

'All countries would be welcome to contribute'

Everyone is talking about what should be done with the World Trade Center site and I think I have a pretty good idea. Since people from other countries also died in the attack, I think the monument should be a World Tolerance Park in which people could come to learn about other people and their cultures. Any country who wanted to contribute a part of their culture to the center would be welcome to do so and information sessions and festivals could be given so that people have the opportunity to get to know other cultures and not be so discriminatory.

Twin Towers of light

Six months after September 11th, two shafts of light were beamed up from Gound Zero in New York as a tribute to those who died. The novel, if transient, memorial was the brainchild of two architects, Gustavo Bonevardi and John Bennett, and two artists, Paul Myoda and Julian LaVerdiere, who

6 Blackstock Mews, London N4 2BT, UK (rhino@dial.pipex.com), 2002, 300pp, ISBN 0 948826 59 2

teamed up after hearing they had all had the same idea independently. In collaboration with the Creative Time arts organisation, the so-called 'Towers of Light' came to fruition, and were lit for 32 days from dusk on March 11th.

• *Kara Fultz is a student at Elon University (ww.elon.edu) in North Carolina, USA.*

A website for data on terrorist organisations and their backers

Todd Putnam

This idea is for the creation of a website called something like, terrorismscorecard.org. Now that terrorism is on everybody's mind, it presents us with an opportunity to focus that attention toward ending terrorist policies. (Terrorism is defined as political violence targeting civilians.) The website would list terrorism-related data, probably by country.

'Data available could include financial backers, arms suppliers, numbers of civilians killed, etc'

Data, organized into a scrollable chart might include: financial backers of terrorism, their arms suppliers, training, numbers of civilians killed, etc. It would put the present narrow discussion into a much broader context, revealing that the US itself might be considered responsible (through the backing of such terror organizations as UNITA, RENAMO, the contras, etc) for deaths due to terrorism. Other data included might be the aims of the terrorists and their backers, and international efforts to end the the terrorist attacks.

Such data would reveal which states have been violating international laws against terrorism for years. Hopefully such a sight would lead to greater awareness of the inconsistency of countries' stated aims and actual policies, and gradually compel policymakers to live by the same rules they are demanding of others. Plus, it would make interesting reading.

• *Todd Putnam (e-mail: toddputnam@hotmail.com). Todd is an activist living in the north-west of America.*

Defining terrorism
Nick Temple

Todd's idea is both an innovative and increasingly necessary idea, but he skips over a rather crucial issue: the definition of terrorism. 'Political violence against civilians' is not really precise enough, because this could include government actions against their own citizens. Indeed, coming up with a definition of terrorism acceptable to all countries and organisations in the world is itself a necessary social innovation, and one that has evaded us for generations (ever since the League of Nations tried in 1937). For how can terrorists be judged, hunted down or tackled if there is no agreement on who the terrorists are? Since the events of September 11th, the debate has erupted again with new vigour: recent publications have included a three-volume discussion of the various definitions, and a book entitled 'Enough of the Definition of Terrorism' (by Omar Malik). Below is a brief discussion of some of the best definitions *[Summarised from an article by Timothy Garton Ash, entitled 'First the biography...', in the Guardian (November 10th 2001), and from various articles on the web from www.terrorism.com, www.terrorismanswers.com and www.ict.org.il]*, and an attempt to amalgamate them:

Timothy Garton Ash says there are four things to consider when deciding whether someone is a terrorist: **biography** (who are they, where do they come from, what do they want?), **goals** (are the goals vague and unrealisable or, in some sense, rational objectives?), **methods** (is violence used, and who is it targeted against: military or civilian targets?) and **context** (what kind of state is the terrorism taking place in? is the violent response in any way legitimate?). He suggests that this fourfold template be used to make an examination of each group: these could then go up on a website such as the one Todd suggests. What he does not do is say how these four areas are actually used to decide what is a terrorist organisation: it is all very well having areas to 'consider' but the point is to be able to decide.

'A moral distinction is drawn between guerilla fighters and terrorists'

Boaz Ganor, Executive Director of the Institute for Counter Terrorism, defines terrorism as simply 'the deliberate use of violence against civilians in order to attain political, ideological and religious aims'. Under this definition, the goals and biography are less important: it is the methods that are crucial (the targeting of civilian rather than military personnel). In this way, a (moral) distinction is drawn between guerilla (or freedom) fighters and terrorists, making it easy to distinguish the two. He adds that states are outside the boundaries of terrorism – attacks on civilians by states or governments are covered by the 'war crime' and 'crime against humanity' definitions. [It is worth noting that the US State Department defines terrorism as 'premeditated, politically motivated violence perpetrated against noncombatant targets by subnational groups or clandestine agents, usually intended to influence an

6 Blackstock Mews, London N4 2BT, UK (rhino@dial.pipex.com), 2002, 300pp, ISBN 0 948826 59 2

audience' – but their noncombatant targets include unarmed or off duty military personnel: anyone not at battle readiness. This might have made the French resistance terrorists....].

What Ganor fails to include is terrorism that does not involve direct violence, by which I mean threats, intimidation etc, for terrorism is, as the Terrorism Research Center puts it, also 'a psychological act conducted for its impact on the audience'. So threats of violence and psychological terror should be included somewhere in our list. Terrorism also always has a political motivation (which distinguishes it from organised crime), which includes religions or social motives, within the wider sense of what is political. Paul Pillar, a former deputy chief of the CIA's Counterterrorist Center, adds that terrorism is premeditated as well, and that this is a key aspect of its make-up.

'Definition is done by specific inclusion, not particular criteria'

Just before drawing together the above into one definitive set of criteria, it is worth adding a brief note about how the UK and the EU currently attempt to define terrorism. The Terrorism Act (2000) in Britain says that terrorism means 'the use or threat of action to influence a government or intimidate the public for a political, religious or ideological cause', which is quite broad; the act gets round the definition problem by listing twenty-one organisations which it is an offence to belong to: definition by specific inclusions rather than general criteria. The EU has proposed legislation which says that terrorism is 'a deliberate attack by an individual or a group against a country, its institutions or its people – with the aim of intimidating them and damaging or destroying their political, economic or social structures'. Again, what stands out is the lack of distinction between civilian and military targets, although this does include the key aspects of intimidation and premeditation which other definitions have missed.

Being definitive about terrorism

Here, then, are my criteria on deciding if a group is terrorist or not:

- A terrorist act is premeditated and deliberate
- A terrorist group uses violence, the threat of violence or other psychological intimidation
- A terrorist group targets civilians and civilian buildings, rather than military ones
- Terrorist acts are politically motivated (including religious, social and more narrowly political objectives)
- Terrorist groups are not states or countries; they are subnational, but can

be supported by governments and nations (hence 'state-sponsored' terrorism) and to these, I would add some footnotes:

• The objectives of groups should be looked at in the context of the state they are in, and to whether their objectives are rational or achievable (this does not condone violence against civilian targets). Are democratic and peaceable avenues available?
• Terrorist groups can change: groups and organisations evolve all the time, and judgements should be flexible and consistently updated

What the above definition does do is make tough decisions about some troublesome issues: for example, violence against civilians is never acceptable and guerilla or 'freedom fighting' is legitimate in some cases. Thus, for example, the above definition to an extent legitimises (whilst not necessarily supporting) Palestinian violence against Israeli military targets, but would label suicide bombing of civilians a terrorist act. Israel's actions, if considered unlawful, would have to be judged under the banners of 'war crimes' or 'crimes against humanity', because they are a state.

World Peace Index

Ricky Chen

This World Peace Index would be similar to indexes like the Human Development Index. The Index will measure quantities like the amount of defence spending, number of large and small scale conflicts, fatalities and injuries from conflicts, the numbers of weapons of mass destruction. It could also factor in the number of organisations promoting peace in a particular country.

• *Ricky Chen (e-mail: rche7182@mail.usyd.edu.au). Ricky is an honours student at the University of Sydney, Australia.*
• *For a different kind of online World Peace Index, see http://www.ngpsp.org/ and the previous item about the 'conflict barometer' in this section.*

Silent walking for peace

Summarised from information on the Peace-by-Peace website (www.walkforpeace.org), and from information from Martin Farrell. The latter item was monitored for the Global Ideas Bank by Michael Norton.

There have been different responses to the violence and conflict erupting around the world in the past year, varying from demonstrations to mass e-

6 Blackstock Mews, London N4 2BT, UK (rhino@dial.pipex.com), 2002, 300pp, ISBN 0 948826 59 2

mailing of the American president. One quieter, more thoughtful response has emerged on both sides of the Atlantic: walking silently for peace. The idea is that people uncomfortable with protesting vociferously at demonstrations can let their feelings be known in a different way, and at the same time have time to think, meditate or pray for peace.

'The women will walk through seven states on their way to Washington'

In the US, a group of women, who call themselves Peace-by-Peace, started a walk on January 21st 2002 (Martin Luther King Jr. Day) from the Peace Wall in Berkeley, California. They will then walk through Arizona, New Mexico, Texas, Oklahoma, North Carolina and Virginia before reaching Washington on September 11th 2002. Along the way, they hope that the walk will prove to be an opportunity for finding inner peace as well as demonstrating their collective will to participate in a world where people can live together harmoniously.

The 'Walk in Peace for Peace' started in London in October 2001, and its intention is to take place on the first Sunday of each month starting at Speakers' Corner in Hyde Park. The idea behind the walk is that more and more people join, and the walk slowly grows until it cannot be ignored. Everyone on the walk walks silently, one after the other, making their point in deed, rather than word.

• *Peace-by-Peace can be contacted at 2121 Kittredge *250, Berkeley, CA 94704, USA (tel: +1 510 496 1260 ext 1661; e-mail: peacebypeace@onebox.com; web: www.walkforpeace.org).*

• *For current information on the London Walks in Peace for Peace, call 020 8755 0353.*

Peace villages to create Israeli-Palestinian co-operation

Anthony N. Tofanelli

To bring peace to Israel and Palestine I see five imperatives within the Peace Village Plan:

1) Israeli Defense Forces would cease incursions into areas of Palestinian settlement.

2) The State of Israel would announce that territory presently non-supportive of human settlement may be set aside for the construction of Peace Villages.

3) The State of Israel would announce that a Peace Village Construction Program was seeking volunteers, both Palestinian and Israeli, to build and populate such projected new settlement.

4) The State of Israel would accept design concepts for self-sufficient Peace Villages which would, as far as technically possible, produce all essential consumables for their inhabitants.

5) The State of Israel would seek a World Bank loan for partial funding of the Peace Village Construction Program. Besides paying for the actual construction of Peace Village settlements, World Bank funding would also support the construction of necessary water, transport and communications infrastructures – as required by Peace Village settlements.

Further Explanation:

Co-operation can be infectious. There are sufficient numbers of Palestinians and Israelis who might actively seek to produce peace by removing themselves from areas of immediate confrontation and building, within secure areas, joint settlements. To provide military security for such a project I would most naively propose a joint effort by the IDF and a Palestinian force specifically assigned to protect Peace Village settlement areas. Possibly the State of Israel would allow United Nations Security Forces to provide security for Peace Village areas, but this is doubtful. Still, such would seem a most creative and pro-active use of UN Security Forces.

'The design for a Peace Village would combine space technology with desert architecture'

The concept design for a Peace Village, in my estimation, would be an earth-bound variant of Mars settlement design blended with the desert architectures of compact, walled towns as seen throughout the Middle East and North Africa. When one combines the on-site production of all essential consumables, as Mars settlement design must, with the practical nature of advanced desert architecture the resulting hybrid would be fully suited to achieving adequate wealth and comfort for its inhabitants. Arid locations within Israel and Palestine would allow current, sustainable energy technologies to produce on-site, energy self-sufficiency for the Peace Village.

And what of water supply? Peace Villages would be designed for maximum water efficiency but the source of water must, in my estimation, be an enlarged desalination capacity within Israel and Palestine. Although solar-driven desalination plants exist I would suggest as ideal the use of cold fusion energy production for this purpose. The prime output from the cold fusion reaction is heat energy-simply made-to-order for desalination. Those who believe cold fusion to be a hoax should research the Japanese Government's successful

6 Blackstock Mews, London N4 2BT, UK (rhino@dial.pipex.com), 2002, 300pp, ISBN 0 948826 59 2

support of cold fusion research and development between the years 1990 and 1995. Although cold fusion-driven desalination would be ideal, the success of a Peace Village Construction Program for Israel and Palestine would not necessarily hinge upon it.

By creating a project whereby Israelis and Palestinians could build and live together, within a secure perimeter, the Israeli Government would demonstrate its commitment to peace through pro-active rather than regressive means. Eventually, it would be hoped, the example of Israeli-Palestinian co-operation within Peace Villages would spread throughout the State of Israel and that the need for secure perimeters would eventually dissipate.

• *Anthony Tofanelli is the author of a Global Peace Plan which asserts that sustainable development is the only secure foundation for peace and prosperity. Mr. Tofanelli was born and raised in Napa, California where he presently resides (e-mail: damatta@saber.net).*

Distribution of targetable assets for increased safety

Summarised from an article by Oliver Morton, entitled 'Divided we stand', in Wired magazine (December 2001 issue; www.wired.com; to subscribe call +1 415 222 6200 or e-mail: subscriptions@wired.com).

Repsonding to the events of September 11th, Oliver Morton suggests one overriding principle to ensure greater security in countries under threat: spread out. He suggests that one of the main lessons to be learned from the Twin Towers attack is that concentrating valuable (and therefore targetable) assets in one place is both risky and unnecessary. This does not only apply to concentrations of people either, but, for example, to a city that relies on only one river as a source of water or on one electricity station as a source of power. The solution to these 'concentration[s] of consequence'? Distribute and diversify. Morton suggests that the 'development of distributed system throughout the national infrastructure should be seen as a priority by all the countries around the world'.

'Relying heavily on imports of oil is a concentration of risk'

Thus, it makes sense in *security* terms, let alone environmental ones, to replace a few major nuclear and fossil-fuel power stations with solar, wind and hydroelectric power. A terrorist group targeting a giant windmill, or even a group of them, is far less of a threat than one targeting a nuclear plant.

Similarly, relying heavily on imports of oil is a concentration of risk in one area: diversifying energy production reduces this concentration. Air travel could also be distributed and made smaller, with greater numbers of smaller aircraft flying from greater numbers of smaller airfields, again spreading the assets out across the country, while not necessarily making it more inconvenient for passengers.

Morton also extends the distribution theme to computing and the internet where, he suggests, the use of the same systems and applications by everyone is a cause for great concern. The world wide web may be a model of distribution and diversity, but if everyone uses Internet Explorer to access it, there are prime issues of security and vulnerability risk; and this again is an area that can be targeted by criminals and terrorists.

'Another way of encouraging diverse small-scale initiatives'

All of this may seem like a very defensive response to an unforeseen security problem, but it can also be seen as another way of encouraging diversity and distribution of small-scale initiatives that many environmental and sustainable development groups wish to see. As well as the examples of energy production, the same principles apply to food production, housing and public health. Security fears could prove to be a side-entrance for groups wishing to see diversity and variety flourish in their country. It will not only be better for us, but it could also be safer.

Exchanging weapons for productive tools, and creating art from the arms

Summarised from a Christian Aid brochure, entitled 'Swords into Ploughshares; Transforming Arms into Art' (January 2002).

A project run by Christian Aid for the last seven years allows the citizens of Mozambique to hand in weapons in exchange for productive tools. No questions are asked about the origins of the weapons, or who owns them. What they receive in return depends on the number, type and functionality of the weapons, and on whether they live in urban or rural areas, but bicycles, hoes, sewing machines, construction tools and school equipment have all been given in exchange. The majority of the arms are destroyed immediately after their collection, under strict safety conditions, but another innovative aspect

6 Blackstock Mews, London N4 2BT, UK (rhino@dial.pipex.com), 2002, 300pp, ISBN 0 948826 59 2

has been added to the project in the last year or so: transforming some of the weapons into art.

'Instruments of war are rendered harmless creatively'

The idea behind transforming some of the weapons into art is twofold: to publicise the project, and Mozambiquan art, throughout the world via exhibitions, and to promote a culture of peace. To see sculptured chairs, birds and jazz instruments made from AK47's and ammunitions has powerful symbolic significance: instruments of war have been rendered harmless by man's creativity, and weapons have been taken out of use permanently by being made into symbols of peace and unity.

• *For further information, see www.africaserver.nl/nucleo , www.iansa.org/ documents/research/TAE or www.christian-aid.org.uk*

POLITICS

Presidential debates judged on ability to solve problems constructively

Ben Moore

It is kind of strange that in a society that values different thoughts and ideas we elect Presidents based on how well they can blow away the other guy's idea. Presidential debates aren't looking for the right answer, they are looking for a way to prove the other candidate wrong. There must be a way to end this. If we had presidential debates where the two candidates had to build off of each other's ideas than we could elect a president based on his desire and ability to look for the right answer, not on his eloquence or stage presence.

My idea is to make the two candidates work together to come up with a better idea. Both candidates could state their ideas for an issue. Then they have to work together to come up with a better way than they had before. Whoever did a better job of working together to find a better way wins the debate. Then we could elect a President that we believe would try to do the right thing.

• *Ben Moore is a student at Elon University (www.elon.edu) in North Carolina, USA.*

Crisis committees for local citizenship power

Summarised from an article by John Papworth, entitled 'Crisis Committees: our world in crisis', in Fourth World Review (Issues 115/116; subs £2 per issue, call 01793 772214).

John Papworth's idea is for a crisis grouping in every locality to re-empower citizens and give them the means to determine their own (human-scale) policies and futures. These 'crisis committees' will not be centred round a particular political viewpoint, such as socialism, anarchism or pacifism, but be a way of uniting people to confront the issues arising from centralised power. Each committee in each neighbourhood will aim to assert that neighbour-hood's power, and to use it for its own rational purposes. In this way, a honeycomb of local groups can build up, gradually growing in number and influence.

6 Blackstock Mews, London N4 2BT, UK (rhino@dial.pipex.com), 2002, 300pp, ISBN 0 948826 59 2

'Crisis committees deal with the root of the problem: who holds the power'

The argument that lies behind the concept of crisis committees is that there are two approaches to the global problems facing the world: challenge them on an issue by issue basis through activist organisations and campaigns, or face up to the bigger issue of power and who has it. Essentially, rather than treating what might be called the symptoms of global political machinations (be they environmental, terroristic or educational etc), crisis committees aim to deal with the root causes of the problems: who holds the power in order to be able to abuse it. What John Papworth is saying is that there is a crisis of democracy in today's society, as citizens have become further and further divorced from participation and decision-making. He points to the Prime Minister's increasingly presidential aspect, in which he often fails to consult the UK Parliament before announcing the country's position; he also points to the ineffectiveness of the current political system in developed countries, in which apathy, disillusionment and discontent are high.

The key, therefore, is to take our destinies in our own hands, by creating the change of course needed in our own local communities. This approach, Papworth believes, is better than attempting to create a mass centralised political organisation to counter the mass centralised political governments. As history has shown, with the French revolution and the labour movement for example, these mass organisations either become co-opted by those they opposed or they become corrupted by power upon replacing the previous regime. So human-scale groupings will work more effectively, and they will be less likely to let power go to their head, because the only power they have will be to change things in their local community.

'Harnessing the increasing awareness of the need for change'

The minority that agree there is a global crisis (of whatever hue or timbre) are undoubtedly growing, and the idea of crisis committees could be one way of harnessing that increasing awareness of the need for change. As John Papworth writes:

'Four or five people meeting in a coffee bar or someone's home to discuss the affairs of the day may appear of trifling consequence, but meeting regularly, with a direct focus on the global crisis, seeking to elucidate its causes and how they might be countered, multiplied around the world can yet, with clarity, vision, persistence, determination and no lack of moral courage, save it.'

Institute for Social Inventions, £15 subs, £17 from abroad by credit card, tel London 020 7359 8391

• *For more information on crisis committees, or to order copies of the Fourth World Review, contact The Fourth World, The Close, 26 High Street, Purton, Wiltshire SN5 4AE (tel: 01793 772214; fax: 01793 772521; e-mail: john.papworth@btinternet.com). The Fourth World Review welcomes comments on the above idea to contribute to a debate on the subject.*

Banning insults in parliament to avoid divisiveness

Summarised from an article by Laurie Copans, entitled 'Israeli lawmaker pushing for ban on insults', in the Seattle Times (June 22nd 2001), monitored for the Global Ideas Bank by Roger Knights.

Israel's parliament could be made to hold its collective tongue if a new legislator has their way. The parliament has been renowned for its freewheeling debates, but this has become more and more characterised by personal, vindictive insults in recent years. The atmosphere has degenerated to the point where speeches are drowned out by others shouting over them, and people run through the chamber finger-pointing at individuals. This has the effect of perpetuating the divisiveness of Israel's political climate and reduces the chance of reasoned debate and policy-making. So legislation has been suggested that would lead to members of the parliament being reprimanded or even suspended for such verbal offences.

'Recent insults included lunatic, Nazi, pig and terrorist'

A list of 68 insults was collated from recent debates in the Knesset, and these included anti Semite, blood drinker, degenerate, fascist, filth, gut ripper, instigator of murder, Jew-hater, lunatic, monster, murderer, Nazi, pig, racist, savage, terrorist and thug. The intention of the new law would be to reprimand first-time offenders for use of any of these words, and suspend persistent offenders for consistent foul language. The list will have to be agreed upon, though, as the list drawn up also included relatively inoffensive terms such as poodle, nincompoop and cheat.

A recent survey in Israel discovered that 50 per cent of those polled found the slanging matches in the parliament embarrassing. The law may be radical, and could be seen to impinge on the right to free speech, but it could help hugely in changing the tone of political debate in the region, which the representatives do much to set and maintain. It might also enable them to set a better example to the younger generation on matters of debate, reasoned argument and representation.

6 Blackstock Mews, London N4 2BT, UK (rhino@dial.pipex.com), 2002, 300pp, ISBN 0 948826 59 2

The Common Good State: the next phase of human societies

Peter A. Zuckerman

Introduction

The philosophy behind the Global Ideas Bank, and its products – such as the annual compendium of ideas – is a good one. The social inventions published '...address issues, and operate artfully on them, at the human scale, often on a neighbourhood level'. However, there are global problems where this approach cannot work.

The most important social invention of the human species was the 'state'. To quote from *Social Inventions* by D. Stuart Conger:

'Social Invention: Government — concept of the state; When: pre 3500 B.C.; Where: Sumer (Mesopotamia); Who: Sumerians; Why: Evolved out of the necessity to have an authority in an area in order to mediate disputes. Was first embodied in one person and later bureaucracy developed around him.'

The state, with all of its faults, over the centuries brought about human civilization and progress. But the human condition is now reaching a stage where the traditional state requires a radical change.

Terrorism and other manifestations of human violence continue throughout our planet. Many of these conditions are caused by underdeveloped countries' negative political, social, economic and environmental conditions. Totalitarian and autocratic governments, combined with powerful military forces, cause major diversion of resources from human needs.

Human societies developed from bands to tribes to chiefdoms, finally reaching the traditional state. But negative social developments resulted in a condition of worldwide political mismanagement. To remedy this situation, we must advance beyond the traditional state to the common good state.

Reaching and implementing the common good state worldwide requires the leadership by the most advanced traditional state, which is the United States of America. With the assistance of such allies as the European Union, Japan and India, the common good state will be adopted throughout the planet. This will result in the elimination of political mismanagement and the reduction of the war institution, thereby advancing human survival and progress.

Institute for Social Inventions, £15 subs, £17 from abroad by credit card, tel London 020 7359 8391

The Problem

The recent terrorist attacks on the United States highlight the new dangers to human progress and survival. The media published many theories concerning the motives and backgrounds of the terrorists. Past manifestations of human violence had their own causes. The genocides of Nazi Germany were based on racism. The mass murders of Stalin and Mao were justified by alleged capitalist exploitation of workers. The terrorists attacking America claimed religious justification for their wicked deeds. But a more realistic explanation is based on the major differences among human societies.

Most of the underdeveloped countries of the world suffer from extreme poverty, ill health, environmental destruction, low quality of life, and a feeling of humiliation when comparing themselves to the developed world. These conditions are exacerbated by the reality that the problems of many countries are not solved, and are even made worse, by incompetent and even corrupt governments. The desperate conditions of existence for many in these societies, as compared to the high standards of living in the advanced countries, then provide a fertile ground for the terror planners and executers.

'Only 41.4 per cent of the world's population live in 'free' societies'

The recently published *Freedom in the World 2002: The Democracy Gap* by the Freedom House (a New York-based think tank that monitors political and civil liberties) explains the causes of the negative human conditions. Of the world's population of 6.1 billion, only 41.4 per cent live in 'free' societies. Of course, there is a strong relationship between political freedom and economic development. The 'partly free' or 'not free' countries control the remaining 58.6 per cent of the human populations, or almost 3.6 billion human beings.

Diversion of resources from human needs

Armed with increasingly powerful weapons, military forces rule or dominate much of the world's population. If we count the totalitarian (not free) and authoritarian (partly free) governments, which could not exist without military force, more than half the world's population lives under direct or indirect military rule. But even in democratic countries huge amounts are spent every year on maintaining their military forces and on weapons research and procurement. These expenditures by necessity are diverted from solving or alleviating the many social and economic problems of the world. Totalitarian and authoritarian leaders of their countries find it more useful to maintain large armed forces than to increase the living standards of their oppressed subjects.

6 Blackstock Mews, London N4 2BT, UK (rhino@dial.pipex.com), 2002, 300pp, ISBN 0 948826 59 2

This diversion of resources from human needs creates the following negative conditions:

- 1.2 billion people live in absolute poverty
- 1.5 billion lack basic health care and sanitation
- Nearly 1 billion people suffer from malnutrition
- 20% of the world's population is illiterate
- There are 50 million refugees from war and famines
- This is accompanied by much environmental destruction — deforestation, soil erosion, desertification

Analysing and understanding the fundamental causes of the support of terrorism enables us to develop the solution. We have reached a situation where we have to shape our future into the right direction with new social inventions.

As we begin the 21st century, the dangers to human survival multiply. A rapidly growing world population is afflicted in many countries with a harmful way of thinking. An emotional mindset, which is conducive to enmity against different clans, tribes, nations, ethnic groups, religions and others is reinforced by logical inventions of technologies. Thus, authoritarian leadership can use communications and military technologies to gain and stay in power, frequently by waging war against domestic opposition or neighbouring countries. Religious fundamentalists are using electronic communications to spread their message of hate. Even in democratic countries some politicians use racial or religious appeals in their election campaigns. This fatal human weakness explains the negative conditions of many societies and nations.

The Development of Human Societies

Physiologist and evolutionary biologist Jared Diamond in *Guns, Germs, and Steel* provides a basic classification of human societies as evolved from the primitive origin of our species.

'Bands are the tiniest societies, consisting typically of five to 80 people, most or all of them close relatives by birth or by marriage. In effect, a band is an extended family or several related extended families.' Chimpanzees and gorillas also live in bands, but today human bands exist only in remote parts of New Guinea and Amazonia.

The next stage of human society development is the tribe. The tribe '...differs in being larger (typically comprising hundreds rather than dozens of people) and usually having fixed settlements'. Both bands and tribes lack a bureaucracy, police force, and taxes. Their economies are based on reciprocal exchanges between individuals or families, rather than on tribute paid to a central authority.

'Chiefdoms emerged in around 5500 BC'

The subsequent stage of human society development took place in the Fertile Crescent around 5500 B.C., with the emergence of chiefdoms. Chiefdoms were considerably larger than tribes, ranging from several thousand to several tens of thousands of people. The problem of potential internal conflict among thousands of people was solved by the appointment of 'one person, the chief, to exercise a monopoly on the right to use force'.

The final stage of society development is the modern state. The first states emerged around 3700 B.C. in Mesopotamia, but today they rule all the world's habitable surface. Central control is more far-reaching, and economic redistribution in the form of taxes is more extensive in states than in chiefdoms. Economic specialization is more extreme. Internal conflict resolution within states has become increasingly formalized by law, a judiciary and police.

All existing societies now have complex centralized organizations. There are several obvious reasons for this human condition:

• Conflict between unrelated strangers requires centralized authorities to monopolize force and resolve conflicts
• Communal decisions in large societies can only be made by a structured and centralized authority
• Large societies require a redistributive economy facilitated by a centralized authority
• Densely populated regions require large and complexly organized societies for proper functioning

While the development of human societies was strongly facilitated by the creation of centralized states, a negative condition emerged in parallel with these developments:

'Considerations of conflict resolution, decision making, economics and space thus converge in requiring large societies to be centralized. But centralization of power inevitably opens the door – for those who hold the power, are privy to information, make the decisions, and redistribute the goods – to exploit the resulting opportunities to reward themselves and their supporters.' Taken to an extreme, this condition converts many societies into 'complex kleptocracies'.

Kleptocracy: a government characterised by rampant greed and corruption.

Kleptocratic governments are very common in authoritative societies. But even in democracies politicians and other powerholders are corrupted by their

6 Blackstock Mews, London N4 2BT, UK (rhino@dial.pipex.com), 2002, 300pp, ISBN 0 948826 59 2

desire to obtain power and maintain it. Their need to gain and hold office (and power) requires contributions from special interests. These in turn expect and receive favourable legislation, government contracts and other economic and financial benefits. This excessive shifting of resources to the well-to-do ensures that many social and economic problems remain unresolved. In effect, a form of mild kleptocracy comes into existence, based on the human weaknesses of greed and hunger for power. An example of this has been the recent Enron scandal in the US.

Negative social developments

While the development of human civilization provided great advances in science, technology and general prosperity, many negative conditions also emerged. As human societies evolved from bands to states, basic human characteristics shared with other primates remained. The many institutions of civilization converted the human savages into intelligent and civilized beings, with ambitions even to extend into space and the exploration of other planets. But frequently the institutions of humankind are controlled by men and women more interested in power and domination than in advancing human survival and progress.

'Centralized decision-making leadership facilitates the keeping of power'

These traits then transform many countries into harmful entities. Centralized decision-making leadership facilitates the keeping of power. The establishment of powerful military forces is supported by modern technology able to develop affordable weapons of high killing power. Such institutions as secret police, supported by the military, can easily control populations and suppress dissent. The leadership of political institutions can use ideologies and other motivations to threaten and even attack other states, if motivated by their quest for power.

Thus the emergence of organized warfare paralleled the development of human societies. As societies emerged into chiefdoms and states, more violence-prone males became available for combat. Economic specialization provided the means to support standing armies. The development of increasingly sophisticated tools for killing, weapons, made the military forces more decisive. The powerholders of the more powerful states find it rewarding to threaten, attack and even conquer their neighbours. To defend against these threats, even relatively peaceful nations need to maintain armed forces, with the resulting wasteful military expenditures.

Institute for Social Inventions, £15 subs, £17 from abroad by credit card, tel London 020 7359 8391

Worldwide political mismanagement

Both democratic and non-democratic governments suffer from a chronic condition of political mismanagement. This is not surprising in authoritarian regimes. Authoritarian leaders use mass propaganda, brutal repression, control of the media, electronic surveillance, secret police and the military to stay in power. They have no mechanism for the orderly transition of authority – in fact, the sole purpose of such regimes is to stay in power, regardless of the costs to their unfortunate subjects. The continuous struggle against their own people leaves few resources to improve the economy and society. Thus the world's environmental and social problems continue to worsen, and human development is even regressing in many places. Only in countries where repressive governments are allowing market forces to emerge is there economic and social progress.

Democratic governments are also becoming the victims of political mismanagement. The need to gain office requires an excessive amount of time for non-governing activities, the courting of special interests, fund raising and the like. In some nations, such as Italy and Japan, links to organised crime exist. Pork barrel politics and political corruption are encouraged, and ethnic and class divisions are fomented. All this contributes to a gradual withdrawal of the electorate from the governing process, which is very damaging to democracy.

'Political mismanagement is intensified by warmongering and militarism'

Political mismanagement is intensified by the war institution and militarism. In non-democratic countries the military either controls the government directly, or provides the means for maintaining the powerholders. In democratic countries the military is under civilian control. But in either situation the war institution and the military divert huge resources from their country's social and economic problems.

Advancing beyond the Traditional State

Jared Diamond's summation of the evolution of human societies discloses the weaknesses of the traditional or conventional state. Powerholders have special access to information, can make decisions and redistribute surplus goods. This centralized leadership and decision-making enables them to reward themselves and their supporters at the expense of the general welfare of their societies. Throughout history this was the common characteristics of authoritarian governments. But even the more democratic and open societies can be tainted by this negative potential. The recent examples of 'crony capitalism' – more accurately described as 'klepto-capitalism' – in Malaysia,

6 Blackstock Mews, London N4 2BT, UK (rhino@dial.pipex.com), 2002, 300pp, ISBN 0 948826 59 2

Indonesia and other Asian countries demonstrate the harm done even by non-authoritarian governments.

To overcome this potentially fatal trend, a new type of state has to emerge. The reinventing and strengthening of institutions to form a civil society will provide the infrastructure of the next development of human societies: the common good state.

Common good: 1. A desirable end for government or public policy, which is good for the whole society.

2. The communal approach to the structuring and operating of a society, to reach an optimum level of economic and moral achievement and satisfaction for its participants.

The Common Good State

The common good state would modify the traditional state's institutions and operations, so that a higher level of civilization would be achieved to ensure continued human survival and progress. The 'Traditional State vs. the Common Good State' table summarizes the changes that should be made to the negative characteristics of the traditional state.

Reaching the Common Good State

Obviously the concept of the common good is highly desirable for the continued survival and progress of humankind. However, a major obstacle remains in reaching it. How can people of highly diverse values, opinions and outlooks reach agreement on what is the common good?

'Reaching the common good state becomes feasible, because rational procedures can be followed'

Reaching the common good state becomes feasible, because rational procedures can be followed in setting up societal goals, and selecting the best public policy alternatives for implementing these goals for the common good. Our considerable intellectual and information resources will provide the means of accomplishment. Only a logical approach can enable us to identify our problems, their costs and the resources available for solving them, without the conflict that all too frequently accompanies major social or economic problems.

For the first time in human history, it is possible to develop and implement economic, social and public policy decisions designed for the needs of societies. An excellent example is the evolution of the conflicting European countries into the European Union. This process was facilitated by such

Conditions	Traditional State	Common Good State
Human characteristic of genetic predisposition toward violence	Targeted against other states and/or minorities; internally as gangs, organized crime etc	Institutions improved or developed to reduce/eliminate internal and external strife and violence
Violence prone males available	Thousands to millions	Control tendencies to male violence by strengthening families and other civic institutions
Levels of specialization to generate food surpluses and services	Intensive, with potentially huge surpluses of food and services	Continue technological and other developments to generate food surpluses, products and services for the common good
Emergence of governing institutions and philosophies	Centralized decision-making leadership, supported by complex bureaucracies	Decentralize decision-making activities to civic institutions and convert bureaucracies into true public servants
Culture patterns formed by means of livelihood - eg cattle nomads, agriculturists etc.	Institutions strongly influenced (through education, propaganda etc.) by culture patterns	Educational and religious institutions revise their teachings to eliminate culture patterns encouraging enmities against other human groups
Ability to make war tools = weapons (high lethality index)	Science, technology, industry and surpluses produce weapons of tremendous lethality	Weapons of mass destruction will be abolished for the common good and survival of humankind
Capabilities for controlling subjects and suppressing dissent	Very powerful technologies and institutions are available (secret police, military etc.)	Citizen-serving leadership has no need for controlling subjects; legitimate grievances are encouraged to solve problems
Self-interest of institutional leadership to make war	Can be very high, depending on ideologies or psychopathic motivations	Citizen-serving leadership only interested in peace and prosperity for the common good
War promotion and conducting capabilities	Intensive war promotion efforts feasible, because of militarism, propaganda	The common good state eliminates the need and capabilities for promoting & conducting war

6 Blackstock Mews, London N4 2BT, UK (rhino@dial.pipex.com), 2002, 300pp, ISBN 0 948826 59 2

policies as the Marshall Plan and various unifying institutions, such as the European Common Market.

Implementing the Common Good State

The common good state, implemented worldwide, is a highly desirable evolution for the human species. But how can such a major change be accomplished?

Exploring the evolution of human societies provides the answer. Our species' social evolution started with bands. Each band occupied a small territory, and was continuously in conflict with other bands. Eventually a powerful band realized that it was more beneficial to absorb a defeated band into their group, instead of killing them. This converted bands into tribes, as other bands realized the benefits of a larger social organization and copied the institution.

As with bands, the tribes continued to struggle with each other for additional territories and resources. Again a successful tribe realized the benefits of uniting with other tribes to form chiefdoms. The success of chiefdoms in expanding their territories caused the other tribes to unite into chiefdoms.

The first government that could be considered the state (or city-state) emerged in Mesopotamia. The Sumerian chiefdom, using the resources of irrigated agriculture, was able to absorb other chiefdoms, and developed such social inventions as bureaucracy, priesthood, law, writing, factories and armies — all the attributes of the traditional state. To survive, other chiefdoms then gradually formed states. While much violence resulted from the interactions of states, they also facilitated the emergence of modern civilization.

The above examples suggest that the evolution of the common good state will follow the same model. The most successful traditional state, realizing the need for human survival and progress, will initiate the first common good state. The benefits of the new form of society will be so obvious that eventually all the failing traditional states will find it necessary to convert to common good states. Of course, the first common good state will find it useful to assist the other states to reach this desirable condition.

World Leadership for the Common Good State

With all its imperfections, the United States is still the most successful of the traditional states. As the remaining superpower, America has all the resources needed for world leadership. Supported by the European Union, and such powerful allies as Japan and India, the United States could initiate a new global regime. Gradually even the most corrupt of the traditional states would change to the common good state, to ensure their own survival. This process would also be facilitated by a reformed United Nations.

The United States, even with its allies, would be faced with a formidable task, in advancing to the common good state. But fortunately a condition is reached when most of the world's problems, and the prevention of their resolution, can be traced to the true causes. The elimination of political mismanagement and the downsizing of the war institution is becoming feasible.

'Existing policies of promoting human rights and democratisation will be intensified'

Existing policies of promoting human rights, democratization and civil societies will be intensified and pursued vigorously. Worldwide military downsizing will achieve substantial multilateral disarmament, including the elimination of the most dangerous weapons systems. The tremendous financial savings from reduced military expenditures could be applied to the alleviation of the problems of humanity. Human needs could be met by transferring military expenditures to economic development, education, health improvement and other deficiencies of less developed countries.

Cutting down the flow of weapons to non-democratic regimes would also speed up the worldwide trend toward democratization and civil societies. Simultaneous efforts will be made to promote the freeing of oppressed minorities, while reducing the levels of ethnic and religious violence. Finally, by eliminating mistrust among countries the massive cooperative efforts needed to restore the global environment could be undertaken. The ultimate goal would be the bringing about common good states throughout the world, thereby ensuring continued human progress and survival.

• *Peter Zuckerman (e-mail: pazpax@earthlink.net)*

The Wisdom Council

Jim Rough

The Wisdom Council is an idea that can be applied to cities, counties and nations, to help those groupings form a wise and responsible 'voice of the people.'

To establish a Wisdom Council, the citizens of your city, county or state should pass the following resolution.

We, the People of '???????', resolve that:

Section 1: Every six months a group of sixteen registered voters shall be randomly selected and assembled to meet for one and a half days. Those who

6 Blackstock Mews, London N4 2BT, UK (rhino@dial.pipex.com), 2002, 300pp, ISBN 0 948826 59 2

attend both days shall form a Citizens' Wisdom Council whose unanimous views are termed 'Statements of the People.'

Section 2: The Citizens' Wisdom Council will present these Statements and how they were developed back to the people in a new ceremony. If possible the ceremony and even the meetings, will be televised.

Section 3: Meeting facilitators shall assure that the conversation in the Citizens' Wisdom Council is collaborative, open-minded and creative. They will assure that the views of each member are respected and help the group reach consensus. Facilitators shall not determine topics nor shall their personal views influence decisions.

Section 4: After the presentation, the (City, County, State) will support and encourage informal dialogues so that all citizens have an opportunity to meet with others and to consider and respond to the Statements. The Statements will be widely disseminated until the next Wisdom Council.

Section 5: A Wisdom Council Oversight Committee will assure the integrity of the process, hire facilitators, and provide expert information when requested.

Section 6: For deciding procedural issues within the Citizens' Wisdom Council, like meeting times and agendas, a majority vote may be used.

'The Council involves all people in a high quality dialogue about the most important issues'

Without challenging the existing structure of an organization, the Wisdom Council establishes a framework for creating a wise and responsible 'We the People.' It involves all people in a high quality dialogue about the most important issues and, over a few cycles of the process, helps them reach consensus decisions on those issues. It does this through a briefly-existing small group process which resonates with the whole system. The small group selects the issues, addresses them in a thoughtful, heartfelt way, articulates consensus Statements, and presents the Statements to all the people. The resulting whole-system dialogue builds community and a powerful political will in the public interest.

• *Jim Rough (e-mail: jim@tobe.net; web: www.wisedemocracy.org). Jim is a corporate consultant, speaker, seminar leader and author in the United States who originated Dynamic Facilitation as a way to assure creative, collaborative thinking in small groups (see www.ToBe.net).*

Instilling the voting ethic

Justin T. O'Conor Sloane

Like the work ethic perhaps a voting ethic too can be learned. In the United States a relatively small number of its citizens are registered voters and fewer yet actually turn out during elections to vote. Granted, many Americans are disillusioned and cynical regarding the current state of politics in the US and have as a result shied away from their civic responsibility but perhaps there is something else at play here as well: a lack of voting ethic having been instilled in Americans.

'Parents should take their children with them to the booth when they vote'

In the U.S, when you turn 18 you are allowed to vote. However, many of these young adults are almost totally unfamiliar with the political process and the importance of voting unless they grew up in a family that was politically engaged and/or they happened to have taken a civics or related class in school. My idea is this: from the 1st grade onwards parents would bring their children with them to the voting booths where their children would be guided through the voting process, either by their parents or by volunteers, using special instructional ballots and material provided at the voting site and casting their votes in kid-friendly booths. In addition, teachers could conduct the same instructional exercise in voting either in their classrooms or as a school-wide activity in their school's gymnasium so that the voting experience would be taught and reinforced both at school, at home and in the community.

As well, kids could be given certificates of voting to further develop their sense of the importance of voting and their sense of accomplishment for having participated. In this way, perhaps a sense of voting ethic, civic duty and familiarity with voting could be invested in the youth such that when they reach voting age they will become active and enthusiastic participants in their country's political process. This idea is obviously applicable to any country wishing to improve its voter turnout.

• *Justin O'Conor Sloane (e-mail: KingOConor@yahoo.com). Justin holds a Bachelors degree in Political Science from the University of Washington and lives in Seattle, Washington, USA.*

6 Blackstock Mews, London N4 2BT, UK (rhino@dial.pipex.com), 2002, 300pp, ISBN 0 948826 59 2

A contract with the planet

Summarised from an item in Positive News (Spring 2002 issue; subs £12.50 by calling 01588 640022, e-mail office@positivenews.org.uk or see web: www.positivenews.org.uk).

A new movement, spearheaded by one of the founders of Ben and Jerry's ice cream, is endeavouring to mobilise American people to reduce world poverty and hunger, promote renewable energy and close the gap between the rich and poor. Based on the theory laid out by Paul Ray that there are 50 million 'cultural creatives' holding similar views on social issues in the US, 'TrueMajority' intends to use e-mail, rock concerts and parades to involve people continually on issues of policy that concern them. It is as Ben Cohen puts it, a switch of strategy "from trying to convince the middle-of-the-roaders to activating the converted".

'The parade includes an eleven-foot pig and a natural gas-fuelled bus'

Already the parade, which includes a giant Earth on wheels that shakes hands with a huge United States as it rolls along, an eleven-foot pig, and a yellow double decker bus powered by natural gas, has travelled to cities in five states. And more are planned. Meanwhile, TrueMajority will monitor issues in Congress and send e-mail alerts to people on its list. By clicking 'reply', the recipients authorise a fax to be sent in their name to their representative, ensuring direct participation in the democratic process [this is a more co-ordinated version of FaxYourMP.com, the British website project, which won the Institute's Politics Award for 2001, but is focused more on empowering individual people].

Behind TrueMajority lies a document which emerged at the end of 2001, after the events of September 11th. It outlines ten parts of a 'contract with the planet' for people to sign up to (and is written from an American viewpoint):

1 Attack world hunger and poverty as if our life depends on it
2 Champion the rights of every child, woman and man
3 Pay our UN dues ungrudgingly and end our obstructionism to the world's treaties
4 Reduce our dependence on oil and lead the world to an age of renewable energy
5 Close the book on the Cold War and end the nuclear nightmare forever
6 Renounce 'Star Wars' and the militarisation of space
7 Make globalisation work for, not against working people
8 Ensure equal treatment under law for all

9 Get money out of politics
10 Close the gap between rich and poor at home

Though the contract alone achieves little, the efforts of Cohen's new movement to actually involve and mobilise people as a unified force (it aims to have several hundred thousand people signed up by the end of 2002) is a practical attempt to try and make these principles a reality. It should not be forgotten that, just as America is pinpointed as the cause of many global problems, it can also be the centre of solutions as well.

• *For more on the 'contract with the planet' and the work of TrueMajority, contact TrueMajority, PO Box 1976, Old Chelsea Station, New York, NY 10113-1976, USA (tel: +1 212 243 3416; e-mail: info@truemajority.org; web: www.truemajority.org).*

The Meta-Federation: rules to avoid conflicts in society

Eric Chen Yixiong

People in our societies often have conflicts, which can turn bloody when they impose their own ways of lives onto another. Since different groups of people have different ways of life, must conflict inevitably exist in our societies? Maybe a better solution can solve this problem.

What if everyone can set up their own societies which compete freely for members who would live in them? To establish the rules that protect themselves and their customers, these societies can join an entity called a Meta-Federation.

Basically, membership only requires a few rules:

1) Members shall not restrict their customers/citizens from leaving their premises.
2) Members shall not interfere in each other's affairs, unless they had received permission from the parties that their such actions would affect.
3) Members can do whatever in their power, to punish those who had interfered in their affairs and entered their premises, as long as these people had received prior warning.
4) Upon violation of these rules, offending societies would no longer remain as a member of the Federation.
 5) These rules only apply to members.

6 Blackstock Mews, London N4 2BT, UK (rhino@dial.pipex.com), 2002, 300pp, ISBN 0 948826 59 2

Rule 1 would prevent dictators or social leaderships from imposing their authoritarian way of life onto those who do not subscribe to such thinking. Rule 2 would inhibit member societies from interfering with each other's affairs. Rule 3 would allow societies to impose penalties for repeated violations of unauthorized access. Rule 5 would prevent the federation from imposing its own rules on others.

This has a potential to provide an acceptable framework for international relationships for our present day problems.

• *Eric Chen Yixiong (e-mail: cyixiong@yahoo.com). The author, a male teenager with a wide range of interests, lives in Singapore. You can visit his website at http://eric.webhop.net*

Eliminating bureaucratic language in official documents

Summarised from an item, entitled 'Declaring war on officialese', on Yahoo News online (June 4th 2002; http://daily.news.yahoo.com).

Italy has introduced a campaign to try and revolutionise the way the state communicates with its citizens: by making bureaucratic language in government documents understandable. The 'Chiaro!' (Clear!) project will particularly look at getting rid of complex clauses and confusing terminology. The civil service minister who is co-ordinating the campaign, Franco Frattini, said that "this is a cultural revolution in our relationship with [our] citizens", which demonstrates how serious the authorities think the problem is at present.

Minister Frattini gave the following example of how bureaucratic language could be simplified:

Before – 'The aforementioned office for economic treatment will cease the distribution of monies commencing from May 1, 2001.'

After – 'Our office will stop payments as of May 1.'

'Citizens can inform on those using an unnecessary number of words'

The campaign also includes a website where citizens who have spotted someone using ten or twenty words where four or five would suffice can inform the ministry. The departments and ministries that achieve the level of clarity aimed at will be rewarded with a 'Chiaro!' stamp on their documentation. The main problem may prove to be retraining personnel to stop them using the incomprehensible language they have written in for so many years. Others worry that simplifying language could go too far, leading to the elimination of nuances and clauses which are necessary, particularly in legal texts. The government is determined, though, and the war on officialese and bureaucracy has begun in earnest.

 • *See www.funzionepubblica.it for further information.*

Re-appraising political decisions with the benefit of hindsight

Mayer Hillman

This is the 13th instalment of Mayer Hillman's Musings for the Institute for Social Inventions. Mayer Hillman is Senior Fellow Emeritus at the Policy Studies Institute.

Central and local government reach decisions, for instance on planning matters following public inquiries, which in due course of time may be seen to have been ill-advised and therefore to vindicate opponents who had presented counter arguments. Insofar as there is any subsequent analysis of such an outcome, the politicians involved are usually treated as if they had simply been misguided or mistaken in their judgement rather than having deliberately ignored the public interest for baser reasons such as short-term electoral advantage. It is commonplace to view a regrettable decision as the consequence of an inevitably imperfect process. In effect, it is written off as a lost cause with nothing to learn about how to make such errors less likely to occur in future. At best, aggrieved opponents may have the minor satisfaction of being able to say at a later date 'we told you so'.

'An independent scrutiny panel would review the outcome of the original decision'

Could something more positive be derived that could lead to better decisions being made by adopting a new process of re-appraising past ones? One method that can be proposed would be to choose by public consultation or voting a limited number of key decisions on contentious issues that were reached in the past. An independent scrutiny panel would review the outcome of the original decision, say two, three or four years later, as appropriate. Its aim would be to reach a judgement as to whether the outcome was as originally

6 Blackstock Mews, London N4 2BT, UK (rhino@dial.pipex.com), 2002, 300pp, ISBN 0 948826 59 2

envisaged and whether the evidence presented at the time had been fair, reliable and objective. It would have similar characteristics to a small House of Commons Select Committee inquiry with all-party representation, but crucially also some co-opted independent members with expertise in any critical aspects of its examination.

Such a procedure could represent an invaluable learning process for politicians, civil servants or council officers, and professional advisers as well as for the general public, especially of course those who represented opposing evidence and views on the issue under review. More optimistically, over time, the experience should result in an improvement of both the process employed and the quality of decision-making.

'Re-appraisal could promote presentation of more carefully prepared evidence'

There can be little doubt too that awareness of the possibility of contentious decisions being re-appraised at some time in the future could encourage all those involved to take their responsibilities more seriously. This would impinge on their consciousness not least owing to their wishing to avoid the risk of exposure of their failure to have acted as they should have done, especially with the prospect of critical media coverage. It could also promote presentation of more carefully prepared evidence from all the parties involved. At present, anyone involved knows that they are unlikely to be held to account for getting things wrong because nobody bothers to 'rake over old coals' and that, even if that were to happen, they would be likely to be out of office, retired or dead by the time that their decisions or the grounds for their objection were evaluated.

● *For an idea similarly focusing on long-term accountability, see the item on Long Bets on page 284.*

SPIRITUALITY

Secular deities: the means to avoiding religious dogmatism and conflict?

Nick Temple

Inspired by, and partly summarised from, an article by Wole Soyinka, entitled 'Faiths that preach tolerance', in the Guardian (May 4th 2002). The full article originally appeared in a set of essays called The End of Tolerance? *(Nicholas Brealey, 2002; ISBN: 1857883179, 274 pages, £12.99).*

The idea of a 'secular deity' would appear to be an oxymoron, so it is perhaps best to start with what is meant by secularism in this context. In his article, Wole Soyinka refers to the secular temper as being 'humanistic', and he also refers to an age-old belief in the 'unity of the human community': age-old is a particularly apt phrase, because secular comes from the Latin 'saeculum', meaning 'a lifetime or generation'. So secularism here is about universal human beliefs dating back lifetimes, and ones that are concerned with unity and indivisibility amongst humans. In particular, the idea of the secular deity is proposed in response to the divisive dogmas and intolerances of existing religions. The premise is that the religions which dominate the world fall all too easily into dogmatism, absolutes and binary oppositions, and that a more open, tolerant and 'human' spirituality could help avoid the myriad conflicts and problems arising from those oppositions.

'People who wander from the path are not criticised or punished'

For his example of a secular deity, Soyinka goes back to his homeland Nigeria, and the world of the Yoruba. Their belief is that when a child is born, he or she bring their own destiny into the world (what they call their 'ori'), and that it is useless to try and change it or to impose a different one upon them. And this aura or destiny can change with the child's growth and life in the world: other guardian deities may be added or replaced. At the heart of this is the Yoruba's belief that all gods are different parts of the giant, universal whole of which humans and humanity is a part. Similarly, their Bible or Koran equivalent, in the form of prognostic verses (known as 'Ifa'), is filled with signs and parables, but also mentions those who decided not to follow the Yoruba

6 Blackstock Mews, London N4 2BT, UK (rhino@dial.pipex.com), 2002, 300pp, ISBN 0 948826 59 2

path: these people are not criticised or punished for their choices; if they suffer misfortune, that is down to their own destiny.

'Truth is called by many names and approached from myriad routes'

It is this concept of truth as being different things to different people that is key here; Soyinka quotes from the ancient India Vedic texts to illustrate the point: 'Wise is he who recognises that Truth is One and one only, but wiser still the one who accepts that Truth is called by many names, and approached from myriad routes.' Something that the proud Muslim Osama Bin Laden and the equally proud Christian George Bush might want to heed. Our beliefs should unite us and be accommodating in spirit, not divisive in their effects. The search for truth should not be confused with the veneration and validation of particular propositions of truth: there lies the path to absolutism, dogmatism and religious conflict. An acceptance of others, and of other 'truths', should be paramount in our spiritual lives, and our deities should be elastic and dynamic: able to change to our own constantly evolving perceptions of the world, and able to be moulded into a personal system of tolerance, faith and understanding. And, of course, this is not so much a new social invention as a rediscovery of a much older one: a unifying, non-competing spirituality from generations ago.

Those who believe in these religions would rightly point to them teachings which urge tolerance of others, loving thy neighbour etc, and they would be right to do so. The issue is more with the institutions and the texts. The former often inexorably leads to factionalism and a concentration on internal politics rather than the religion's ideals (helping others, supporting fellow believers, providing a sense of belonging and a place in the world, helping things make sense etc). The latter are, like any text, open to a huge variety of interpretations, allowing any particular group to cite parts of them as justification for their own particular version of the religious beliefs – this is then reinforced by the institutionalising of this version or interpretation. Then the arguments over who is right, or who follows the one true way, inevitably follow.

'A personal spiritual connection on individual terms, with unity at its core'

What I would like to see emerging is something close to transcendentalism – a belief in spirituality, in the divine in all things, in communion with nature and others, but with no regulations, texts, canticles, absolutes, buildings, or intermediaries. A personal spiritual connection on individual terms, everchanging, and always holding unity at its core. This may be a little away from Soyinka's 'secular deity', but there are similarities: openness, understanding, the ability to evolve, a belief in unity, tolerance of other opinions, and a strong faith in a world above and beyond our own. A religion that accommodates not divides; a spirituality that strengthens and evolves, rather than dwelling on one path that has been followed for centuries.

• *Nick Temple, the Institute for Social Inventions, 6 Blackstock Mews, Blackstock Road, London N4 2BT (tel: 020 7359 8391; fax: 020 7354 3831; e-mail: rhino@dial.pipex.com; web: www.globalideasbank.org).*

Aggregating God's characteristics for a global deity

Aaron Campbell

I think we should try to see if we can come up with a global term for God, one that we can all agree on more than we have up to now. It is clear that we as humans have been having problems with our concept of God: we seem to disagree so vehemently about who or what God is that we often kill each other to prove how right we think we are.

'Developing a dynamic database in as many languages as possible'

The internet could be used to aggregate God's characteristics and directives and develop a dynamic database in as many languages as possible to get a clearer picture about how differently we perceive or believe or worship our own God. This would include a collection of quotes, a collection of poems, myths, and stories about miracles.

Even though only a fraction of the world has internet access, the collective understanding of God/Spirit/Creator would increase if we were able to see a non-partisan attempt to sum up our feelings and definitions of God. In this way, we could use the new technology that connects and unites us electronically to connect and unite us spiritually and ethically.

• *Aaron Campbell (aaron@merc.net). Aaron is an innovator and writer living in Chicago.*

6 Blackstock Mews, London N4 2BT, UK (rhino@dial.pipex.com), 2002, 300pp, ISBN 0 948826 59 2

A Universal Code Flag – a moral banner for us all

Stephen de las Heras

A positive symbol for the new century

Inspired by the tragic events of September 11th 2001, the Universal Code Flag is an attempt to create a moral banner for our time. In these difficult days it seems that an international rallying symbol is missing in the world, and this flag is an attempt to fill that void.

The Universal Code Flag stands for various commonly held beliefs which already guide most morally intelligent people in their behaviour. It is meant to be compatible with most widely held religious beliefs, though not specifically associated with any of them. Many people in the world today believe that the major religions are simply different expressions of the same fundamental truths. And many people who do not adhere to any particular religion still believe strongly in these ultimate moral truths.

Institute for Social Inventions, £15 subs, £17 from abroad by credit card, tel London 020 7359 8391

The various elements contained within the code are meant to form a greater whole, interact with each other, creating a firm foundation for an individual's character, and for a just and prosperous society.

'There is a need for a symbol the whole world can unite behind'

There is nothing wrong with national flags, and taking pride in where you live. There are many wonderful countries in the world, with many beautiful flags. But ultimately, country flags represent a geographical area, and not a broad scope of ideals. In a global world we need a symbol that people everywhere can unite behind. It's also important to remember that in the history of mankind many innocent people have been killed in the name of nationalism.

This flag is an experiment that could succeed with your help. If this flag speaks to you, then feel free to download it, copy it, recreate it, and share it with others. Perhaps this symbol can make the world a better place.

To see if the flag really stands for moral truths you already believe in, read the following work in progress definitions for the various elements, and see if you agree with all of them:

Strength: I believe that individuals and societies must be mentally and physically strong enough to endure the challenges generated by a dangerous and unpredictable world.

Wisdom: I believe that the truth can be both complicated and simple, and to understand it one should have an open mind and the ability to see things from different points of view.

Knowledge: I believe that responsibly used knowledge will result in progress for humankind, increasing our ability to shape the universe in life-affirming ways.

Courage: I believe that when necessary one must be prepared to fight and die for a truly just cause.

Love: I believe that caring deeply for others is one of the keys to bringing about true peace and happiness.

Liberty: I believe individuals have the right to live their lives in freedom, pursuing happiness as they see fit, so long as they don't infringe on the rights of others.

6 Blackstock Mews, London N4 2BT, UK (rhino@dial.pipex.com), 2002, 300pp, ISBN 0 948826 59 2

Justice: I believe in society's right to protect the safety of its citizens, to enforce just laws, and in an individual's morally justified right to self defence.

Unity: I believe that we are all children of this earth, and that coexisting in harmony with one another and the planet will bring about the greatest possible good.

Equality: I believe that no man or race is born better than any other, and that wealth and possessions accumulated by some should not come at the excess detriment of others.

Peace: I believe that wherever possible the path of nonviolence and respect for all living things is the very best path to follow.

• *For more information, and to download the flag, go to www.universal-code.net, or contact Stephen at tragula1@aol.com*

Detecting a global consciousness

Summarised from information on the Global Consciousness Project website (http://noosphere.princeton.edu), from an article, entitled 'Did Sept. 11 events refocus global consciousness?', in USA Today (December 6th 2001), and from a report by Roger Nelson in the Arlington Institute's FUTUREdition Volume 5, Number 12 (June 27th 2002; www.arlingtoninstitute.org).

The concept of a global consciousness is not a new one: Jung referred to something called the 'Collective Unconsciousness', while Teilhard de Chardin called this unified human consciousness the 'noosphere', to distinguish it from the geosphere (the non-living world) and the biosphere (the living world). With the advent of the internet and random-generation computer technology, though, a project to try and detect global consciousness has been made possible. The Global Consciousness Project (GCP), based at Princeton University in the US, uses a network of random event generators (REGs) located around the world. The random data from these generators is then analysed at the host server in Princeton. Any substantial world events or happenings are then measured against the data to see if there are any anomalies from the randomness. That is to say, the machine notes correlations between major events and coherence or patterns emerging in the data. These correlations, the project speculates, are due in some way to the effect of a global consciousness: human emotions and responses giving structure to the randomness.

'The chances of the predicted deviations all occurring are a combined ten million to one'

The REGs are, esssentially, advanced coin-tossers, and they send in their results (how many heads and tails, to continue the analogy) to the host machine in Princeton. The analysis of the random data then notes any patterns emerging which deviate significantly from a random path: ten or twenty 'heads' in a row, for example. Armed with the concept of the global consciousness, the researchers predict when such patterns might emerge: such events as the World Cup final, Princess Diana's funeral, or the minutes around the start of a new year. They then analyse the data to see if any patterns emerged at that particular time, to see if focused human attention can affect the data in some way. Over 100 of these analyses have been done thus far, and the correlations have always occurred: the chances of these predicted deviations happening in this way is, the researchers say, a combined ten million to one.

The researchers have no knowledge of how or why these correlations occur, merely stating that there are signs of subtle communication on a global scale. The possibilities of electrical charges affecting the numbers is avoided by the REGs being located around the world. Thus, millions of people in the UK phoning each other on mobile phones or switching on the television to watch Diana's funeral could have no physical electronic effect on a REG in India, for example. But no-one is sure how the human brain could affect the creation of the random data. Matt Pilkington, of the *Fortean Times* in London, suggests that because the brain is an electrical device, it is not inconceivable that it might have an effect on magnetic fields. This would account for the electronic REGs being affected by shared moments of emotion and focus.

'The most striking correlation took place on September 11th'

The most compelling piece of evidence the project has amassed thus far, the most striking correlation between a major event and a structure occurring to the random data, occurred on September 11th. On that day, the data was non-random to the point that the researchers said that, "if you had not known September 11th was unusual, you would've settled on September 11th as being an unusual day", purely because of the structured results which lasted for several hours. The project's website contains a detailed analysis of the day's data, and explains its methodology of data collection and analysis.

The general consensus of the researchers of the project and 'anomaly' experts worldwide is that it is far too early to say what, if anything, this all means. The power of the internet and new technology has provided the means

6 Blackstock Mews, London N4 2BT, UK (rhino@dial.pipex.com), 2002, 300pp, ISBN 0 948826 59 2

by which an approach can be taken to attempting to detect a global consciousness, but the analysis (and methodology) is still at a fledgling stage. It remains to be seen whether De Chardin's statement about the 'noosphere', the part of the world of life created by human thought and culture, will ever be proven true:

'Pushed one against the other by the growth of their number and by the proliferation of their connections, approached one to the other by the reawakening of a common force and by the feeling of a common anxiety, the future human kind will form nothing but an unified consciousness'

The only conclusion for now is that anomalies do seem to correspond to the unusually coherent focus of humans at times of extraordinary events. These could be the first faint, detectable signs of this 'noosphere', our global consciousness.

• *For more information on the Global Consciousness Project, contact Roger Nelson (rdnelson@princeton.edu) or see the website at http:// noosphere.princeton.edu*

• *For articles on a similar theme in previous Institute books, see 'The 21st century guru as a collective cyberspace entity' in* DIY Futures *(ISI,1996), and 'The history of the evolution of consciousness' in* Creative Speculations *(ISI, 1997). See the back of this book for ordering details.*

OLD AGE

Communal apartments as meeting places for the elderly

Summarised from an e-mail to the Global Ideas Bank by Alain Blomart (October 4th 2001).

My idea relates to the old people in our industrialised societies, who very often end their lives alone. Old people's homes can be expensive and the majority die soon after entering these institutions. I think it is better for them to remain in their apartments as long as possible, in order to retain more independence.

'The flat could be rented out collectively'

My proposal also aims to avoid the anonymity of large buildings (blocks of flats etc). The suggestion is that, when there are quite a few older people in a building, they rent a flat collectively to use as a communal space. This apartment would then function as a meeting place for all the people in the building who are interested (old and young), and would not cost a great deal (a flat rented at £600 a month would cost 30 people £20 each month). People could play cards, spend afternoons there, and talk to others, reducing the isolation and anonymity that can occur in such buildings. There would need to be some sort of organising committee to arrange collection of the rent and maintaining the apartment in a good condition, but these issues should not be insurmountable.

Build elementary schools next to retirement homes for generational interaction

Submitted to the Global Ideas Bank by Robyn and Lisa, two students at Elon University in North Carolina, USA. The latter item is summarised from an article by Debbie Macklin, entitled 'Young at Heart', in Resurgence magazine (September/October 2001 issue; to subscribe, call 01208 841824 or e-mail: subs.resurge@virgin.net).

Our idea is to try and combat the process of discarding the elderly that seems to go on in our society. To effect this change, retirement homes could be built

6 Blackstock Mews, London N4 2BT, UK (rhino@dial.pipex.com), 2002, 300pp, ISBN 0 948826 59 2

by elementary schools, so that when the children have story time or recess, the elderly can be invited to join them and interact. Programmes can be built around these ideas to help include the elderly in the school environment. This way children are taught at an early age to respect and care for the elderly, and they benefit from being around wise and experienced people. The elderly would feel included and needed because they would be helping our future generations.

Inter-communal residence in France

In a project with similar intentions to the one above, a new inter-communal residence, in Saint Maur in France, houses over a hundred retired people and also a creche and nursery school. There is no obligation for the two groups, at opposite ends of the age spectrum, to mix, but most look forward to the time they spend together. This occurs over lunch or during joint activities, like drawing and painting, in the afternoons. Many of the senior citizens also enjoy reading stories to the pre-school children.

'The elderly residents have a greater dynamism when the children are there'

The director of the 'halte-garderie' (a combination of nursery school and day-care centre), Stephane Reyes, believes that the children's concentration improves because the "older people have more time for them". Meanwhile, the nursing manager of the retirement home, Agnes Vincen, has noticed a dynamism to the residents when the children are there, and an improvement in "psychology and morale". What is certain is that such schemes, of which there are a few in France and other European countries, help to break down prejudices about age and the elderly. Indeed, such places of generational interaction could prove to be a sign of a more open attitude towards old age, one that is less predicated on viewing old age as an illness and that remembers that the elderly are people who still have much to contribute to society. The scheme can also work particularly well for those older people whose grandchildren live far away, or for those who don't have grandchildren, and vice versa for children who have no grandparents.

Institute for Social Inventions, £15 subs, £17 from abroad by credit card, tel London 020 7359 8391

Social Inventions
An ideology cup final: quizzing the world's thinkers

Gary Rowe

I'd like to see two teams of say 10 to 20 of the world's most influential scholars, journalists, and thinkers (both liberal and conservative) pose questions and answers to each other in an effort to tackle the world's most profound questions.

'Starter questions to include 'What is Democracy?' '

Starter questions that neither side could avoid would include: ' How much time does the Earth have left?' 'Which Ideology could actually do the best job of sustaining what's left of the Earth?' What is democracy? Is it 'The Best for the Most?' or is it a 'Winner takes all society?'

A moderator (or team of moderators) could base this on the 'SuperBowl' idea with penalties for slander and such being assessed (for fun) and real-time Internet use to find support data helping (or hurting) each side of the debate. We could even show how other countries or individuals are reacting to the discussion in real-time to one another, but I believe that waiting, say a week, to respond would be a better alternative for viewers giving them time to digest what has been already said. Perhaps a follow-up broadcast could aid this process.

I guess corporate sponsors could help underwrite this and provide the necessary exposure, I'd like to see it as an alternative to watching the real 'Super Bowl' [or similar event in non-US countries]

Of course the Earth would be the real winner, with a debate independent of governments leading to a consensus on questions of importance. As well as fostering debate and interest among the public, it would also have the potential to be seriously entertaining.

• *Gary Rowe (e-mail: growe@bellatlantic.net). Gary is a cashier in a large supermarket chain in the US, and 'a citizen of the Earth with a vested interest in the future of life'.*

6 Blackstock Mews, London N4 2BT, UK (rhino@dial.pipex.com), 2002, 300pp, ISBN 0 948826 59 2

Make Boxing Day a 'giving' day again

Summarised from a letter from Liam Robb, entitled 'Last gifts of the season', in the Guardian (December 28th 2001).

Liam Robb suggests a return to the traditions of Boxing Day, in which unwanted possessions were 'boxed' up and distributed amongst the poor, needy and those in service industries. He suggests that a box could be distributed to every household in Britain to be filled with unwanted presents and uneaten (unperishable) food post-Christmas Day, and that these things could then be distributed in the UK and abroad to appropriate organisations and groups. As Christmas has become more commercial and frenzied in its excess, such a new Boxing Day tradition could provide a welcome (and worthwhile) antidote on the following day.

'The giving aspect emerged from the aristocracy giving presents to servants'

Boxing Day is thought to have originated in the Middle Ages, and the giving aspect of the day may have emerged from the aristocracy giving Christmas gifts to their servants (who had to work Christmas Day, but not the following day) or from priests distributing the money collected for the poor at churches over the Christmas period. Boxing Day takes place not only in the UK, but also in Australia, Canada and New Zealand. The charitable aspect of the day, at least in the UK, was lost sometime ago, and the day is now better known for being 'the day when you visit the grandparents' or 'the day when the football matches are played'. It could be time to make it a day for 'boxing up' again.

'Long Bets' – fostering accountable long-term thinking

Summarised from an e-mail to the Global Ideas Bank by Paul Spinrad (September 2001) and from an article, entitled 'Wanna Bet?', in Wired magazine (May 2002 issue; www.wired.com; to subscribe call +1 415 222 6200 or e-mail: subscriptions@wired.com). The latter item was monitored for the Global Ideas Bank by Roger Knights.

'Long Bets' are long-term, serious, measurable, public forecasts on what the future will hold, backed up by a monetary contribution based on the participants' certainty about their particular prediction. The Long Bets Foundation (a collaboration between the Long Now Foundation and Wired magazine) will hold the funds, maintain records and administer the agreement until it has reached its term. The purpose of the idea is to foster serious long-term thinking, in an age of short-termism and minute attention spans, and to make those making (grandiose) claims about the future more accountable: essentially, putting their money where their mouth is. In time, it also expects to help us understand what kinds of truths are easier (and which more difficult) to forecast, and what people from which fields are right (or wrong) more often. In general, the idea hopes to improve our collective ability to foresee what will happen by including money and public accountability in the predicting process. And the winner's money? Goes straight to a designated charity or non-profit.

The basic rules of Long Bets are as follows:

- the minimum bet is $1,000
- the minimum period for the bet is two years
- odds are always even
- the subject of the bet must be of importance, socially or scientifically; the terms of the bet should be such that there can be a clear outcome; the terms of the bet, and those making it, are made public
- each bettor must supply a succinct argument along with the bet, stating why they will win and why the bet is of importance; these arguments will also be made public
- each bettor must designate a charity to which they wish the collective stakes of both bettors (plus interest) to go to at the time of the bet's consummation
- members of the public are welcome to make their own bets

'The victors of particular bets will be publicised as and when they win'

All of the Long Bets will be placed on www.longbets.org, and the organisation will also publicise the consummations and victors of particular bets as and when they occur. The stakes of each bet will be treated as a charitable donation to the Long Bets Foundation, making them tax deductible, and the Foundation will use half of the growth of each stake to administer the site and all the different bets. All outcomes of the bets are binary; that is to say that there will be a winner and a loser, no apportioning of the money by percentage. If the bettors cannot agree on who has won, or if one or both of them has died, experts at the Long Bets Foundation will decide the outcome, explaining why the facts are closer to one side or another.

6 Blackstock Mews, London N4 2BT, UK (rhino@dial.pipex.com), 2002, 300pp, ISBN 0 948826 59 2

Examples of bets already made

- 'A computer will pass the Turing test by 2029' – a $10,000 bet between Ray Kurzweil (entrepreneur, technologist; says YES) and Mitchell Kapoor (founder of Lotus, investor; says NO). The Turing Test is a famous test invented by Alan Turing in 1950, in which a judge has to discern which is the person and which the machine answering questions via text.
- 'Commercial airline passengers will routinely fly in pilotless planes by 2030' – a $1,000 bet between Craig Mundie (CTO, Microsoft; says YES) and Eric Schmidt (CEO, Google; says NO).
- 'By 2010, more than 50 per cent of books sold worldwide will be printed on demand at the point of sale in the form of library-quality paperbacks' – a $1,000 bet between Jason Epstein (former editorial director, Random House; says YES) and Vint Cerf (internet innovator; says NO).

The Long Bets Foundation encourages the public to join in with their own bets, and there are Open Bets on their website (bets made by people looking for someone to take them on and match their stake). And the rest of us can sit back, relax and, in the words of the Long Bets Foundation, use time as a teacher.

- *See www.longbets.org for more information.*

The most common forecasts for the future

Summarised from an article by Kermit Pattison, entitled 'Futurists utilize statistics, analyses to illuminate where we're headed', in the Seattle Times (July 30th 2001), monitored for the Global Ideas Bank by Roger Knights.

Predicting the future is one way of brainstorming for social inventions, of ways in which things can be improved for society in the years to come. The editors of the Futurist magazine picked out some of the predictions for the future which they had come across most in 2001, and they make interesting reading. They include:

'The rise of singleness will continue unabated'

- The continued rise of singleness, which will lead to a wider range of services for single people, including housecleaning, pet care and financial services
- Leisure-oriented business will come to dominate the world economy in the next decade and a half

- Workers will become more dependent on their employers for social services, to the extent that they will find it increasingly difficult to break away from these corporate families
- A 'career pill' may be invented for women, allowing them to postpone the menopause till they are 70, effectively resetting their biological clocks
- Gene therapy could be used to reverse the effects of aging on the memory, and therefore improve people's learning abilities

- *For more futurist predictions see www.wfs.org*

Low-level disruptive innovation is the key to change

Summarised from an article by Edward Rothstein, entitled 'The Unforeseen Disruption of Moving Ahead', on the New York Times website (December 22nd 2001; www.nytimes.com).

The model of a dominant leader facing an insignificant challenge from an unexpected direction, not giving that challenge due attention, and then being toppled is a classic of political and military history. But it is also one that can increasingly be applied to the way in which innovation can change our culture and marketplace. Small innovations can often end up having substantial consequences that were never even imagined at the time of the invention. It is the surprise of the impact of the disruption that is the key to its effect: an inventor may have had one purpose in mind for his idea, but its ripple effects can be unpredictable and far greater.

'What may seem an insignificant innovatory advance can have massive effects'

This is what Clayton Christensen, a business professor at Harvard, looked at in his book *The Innovator's Dilemma*, in which he pointed out that 'disruptive innovation' is not only impossible to foresee, but also essentially unavoidable. Focusing on a business model in particular, Christensen points out that the more dominant the leader in a field is, the more comfortable and secure it feels, the more effective disruptive innovation can be. That is when it is least likely of all to pay attention to what may seem an insignificant challenge, or a small innovatory advance; that is the time when disruptive innovation can have its most powerful effects.

There are countless business examples to back up the theory: IBM and the disruptor (turned leader) Microsoft in the early 1980's, Kodak failing to appreciate the powers of digital reproduction early enough etc. Similarly,

6 Blackstock Mews, London N4 2BT, UK (rhino@dial.pipex.com), 2002, 300pp, ISBN 0 948826 59 2

seemingly small technological inventions can have much wider social impacts. It was thought that the telegraph would create stronger communities, but it had the opposite effect, allowing a much wider population dispersion. The inventors of text messaging cannot have imagined the myriad uses it would have: informing parents of truant children, combating credit card fraud instantly, or allowing deaf people to communicate much more easily and swiftly.

'It was the skill of Nicholas Albery to be flexible with his vision'

Social innovation can work in similar ways. When Nicholas Albery, the Institute's founder, started up the Natural Death Centre in 1991, it was intended as being analogous to the natural birth movement, viewing death as part of the natural process of life. Thus its initial focus was on death education and allowing people to talk about the subject openly. What emerged from the public, though, was a particular interest in alternative funeral arrangements, and it is this part of the Centre's work that has expanded massively, with it running an association of woodland burial grounds, publishing the comprehensive guide to the subject and conducting surveys on environmentally friendly funerals. While the education aspect continued (and is indeed flourishing again), it was the skill of Nicholas Albery to be flexible with his vision; and, in doing so, his original small-scale innovation has had, and is having, a much wider impact on people's lives than otherwise might be the case.

What this idea of low-level disruptive innovation boils down to is essentially two well-worn clichés: 'what mighty oaks from acorns grow' and 'expect the unexpected'. The concept is both an inspiring and a troubling one, though. For what the theory says is that small numbers of people can change the world and society, but it does not state that this must always be a constructive process rather than a destructive one. That decision, as always, lies with the people choosing which path to follow.

• *For more information, see* The Innovator's Dilemma *by Clayton Christensen (Harperbusiness, 2000; ISBN: 0066620694, 320 pages, $16) and* Why Things Bite Back: Technology and the Revenge of Unintended Consequences *by Edward Tenner (Vintage, 1997; ISBN: 0679747567, 368 pages, $14).*

• *For more on the Natural Death Centre, contact NDC, 6 Blackstock Mews, Blackstock Road, London N4 2BT (tel: 020 7359 8391; fax: 020 7354 3831; e-mail: rhino@dial.pipex.com; web: www.naturaldeath.org.uk).*

Michael Young – a life of innovation

August 9th 1915 – January 14th 2002

Information taken from a variety of obituaries from major UK newspapers, and from the biography of Michael Young by Asa Briggs.

Michael Young, the foremost social inventor of his generation, died earlier this year aged 86. Best-known for creating the Open University and the Consumers' Association, he started off hundreds of other projects, from the National Funerals College to the School for Social Entrepreneurs, improving the lives of millions of people. Renowned for his personal energy and charm, Michael Young, later Lord Young of Dartington, was a master of initiating schemes and then persuading other people to get involved in the administration and implementation in the long-term, leaving him free to pursue his next innovation.

Born in Manchester to an Australian violinist father and a painter-author mother, Young's life changed irrevocably when he was sent to the experimental progressive school in Devon, Dartington Hall. The Institute for Social Inventions' founder Nicholas Albery, who greatly admired and was greatly influenced by Young, wrote last year that the school provided 'superb training for entrepreneurial activism'. The school had been set up around the idea of small and large groups of people creating the future, with education being a key foundation of that. Whilst a pupil there, Young ran any number of small business initiatives and innovative projects, with the backing and support of his teachers and mentors. It was this background that was crucial to his later successes.

By the age of 29, Young was already a director of research for the Labour party, and wrote the party's manifesto, *Let us Face the Future*, in 1945. Just five years later, he left the party, due to infighting and a poverty of ideas, but he

6 Blackstock Mews, London N4 2BT, UK (rhino@dial.pipex.com), 2002, 300pp, ISBN 0 948826 59 2

had been involved in one of the most reforming governments this century. Two years after exiting party politics, Young founded his Institute for Community Studies (ICS), which was to prove, over the years, an effective central base from which other projects could be launched. Many of his early initiatives were directly concerned with people at the local level being empowered and helped, and given more rights to improve their own lives, demonstrating this focus on community and its ability to change for good, a lesson instilled at Dartington Hall.

'The Open University presently has 200,000 students on its books'

1964 saw the beginnings of the Open University on Anglia Television, with Harold Wilson taking inspiration from Young's 'dawn university' and National Extension College, and this revolutionised the traditional process of learning for many people. The first students were enrolled in 1971, and the Open University presently has 200,000 students on its books in the UK, and a further 16,000 abroad. Young continued to open up learning to new people through several other distance learning projects, including the International Extension College, the Open College of Arts and the Open School.

The Consumers' Association, best known in its guise of the 'Which?' magazines, was launched in 1957, and has since become widely trusted as a people's watchdog and champion. Again, the emphasis was on empowering people (in this case, to make informed decisions) through a means independent of government or business. Later, Young would also become chairman of the National Consumer Council, helping oversee improvements to public services.

'His book is credited with causing the abolition of the eleven-plus system'

His greatest literary success was his book *The Rise of the Meritocracy* which was published in 1958 and sold half a million copies. As well as giving rise to a new word, it led to a much more in-depth and reasoned debate on issues of opportunity, pluralism and elitism, particularly among the influential political left. It is said that the book had such an impact that it contributed to the abolition of the eleven-plus system of examination in schools.

The links to the work done here at the Institute for Social Inventions by Nicholas Albery and others had been strengthened in recent years, following the creation of the School for Social Entrpreneurs (SSE) in 1997 (Lord Young had been a consultant of the Institute for many years). It aims to foster the spirit of innovation and couple it with business sense, so that those students at the school become not only thinkers, but 'doers', as he himself was. His influence continues there, as it does in so many aspects of public life in this country. Even aside from the many organisations, charities and voluntary projects he has helped to found or start, his influence will live long in the minds, memories and actions of others whom he inspired and assisted.

These are words from a speech Michael Young gave to students at the SSE just prior to the millennium:

"I had to decide...what I was going to say to you, as an old man of the twentieth century, to you people of the twenty-first century. And I think what I would say is 'Go for it'...

'I am shouting "Go for it! Don't be put off! Be persistent!" '

It is perhaps a metaphor of a ship leaving the dock. It's the ship of the next century and there I am on the dockside, waving a message, shouting out 'Go for it! Don't be put off! Be persistent, persistent, persistent!'

Anyway, that is my message to you of the next century, from me in this century. And I don't think the next century will be any different. The resistance to new ideas will be much the same – and the means to overcoming it will be the same. You will need all the guile you can muster and all the persistence. Don't dismiss all your good ideas if they don't seem good ideas to your friends and other people. Believe in yourself. Go for it. That's what I'm shouting from the dockside."

- *The Open University, PO Box 724, Milton Keynes MK7 6ZS (tel: 01908 653231; fax: 01908 655072; e-mail: General-Enquiries@open.ac.uk; web: www.open.ac.uk).*
- *The Consumers' Association, 2 Marylebone Road, London NW1 4DP (web: www.which.net).*
- *The School for Social Entrepreneurs, 18 Victoria Park Square, Bethnal Green, London E2 9PF (tel: 020 8981 0300; fax: 020 8983 4655; e-mail: info@sse.org.uk; web: www.sse.org.uk).*
- The Rise of Meritocracy *by Michael Young (Transaction, 1994; ISBN: 1560007044, 180 pages, £23.50).*
- Michael Young – Social Entrepreneur *by Asa Briggs (Palgrave, 2001; ISBN: 03337502323, 411 pages, £52.50).*

6 Blackstock Mews, London N4 2BT, UK (rhino@dial.pipex.com), 2002, 300pp, ISBN 0 948826 59 2

Sir Peter Parker – a patron remembered

August 30th 1924 – April 28th 2002

Summarised from a number of obituaries online, particularly the one in the Guardian written by Prue Leith.

Sir Peter Parker, a patron of the Institute for Social Inventions, sadly died on April 28th 2002. He was renowned as a different type of businessman, one who thrived on imaginative solutions, emphasised communication and showed concern for others. He became most widely known during his time as chairman of British Rail, a post he held from 1976 to 1983, but was also heavily involved in a number of other businesses, artistic ventures and charitable projects.

Born in Dunkirk in 1924, Parker's family moved to China in 1931 at the time of the Sino-Japanese war, and subsequently stayed in Hong Kong before settling in Wimbledon back in England. He studied Japanese in London, as interpreters were in short supply at the start of the second world war, and went on to join the intelligence corps in 1943. During his time in intelligence, he worked in India, Burma and America, and also lost both his brothers who were in the RAF. After the wars end, he went to Oxford and became well-known as, among other things, an actor. He also studied in America and stood as a Labour candidate before finally entering the business world, still not even 30.

He went on to work for a number of businesses throughout the 50s and 60s, always combining what have been called his 'twin drives of social concern and relentless ambition'. From 1976 onwards at the helm of British Rail, Parker persuaded a succession of government ministers for greater state investment in the railways, alongside a modernising drive aimed at greater productivity. He was always interested in the intellectual and artistic side of management and business, in trying to achieve the difficult reconciliation of greater efficiency with the community's social imperatives.

He also campaigned vigorously for the introduction of Japanese as a language to be taught in schools, and many of his closest business relationships were with the Far East, particularly in his time at Mitsubishi. He was a key figure in fostering artistic and business collaborations between Japan and England throughout the 1980s and 90s, and promoted Anglo-Japanese friendship right up until his death. This commitment to promoting greater capability in other languages, and encouraging closer links with foreign countries stemmed from his cosmopolitan background and childhood, but also from an openness to possibilities. His strong belief in the importance of education also permeated his tenure as chairman of the London School of Economics from 1988 to 1998.

'A commitment to imagination, innovation and people-centred business'

As Prue Leith wrote in her obituary of Sir Peter, he was 'impatient with narrow-mindedness, neat boxes, and imagination-free leaders. He liked the space where business meets the arts, where education meets politics, where ethics meets the bottom line'. It is in this sense that he was a perfect patron for the Institute, with his commitment to innovation, imagination and people-centred business. After Nicholas Albery's death, he was one of many who offered support, both financial and practical, to the setting up of the Nicholas Albery Foundation, and promised to continue as a patron in the future. He will be sorely missed.

Sir Peter Parker also contributed to the Institute's book of inspiring advice from extraordinary people, *Seize the Day*, in 2001, and these were his tips for future generations:

Rules for good management

• Eat and drink less, and laugh more: don't think you have to be unpleasant to be strong
• Somehow find a way of sleeping twice a day
• Do all your sums, look hard, but don't forget you have to leap
• Hire people cleverer than you are and delegate more than you think is good for you. And take the blame
• Learn one other language at least; appreciating another culture will help you understand your own, and it's never too late

6 Blackstock Mews, London N4 2BT, UK (rhino@dial.pipex.com), 2002, 300pp, ISBN 0 948826 59 2

• Find things to praise in people but don't too easily trust yourself about yourself – you're such a flatterer

'If you're in a hanging mood, hang people like pictures – in the best light'

• If you're in a hanging mood, hang people like pictures – in the best light
• One minute of your time could be somebody else's day, good or bad, courtesy or curse
• Round tables for meetings do make a real difference
• Take your problems home – the family has shrewdly sized them up in general terms anyway, but without the detail it is even more worrying for them
• Organise into the smallest group you can – that way people are real to one another
• Ask people to do what they do best – don't ask Sinatra his view of the atomic bomb

[Sir Peter added: I have always used these simple rules (which appear in my autobiography *For Starters*) to underpin whatever professionalism I have. I want managers to renounce the stereotypes. There is no need to be half a man, or woman, to be a manager. As Hamlet said to Horatio, 'every man hath business and desire'.]

• *National Languages for Export Campaign, Trade Partners UK, Bay 905, Kingsgate House, 66-74 Victoria Street, London SW1E 6SW (tel: 020 7215 8146; fax: 020 7215 4856 ; e-mail: duncan.lillywhite@tradepartners.gov.uk; web: www.tradepartners.gov.uk/national_languages/about/introduction/ introduction.shtml).*
• *For more on the UK-Japan 2000 Group, see www.jcie.or.jp/thinknet/ forums/uk/forum.html*
• For Starters *by Peter Parker (Jonathan Cape, 1989; 326 pages, £16.95; currently out of print).*
• Seize the Day *edited by Nicholas Albery and Stephanie Wienrich (Chatto and Windus, 2001; ISBN: 0701169389, 384 pages, £12). This book can be bought mail order from the Institute for Social Inventions, 6 Blackstock Mews, Blackstock Road, London N4 2BT (tel: 020 7359 8391; fax: 020 7354 3831; e-mail: rhino@dial.pipex.com; web: www.seizethe day.org.uk).*

ONE-LINERS

This is a new section in the Institute's annual compendium especially for all those one-line bright ideas which have not always been fully thought through, or are at the earliest stage of development. Nevertheless, from small nuggets, a golden future can be created, so pan for gold amongst the following:

Books with an accompanying soundtrack CD for each chapter – Jim Richards, from the Idea-a-day website (www.idea-a-day.com)

Fill every available space in an automobile with helium. Or, even, create space to be filled to reduce automobile weight – James E Williams (tidyhoot@att.net)

A 'people library' where people can ask assorted experts for advice on particular subjects – Mike Ruddy, from the Idea-a-day website (www.idea-a-day.com)

Gun buyers have to be shot once non-fatally by every weapon they purchase – Richard Murnane, PO Box 1247, North Sydney, NSW 2059, Australia

Bomb Afghanistan...with butter, rice, medicine and hope – Kent Madin, www.globalmeditations.com

Fit wing mirrors to blackboards so teachers can see what pupils are up to – 'Googler D', from the Idea-a-day website (www.idea-a-day.com)

A Trans-African pipcline to provide water for the whole continent where needed – Julie Macdonald (M00cvz00@btinternet.com)

Use giant airships to transport Antarctican ice blocks to countries in need of water – Dave Parkin, 20 Riverside Rd, Penwortham, Preston PR1 9RE

Give police powers to arrest someone they are convinced is too tired to drive (as for drink/drugs) – Chas Bayfield, from the Idea-a-day website (www.idea-a-day.com)

A 'Transvestite Day' when men and women swap roles for the day, including all duties, chores and work – Julie Dalrymple (julie420@kidrock.com)

6 Blackstock Mews, London N4 2BT, UK (rhino@dial.pipex.com), 2002, 300pp, ISBN 0 948826 59 2

Customers must have a mandatory basic knowledge of how something works before buying it – Darrin Gray (ditirmind@excite.com)

Laughter should be used to control riots (by broadcasting it to crowds) – William Taylor (wftaylor@adelphia.net)

Taxing brands and shops that overpackage unnecessarily – Becky Clarke, from the Idea-a-day website (www.idea-a-day.com)

Prisoners to write essays on their (criminal) motivations to create an educational resource – Bill Jordan (bjordan@vicnet.net.au)

Changing classroom locations to keep things fresh and interesting – Behzad Rassuli (bazurd@hotmail.com)

Recycle old windows as picture frames – Kirstin vander Giessen-Reitsma (kirstin@studiou.com)

Temporary tattoo by law for a year before making it permanent – Sarah Wilburn and Kaitlin Gruley (Elon University)

Publications available

Orders can be placed by cheque or (using Visa or Mastercard) by phone, fax, letter, e-mail or securely online (at www.globalideasbank.org/bookorder.html).

• **I wish to be sent the following <u>ticked</u> PUBLICATIONS** – (UK p&p included. Add 9% for European p&p, 32% for airmail p&p for the rest of the world. 10% off for Institute subscribers, except for those books marked [*])

[*] '**The New Natural Death Handbook**', 120+ woodland burial grounds, cardboard and regular coffins, best buy funeral directors, legalities of funerals, caring for the dying at home. £13.50 first class.

[*] '**How to Organise a Woodland or Inexpensive Funeral**'. For a credit card phone or web donation of £6.99, this summary (less detailed than the handbook above) can be e-mailed to those with e-mail and web access who are in urgent need. It is only available as an e-mail.

[*] '**Living Will & set of forms**'. Living Will, Life Values Statement, Death Plan and Advance Funeral Wishes form. Set of forms for a donation of £5 or more.

NEW! [*] '**After Life**', reports from the frontline of death, £6.50 first class.

[*] '**Progressive Endings**', complements the New Natural Death Handbook, with more in-depth articles and items on death and dying, £6.20 first class.

[*] '**Poem for the Day – 366 Poems, Old and New, Worth Learning By Heart**', with foreword by Wendy Cope. 400 page book with a poem for each day of the year. £11.97 (incl. p&p.).

NEW! [*] '**Seize the Day**', a calendar of tips for living, a hardback companion to 'Poem for the Day'. £13.99 (incl. p&p.).

[*] '**Time Out Book of Country Walks**' by Nicholas Albery. The new blue cover revised 416-page calendar of walks easily reached by train as day outings from London, with a pub lunch and a tea place afterwards. £11.99 (incl. update sheets, train times for Saturday Walkers' Club, p&p.).

• '**Alternative Gomera – Guide to a fortnight's walking round Gomera Island near Tenerife**' by Nicholas Albery, 6th edition. £9.99 incl. first class p&p. Map £5.85 extra.

• '**Future Workshops - How to Create Desirable Futures**', by Robert Jungk, used by groups throughout Europe as a manual. £8.99.

• '**The Forest Garden**' by Robert Hart, How to establish a food-growing permaculture Forest Garden, in town or country. £3.50. 4th edition.

• '**Cornucopia of Ideas – a global ideas bank compendium**', best project and schemes displaying human imagination, £15 incl. p&p.

• '**Book of Inspirations – a directory of social inventions**', preface by Brian Eno, £15 incl. p&p.

6 Blackstock Mews, London N4 2BT, UK (rhino@dial.pipex.com), 2002, 300pp, ISBN 0 948826 59 2

• 'Social Dreams & Technological Nightmares – a global ideas bank compendium', predicting the next 500 years, £14.85 incl. p&p.
• 'DIY Futures – people's ideas and projects for a better world', 250 new social incentives and schemes. £14.85 incl. p&p.
• 'Creative Speculations – a compendium of social innovations', 'An amazing book, ambitious and successful' (Stewart Brand). £14.85 incl. p&p.
[*] 'Social Dreams', 'DIY Futures' and 'Creative Speculations' (all £14.85) – these three books for £34 incl. p&p (if ordered by a new Institute subscriber): a saving of over £10.
• '1,001 Health Tips – from recent medical research'. FREE! to new Institute subscribers. Get well and stay well.
• 'How to Feel Reborn? Varieties of Rebirthing Experiences' an investigation of primal and rebirthing therapies by Nicholas Albery. The 1985 edition is now available only in a non-paper, digital version which can be downloaded and printed out. 260 pages, £9.99. Go to www.globalideasbank.org/rebirthing.html for free chapter and ordering details.
• 'Community Counselling Circles' by John Southgate, for improving the atmosphere in groups. £6.95.
• 'The Solution for South Africa', an influential cantonisation scheme. £6.95.
• 'The Problem Solving Pocketbook', an overview of the main ways to solve problems, plus some wilder alternatives. £3.50.
• 'Being True to Yourself', by Margaret Chisman, insight exercises for groups. £4.95.
• 'Auction of Promises – how to raise £16,000 in one evening', for church, school and community groups. £1.95.
• The original Institute journals from the 1980s. £10 for a random selection of five issues.

Institute subscriptions

• Enclosed is £15 for an Institute subscription. (Outside UK £17 by credit card.) Members and subscribers receive at least one large book per annum in August or September - *state if you want this year's or next year's* - plus 10% off most Institute publications, except those with [*]. Those supplying an e-mail address may be sent occasional interesting mailings. Subscribers can also join in Social Invention events via the Institute's www.DoBe.org website.)
[The cheapest way to pay from outside the UK is by credit card securely online at www.globalideasbank.org/bookorder.html, or by credit card through phone or fax.]

NAME (caps) ....

ADDRESS...

....

....

TEL. No..

E-MAIL ....

Please photocopy and return this form with cheques payable to: '**Institute for Social Inventions**', 20 Heber Road, London NW2 6AA, UK (tel 020 8208 2853; fax 020 8452 6434; e-mail: rhino@dial.pipex.com; web: www.global ideasbank.org/bookorder.html).

━━━━━━━━━━━━━━━━━━━━━━━━━━━━━━

UK STANDING ORDER FORM – please fill in and return to Institute for Social Inventions, 20 Heber Road, London NW2 6AA. USE CAPITALS.

MY BANK...

BANKADDRESS ....

....

MY ACCOUNT NO. ....

Please pay to the Institute for Social Inventions £........**annually**, starting on

the ...... day of ....20....... (or as soon after this date as possible).

Their account is bank number 60 13 34, account number 38843803, bank

address: National Westminster Bank, 298 Elgin Avenue, London W9, UK.

NAME (caps) ....

ADDRESS...

....

TEL. No..

SIGNATURE...

DATE...

6 Blackstock Mews, London N4 2BT, UK (rhino@dial.pipex.com), 2002, 300pp, ISBN 0 948826 59 2

THE NICHOLAS ALBERY FOUNDATION

The Institute for Social Inventions

The core project of the Foundation, the Institute promotes and disseminates good ideas to improve society around the world. This is achieved through its publications, its annual awards and its website, the Global Ideas Bank. The website, the online arm of the Institute, also plays a key role in encouraging public participation in creative problem-solving. The Institute is further intended to be an idea generator for new projects to be run under the Foundation's umbrella. See www.globalideasbank.org for more.

The Natural Death Centre

The Natural Death Centre, founded in 1991, gives urgent advice and information on alternative funerals, woodland burials, biodegradable coffins, DIY funerals and private land burial. It educates on the subject of death and dying with workshops, publications, seminars and an annual Day of the Dead. More generally, it aims to improve the 'quality of dying'. See www.naturaldeath.org.uk for more.

The Poetry Challenge

The Poetry Challenge provides information and resources (sponsorship forms, certificates, etc) to schools and other organisations wishing to hold a fund-raising event. At a challenge, participants are sponsored to learn poems by heart to raise money for a charitable or non-profit cause. See www.poetrychallenge.org.uk for more.

The ApprenticeMaster Alliance

The ApprenticeMaster Alliance matches up graduates, school-leavers and those wishing to learn a trade with masters willing to teach it. This is done via an online database, and is a free service. In the ideal apprenticeship, there is a beneficial exchange of skills, knowledge and time. See www.apprentice.org.uk

www.DoBe.org

DoBe.org is a website for posting, and signing up to, participatory events in every city in the world. Its aim is to foster real-world interaction and to combat urban isolation; to retribalise the cities using the power of the internet.

• *For more information about any of the above, contact The Nicholas Albery Foundation, 6 Blackstock Mews, Blackstock Road, London N42BT, UK (tel: 020 7359 8391; fax: 020 7354 3831; e-mail: rhino@dial.pipex.com)*